50 Hikes in New Jersey

Scarlet Oak Pond, Ramapo Valley County Reservation

50 *Hikes*

In New Jersey

Walks, Hikes, and Backpacking Trips from the Kittatinnies to Cape May

BRUCE C. SCOFIELD, STELLA J. GREEN, AND H. NEIL ZIMMERMAN

Third Edition

The Countryman Press
Woodstock, Vermont

AN INVITATION TO THE READER

Over time trails can be rerouted and signs and landmarks altered. If you find that changes have occurred on the routes described in this book, please let us know so that corrections may be made in future editions. The author and publisher also welcome other comments and suggestions. Address all correspondence to:

Editor
Fifty Hikes™ Series
The Countryman Press
P.O. Box 748
Woodstock, VT 05091

Note:
Many water sources are identified for hiker convenience, but this is not an endorsement of their purity. All sources should be treated before consuming.

LIBRARY OF CONGRESS CATALOGING-IN-PUBLICATION DATA
Data has been applied for.

ISBN 10: 0-88150-702-4
ISBN 13: 978-0-88150-702-7

Series and cover design by Glenn Suokko
Composition by Doug Porter, San Antonio, TX
Interior photography by the authors, as noted
Cover photograph of the white-blazed Shore Path on the Hudson River © Stella Green
Updated maps by Mapping Specialists Ltd., Madison, WI

The authors and publisher have made the information in this book as accurate as possible. They accept no responsibility for any loss, injury, or inconvenience sustained by anyone using it.

Published by The Countryman Press
P.O. Box 748
Woodstock, VT 05091

Distributed by W. W. Norton & Company, Inc.
500 Fifth Avenue
New York, NY 10110

Printed in the United States of America
10 9 8 7 6 5 4

Acknowledgments

Christian M. Bethmann
Daniel Chazin
Cynthia L. Coritz
Dean Cramer
Rebecca Fitzgerald
German Georgieff
Robert E. Green
Warren Hale
Joan D. James
Bob Jonas
John Jurasek
Devin McCarty and Jennifer Taggart
John Mack
Jim Mershon
Kathleen Meyer
Gill Mika
John Moran
Martina and Peter Moss
Barry Orr
Estelle Parsons
Brian Sniatkowski
Bob Torres
Douglas Vorolieff
Larry Wheelock

50 Hikes in New Jersey at a Glance

HIKE	COUNTY	DISTANCE (miles)	DIFFICULTY
1. South of High Point	Sussex	6	M/S
2. Rattlesnake Swamp to Catfish Pond	Warren	5	M
3. Mount Tammany	Warren	4	M/S
4. Appalachian Trail Backpack	Sussex	28.2	S
5. Schuber Trail, End to End	Passaic/Bergen	7.2	S
6. Ramapo Lake, Ramapo Mountain State Forest	Passaic/Bergen	5.5	M
7. Ringwood Manor Circular	Passaic	3	E
8. Skylands Manor	Passaic	6.25	E/M
9. Governor Mountain	Bergen	5.5 or 2	E
10. Wyanokie Circular	Bergen	7.3	M/S
11. Carris Hill	Passaic	5	M/S
12. Torne Mountain–Osio Rock	Bergen	2.2 or 3.7	E/M
13. Terrace Pond	Passaic	4.5	M
14. Bearfort Ridge	Passaic	7	M/S
15. Pequannock Watershed	Passaic	8 to 9.5	M/S
16. Wawayanda State Park	Sussex/Passaic	7.5	E
17. Appalachian Trail Stairway to Heaven	Passaic	5	M/S
18. Pyramid Mountain	Morris	3	E/M
19. Mount Hope Historical Park	Morris	2.5	E
20. Mahlon Dickerson Reservation	Morris	4.3	E/M
21. Jenny Jump State Forest	Warren	4.5	M
22. Point Mountain	Hunterdon	3.5	M
23. Schooley's Mountain County Park	Morris	3	E
24. Black River Trails	Morris	6.6	M/S
25. Merrill Creek Reservoir	Warren	8.5	E

RISE (feet)	TIME (hours)	VIEWS	KIDS	CAMPING	X-C SKIING	FALLS	SHUTTLE	NOTES
300	4	★	★					Open ridges with views
500	3.5	★	★					Rugged and remote trail, good views
1,200	3	★						Steep climb and descent, views, heavily used
2,750	3 days	★	★			★	★	3-day backpack or walk as day hikes (use 2 cars)
800	5	★	★	★	★	★		Streams, rivers
700	3.5	★				★		Views, lake, ruined estate
250	2	★	★					History, Manor House
1,000	3	★				★		Manor house, gardens
430	3.5 or 1.25	★	★					Views
1,200	6	★						Two peaks and two mines, rock scrambling
580	4	★				★		Steep, rocky sections, good views
525–850	2+ or 3.5	★						Stunning, 360-degree views
350	3.5	★						Rock scrambling, glacial lake
1,200	5.5	★						Great views, rock ledges
400	6	★				★	O	Historic features, views, deep woods
530	4	★		★				Rhododendron stands, lakes, history
1,000	3	★						Fabulous views
390	2.5	★	★					Unusual boulders
350	2							Historic Mines, wildlife
238	3		★	★	★			Great cross-country skiing
900–950	3	★						Glacial boulders, good views
535	2–3	★				★		River, farm fields, rocky ridge
500	2.5	★				★		River gorge, history
400	4					★	★	Grist mill, river walk, meadows
800	4	★	★		★			Friendly footing, wildlife viewing

50 Hikes in New Jersey at a Glance

HIKE	COUNTY	DISTANCE (miles)	DIFFICULTY
26. Jockey Hollow	Morris	5.6	E/M
27. Scherman-Hoffman Wildlife Sanctuary	Morris	3	E
28. Palisades	Bergen	5.75	E
29. South Mountain Reservation	Essex	8.25	M
30. Watchung Reservation	Union	6	M
31. Washington Valley Park	Somerset	4	M
32. Sourland Mountain Preserve	Somerset	3.3	E/M
33. Washington Crossing to Scudder's Falls	Mercer	6	E/M
34. D & R Canal, Bull's Island to Prallsville	Somerset	3 or 6	E/M
35. D & R Canal, Kingston to Griggstown	Somerset	5 or 10	E/M
36. D & R Canal, Weston to East Millstone	Somerset	4.2	E
37. Six Mile Run Preserve	Somerset	3.5	E/M
38. Sandy Hook	Monmouth	4 or 8	E
39. Cheesequake State Park	Middlesex	4	E/M
40. Hartshorne Woods Park	Monmouth	2.5	E/M
41. Allaire State Park	Monmouth	4.5	E/M
42. Cattus Island	Ocean	3	E
43. Island Beach State Park	Ocean	3.5	E
44. Wells Mills County Park	Ocean	4.5	M
45. Bass River State Forest	Burlington/Ocean	3.7	E
46. Brendan T. Byrne (Lebanon) State Forest	Burlington	8.5	M/S
47. Carranza Memorial to Apple Pie Hill	Burlington	8.2 or 5.2	M/S
48. Mullica River Wilderness	Burlington	6 or 7	M/S
49. Parvin State Park	Salem	5	E/M
50. Belleplain State Forest, East Creek Trail	Cape May	7.2	M

RISE (feet)	TIME (hours)	VIEWS	KIDS	CAMPING	X-C SKIING	FALLS	SHUTTLE	NOTES
670	2–4	★		★				Revolutionary War historic sit
416	1.75							Open woods, history, river, some route-finding, bird watching, formal gardens
1,100	3	★	★		★			River walk, history
750	6	★		★	★			Friendly footing, Rahway River views, history. Hike can be easily shortened.
500	4			★			O	Suburban park, wildlife, museum
200	2–3	★			★			Many intersecting trails, bikes
360	2	★	★					Varied terrain, bikes
100	3		★		★			Historic features, towpath
M	2 or 3.5		★			★		Historic canal area
M	2.5 or 5	★		★				Historic features, water, easy walking
M	2		★	★			O	Good introduction to the D&R Canal
M	2		★					Brook crossing, views over farm fields
M	3 or 6	★					C	Beach and dunes walk, history
200	2	★	★	★				Mixture of forest types
160	1.5							Graded trails, varied vegetation
120	2.5		★	★				Historic bog-iron mining area, camping
M	1.5–2	★	★					Views of marsh and bay
M	2.5	★	★					Ocean and bay views
200	2							Hills in the pinelands
M	1.5–2	★		★				Sand roads, cedar bog
M	5	★		★				Explores cedar swamps and cranberry bogs
166	4–5	★		★			O	Classic Pine Barrens hiking with a view
M	4–5							Deep in the Pine Barrens
M	3		★					History, lake
M	4.5	★	★	★				Lake, fishing, beautiful woodlands

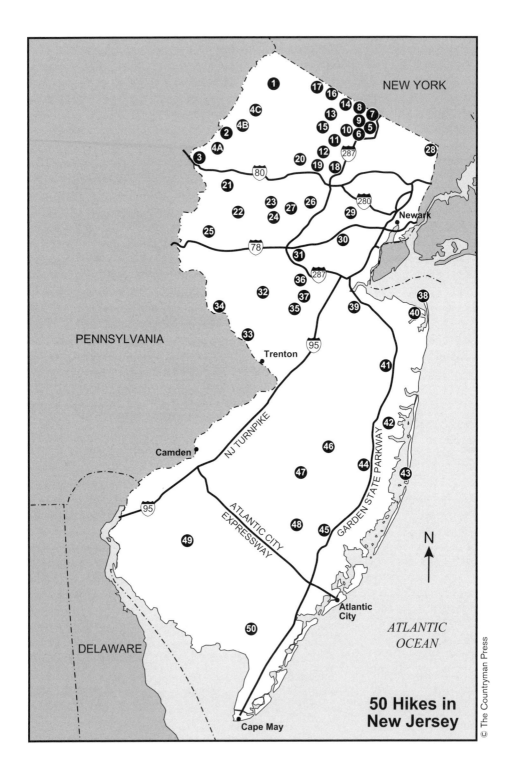

**50 Hikes in
New Jersey**

© The Countryman Press

Contents

Introduction

New Jersey boasts an abundance of fine hiking trails. The famous Appalachian Trail crosses the northern part of the state, as does most of the 150-mile Highlands Trail; the 60-mile Delaware & Raritan Canal State Park Trail crosses from New Brunswick to Raven Rock, north of Trenton; the 50-mile Batona Trail traverses the New Jersey Pinelands; and the Long Path commences its journey northward on the Palisades at the George Washington Bridge. Some trails are located on old roads and footpaths that existed prior to the acquisition of the land for public use, and some date back to the Depression and the federally funded Civilian Conservation Corps, whose members built park and recreation facilities still used today. Many trails, including the Appalachian Trail, are maintained by volunteers, whose dedication is evidenced by the fresh paint marks, water bars, and trails cleared of blowdowns and other hazards.

Hiking in the Garden State is varied, from the flat sandy trails in the southern part of the state to the hilly and rocky highlands in the north. There are swamps, beach areas, woods, and grasslands. Nine-tenths of New Jersey borders on water; of its 480 miles of boundary, all but 48 are along either the seacoast or a riverbed. Except for the northwest section, the typical New Jersey landscape is a low, flat plain filled with meandering streams; four-fifths of the state is no more than 400 feet above sea level, and most of it is less than 100. The high point, in the northwest corner, is 1,803 feet above sea level.

THE GEOLOGY AND TOPOGRAPHY OF NEW JERSEY

Geologists divide New Jersey into four primary provinces. In the northwest, running roughly southwest to northeast, is the Appalachian Ridge and Valley Province, containing the highest elevations in the state. Here, in what was once a major mountain range (since leveled by erosion), is a series of parallel valleys and ridges composed of faulted and folded Paleozoic (Cambrian to mid-Devonian) sandstones and conglomerates 540 to 375 million years old. The mountains we see today are former marine basins of sandstone, shale, and limestone, tipped by the compression of moving continental plates, which have eroded at varying rates, creating a series of parallel ridges and shallow valleys. The Ridge and Valley Province extends for more than 1,200 miles from Alabama to Canada and, because of its regularity, is used as a navigational landmark by migrating birds. Hawk sightings along the main ridges are frequent during the fall migration. The Delaware Water Gap National Recreation Area, Worthington and Stokes State Forests, and High Point State Park together preserve nearly all the mountainous portions of this province. The Appalachian Trail follows the crest of the main ridge, Kittatinny Mountain, for more than 40 miles on its way from Georgia to Maine. The hiking in this province can be challenging because of steep inclines and extremely rocky footing.

Southeast of the Ridge and Valley Province and paralleling it lies the New Jersey

Bearfort Ridge

Highlands Province. This mountainous area is composed primarily of Precambrian gneisses, granites, and schists, which formed between 750 and 1,300 million years ago. They were formerly at the bases of mountains far more ancient than those of the Ridge and Valley Province and were formed from high pressures and temperatures deep within the Earth. From a distance, the Highlands appear as a mass of elevated land at a constant elevation. But the Highlands have a very rugged topography with erratic and disconnected ridges and deep valleys between them. The elevations of the flat-topped summits characteristic of this province lie only a few hundred feet lower than those in the Kittatinny Mountains. The range extends north into New York State as the Hudson Highlands and south into Pennsylvania as the Reading Prong. Hikers will find not only more trails in this province than in any other in the state, but also numerous lakes and reservoirs. The province includes the large Wawayanda State Park and the vast holdings of the Newark Watershed Conservation and Development Corporation, which supplies drinking water to New Jersey's largest city. A number of other state and county parks and forests preserve segments of the natural features of the area.

Comprising most of northeastern and central New Jersey, the Piedmont Lowlands Province is a low-lying plain composed mainly of Mesozoic (Triassic and Jurassic) sandstones and shales dating 190 to 240 million years old. It is separated from the Highlands by a fault line that runs from Mahwah in the north to Milford on the Delaware River. The Ramapo Fault in the northern part of the state shows this distinction dramatically, the boundary being apparent to the discerning eye on both road and contour maps. The more erosion-resistant Highlands rise above the Piedmont by as much as 800 feet in this region. Within the Piedmont Province evidence of former rifting is found in a series of old lava flows that have withstood erosion better than the shales and sandstones and now stand as mountain ridges. Following the deposition of shales and sandstones, rifting of the the North American plate occurred in several places. Rifts are where a series of openings forms between the Earth's surface and the hot mantle miles below the surface. Basalt and related rock is formed from such mantle extrusions. One such rift, to the east of present-day New Jersey, continued to expand and became the Atlantic Ocean. The rift that is now in New Jersey failed to open, leaving behind a number of igneous flows and intrusions. Just across the Hudson River from New York stand the Palisades, the eastern edges of a sill of igneous rock that in places rises more than 500 feet above the river. Farther west are the Watchung Hills, roughly parallel ridges made up of the resistant edges of westward-sloping, basaltic lava flows, which also rise about 250 feet above the surrounding plans. Cushetunk Mountain and others near it are somewhat similar features called *dikes*. Composed of diabase, related to basalt, they are found in the southwestern portion of the province where it extends into central New Jersey.

Extensive development has marred much of the natural aspect of the Piedmont Lowlands Province, though a few parks offer an opportunity to explore what was once the forest frontier of the New York region. Palisades Interstate Park preserves much of the northern portion of the rock ramparts overlooking the Hudson. Several reservations along the crest of the first Watchung Ridge and the Round Valley Recreation Area on Cushetunk Mountain preserve some of the remaining high woodlands. In this province are also found several tracts of land that, although low and flat, offer some interesting hiking possibilities. The federally owned Great Swamp Wildlife Refuge and neighboring county parks have miles of trails, some on boardwalk, that penetrate the wetlands of a former glacial lake of immense proportions. From Raven Rock on the Delaware River to New Brunswick on the Raritan, the towpath of the old Delaware

& Raritan Canal (now a state park) offers the hiker 66 miles of wooded walkway along a quiet but very alive body of water. During its heyday, the canal was the scene of intense activity. In fact, for a while, the Delaware and Raritan Canal did more business than the much better known Erie Canal in New York State.

Encompassing nearly all of New Jersey south of a line drawn between New Brunswick and Trenton is the Coastal Plain, the largest geomorphic province in the state. This entire area is composed of ocean and stream deposits of sands, silts, and clays laid down during the late Mesozoic to the early Cenozoic (late Cretaceous to Miocene), 50 to 80 million years ago. The lowest elevations in the state are here, ranging from only a few hundred feet inland to water level on the seashore. From the gently rolling topography of the Pine Barrens to the sandy beaches along New Jersey's 127-mile coast, this province offers the hiker an environment very different from that found in the rest of the state. The Pine Barrens, a sparse pine and scrub oak forest of about 1 million acres, has been saved in large measure from the pressures of development. The heart of the Pinelands is preserved in several state forests, the largest of which is Wharton, headquartered at the old bog-iron-mining town of Batsto. The Batona Trail (named for the BAck TO NAture Club of Philadelphia) penetrates the forest for some 50 miles from Lake Absegami to Ong's Hat. This marked footpath passes deep cedar swamps, parallels rivers of cedar water, and climbs Apple Pie Hill, at 205 feet the highest summit in the Pine Barrens. Throughout the Pinelands are sand roads—some more than 200 years old—that make for excellent walking through this wilderness of pines.

Several areas along the Jersey coast have been preserved in their original state, in tremendous contrast to the overdevelopment that has occurred elsewhere. Here dunes, marshes, and moving sands pushed by the ocean currents present interesting walking opportunities. The New Jersey coast lies along the Atlantic Flyway, the route taken by migrating birds as they wing their way toward warmer climates. To avoid crowds, we recommend that the coast be hiked during the off-season.

LONG-DISTANCE TRAILS

Two long-distance trails pass through New Jersey, and a third is under construction. The Appalachian Trail (AT), a National Scenic Trail, enters from Pennsylvania at the Delaware Water Gap on its 2,152-mile journey from Georgia to Maine. It runs across the northwest corner of the state for approximately 80 miles and exits just east of High Point. Through-hikers are those hiking the AT's entire length; most require about 6 months on the trail and adopt trail names for the journey. Marked with white rectangles, the AT is administered by the Appalachian Trail Conservancy headquarters in Harpers Ferry, West Virginia. The name was recently changed from the Appalachian Trail Conference to the Appalachian Trail Conservancy. Originally the AT did not extend over the whole length of the Appalachian Mountains, and in the early 1990s, Dick Anderson, a former Maine Commissioner of Conservation, set in motion a move to extend the existing AT to the north, into Canada. The International Appalachian Trail (IAT) was dedicated in 1999. This trail of 690 miles to Cape Gaspé links the highest peaks in Maine, New Brunswick, and southern Quebec. The suggestion has also been made to extend the AT to the south.

The Long Path, (LP) marked in parakeet aqua, begins its northward journey at the George Washington Bridge. For years, its northern terminus was at Windham in the Catskills, but it has now been extended as far north as the Mohawk Valley. It is administered by the New York–New Jersey Trail Conference; the plan is to extend the trail into the Adirondacks. Volunteers maintain both the AT and the LP. The Shawangunk Ridge Trail (SRT) was established as a trail alternative to the LP road walk through Orange County. Only 3.1 miles are located in New Jersey—the remaining miles are in New York.

In addition, the new 150-mile Highlands Trail (HT) will link the Delaware and Hudson Rivers. It uses established trails, and some new footway is being constructed for it; where necessary, connections are made by short sections of paved road. As this book went to press, approximately 75 miles of trail were in place. When finished, the system will link 26 county, state, and federal parks, as well as forests and open spaces. It is the result of cooperation among the New York–New Jersey Trail Conference, the New Jersey Conservation Foundation, and the National Park Service. A proposal surfaced in 2005 to extend the HT into Connecticut.

THE NATURE OF HIKING

Being out in the woods does carry a certain element of risk. All hikers should be prepared with emergency gear and be able to look after themselves. Taking minimum precautions will ensure that your trip is pleasant. Enjoy your hobby.

The hikes here have been assigned a hiking time based on an average pace—perhaps with an edge toward a slow one. Every hiker develops a pace at which he or she feels most comfortable. The slow amble with frequent stops that most beginning hikers adopt soon gives way to a more rhythmic stride. It is usually best to adopt a pace that can be maintained whether the trail ascends, descends, or is level. Begin with

Ramapo Lake

short walks on a regular basis and, as skills and muscle power build, move on to more challenging hikes. In addition to the physical elation of exercising in the outdoors, hobbies such as bird-watching, tree and flower identification, wildlife observation, photography, and local history can be made a part of almost any hike.

To enjoy the outdoors requires a certain amount of planning. Study the route and allow sufficient time to complete the trip before darkness falls. It is not sensible to hike alone. A group of four people is safe and enjoyable. If someone is injured, two of the hikers can go for help while one stays with the injured party. Large groups tend to destroy the feeling of isolation obtainable in wildlands, but if you are going to hike alone, tell someone dependable where you are hiking and when you expect to return, and do not deviate from the established plan.

As a hiker, your body is your resource. It needs enough food to keep energy levels high; it needs water, above all, and it should not be pushed to the point of exhaustion. Hiking is pleasurable if adequate preparations are taken to make it so. Keep your body at a comfortable temperature—neither so warm that excessive perspiration occurs, nor so cold or wet that hypothermia becomes a problem. Getting wet, whether from rain or sweat, should be avoided. Hypothermia (once called exposure) can creep up unawares. The outdoor temperature does not have to be very low. You can become hypothermic in 50-degree weather if there is rain or wind and you are unprepared. Watch your companions for signs of poor reflex actions—excessive stumbling, the need for frequent rest stops, or a careless attitude toward clothing and equipment. Once uncontrollable shivering has started, it may only be a matter of minutes before the body temperature has cooled beyond the point of recovery. Immediate warmth for the afflicted person is the only solution.

Suitable clothing and equipment are essential as safeguards against emergencies. It is assumed—and highly recommended—that new hikers will start their hiking careers during the warmer months, so the pieces of equipment discussed here are only the basics. Winter hiking is superb, with fewer people in the woods, no bugs, and a completely different feeling from summertime hiking, but remember: Rocks may be icy, wet leaves and lichen make rocks slippery, and clothing and equipment must be adjusted to fit the conditions. Some companies now offer extremely lightweight clothing and gear.

Clothing

This is largely a matter of personal choice and the temperature of the day. We do not recommend jeans or other all-cotton pants. When cotton becomes wet, it is heavy, dries slowly, and does not retain warmth. Your breathing will be impaired if your waistband or belt is too tight. Some hikers prefer suspenders to a belt for this reason. We prefer layering as the method of dress—possibly a long-sleeved shirt over a short-sleeved T-shirt for the upper body. Be certain that clothing is loose enough not to chafe. Whatever you wear, though, avoid becoming wet with perspiration; remove layers as needed. You should also add a layer at rest stops to prevent getting chilled. For emergency use we recommend you carry a wool shirt or sweater, wool or polypropylene hat and gloves, a small flashlight, a simple first-aid kit, a pocket knife, toilet paper, and—in summer—bug repellent. In winter, you should also bring instep crampons for icy portions of the trail.

If you would be helpless without your eyeglasses, carry an extra pair.

Boots

First of all, feet must be comfortable. A few hikes in New Jersey can be walked easily in running shoes or sneakers; these may be the preferred footwear of young people for all hiking in the Garden State. However, we strongly recommend that you wear a lightweight hiking boot with effective ankle support. If you need new boots, to ensure a good fit take with you to the store the socks you plan to wear on the trail (see below). There should be ample room in the boots so your toes are not cramped, and there should not be much forward movement of your feet in them. Most good outdoor stores employ salespeople experienced enough to advise on boot choice. If possible, walk around in your home or office for several days before deciding that this is the pair. Your first hike in new boots should be a short one, and should a "hot spot" develop, stop immediately and apply moleskin or molefoam to protect the area against developing a blister.

Socks

Wear two pairs to prevent blisters: an inner pair of lightweight polypropylene or wool and an outer of thicker wool.

Rain/wind protection

Ideally, your coat should have a hood and be waterproof. The hood will prevent cold wind from penetrating between your collar and neck. There are many varieties in the stores. Remember, though, that hiking will generate perspiration, and some parkas will generate rain inside a garment even if it is not raining outside. Many hikers favor waterproof, breathable fabric such as Gore-Tex.

Pack

A lightweight day pack is indispensable for carrying those pieces of equipment essential to happiness on the trail. Most day packs are basically small backpacks that ride high on the back. Some of the newer fanny packs, as well as a hybrid called a lumbar pack, will hold nearly as much as a small backpack and may be more comfortable.

The following items are always in our packs, even for a short hike:

Water

The time has long since passed when you could be refreshed at that beautiful stream by drinking the pure, cold water. *Giardia lamblia* and other intestinal parasites and bacteria have destroyed that pleasure. Always carry a minimum of a quart of water per person, and drink it, even if you are not aware of feeling thirsty. Monitor your urine, and if it is dark, increase your water intake, particularly in colder weather when thirst is not as apparent as it is in hot.

Lunch

Even if lunch is not planned on the trail, take an emergency ration—fruit (hard fruits like apples don't bruise easily), some trail mix, a chocolate bar, or gorp (good old raisins and peanuts—with M&Ms, if you wish).

Maps

The maps in this guide, along with the text, are all you really need for these hikes. As you become experienced, though, you may want to explore areas in more depth. Each hike refers you to other maps, as keyed at the end of this introduction. For hiking in New Jersey, it is not usually necessary to carry a compass, particularly if you are on a described hike; however, if you stray from the trail, having a map and compass—and knowing how to use them—can return you to the path or to civilization. Today, the Global Positioning System (GPS) is an additional navigational tool. When used in conjunction with mapping software, a GPS unit can produce a map of the hike just walked. You will need a good New Jersey road map to find your way to the trailheads. Each hike tells you how to reach the trailhead itself, but getting to the nearby town is often up to you. New Jersey, like most states, issues an official highway map, and it is free. Write to the New Jersey Division of Travel and Tourism, PO Box 820, Trenton, NJ 08625; call 609-292-2470 or 1-800-VISITNJ (1-800-847-4865) or on the Web at www.state.nj.us/travel.

Geocaching

This is a high-tech treasure hunt. In 2000, a new dimension was added to the adventure of being outdoors. A new game called Geocaching, which uses the Global Positioning System (GPS), was designed and developed in the Seattle area and now delights more than 15,000 active participants. Caches are mostly hidden containers, sometimes plastic, sometimes metal, that contain a log book and trinkets, with its coordinates posted on a log page accessed on the Web at www.geocaching.com. Players choose code names for themselves, enter a zip code, and find listed the names and coordinates for caches in their vicinity. Then it's up to the skill of the player to use a portable GPS unit to find the treasure. The pleasure is in the hunt, though, with the cache found, the cacher signs the log using his nom de plume, replaces what he removes from the cache with an item of equal value, and then logs his find on the cache page, which keeps track of the number of "finds." It is estimated that caches exist in every US state and in more than 200 countries, and there are many variations on the main theme.

Letterboxing is a similar pastime (www.letterboxing.com) but instead of a GPS using satellites to obtain coordinates, this game uses instructions and puzzles to locate the treasure, and you need a rubber stamp and pad to validate the find. Other sites such as navicache.com are also available.

FACTS FOR HIKERS

Trail markers

The trails in the Garden State are mostly color coded with paint blazes on convenient trees. Sometimes metal or plastics tags held on by nails substitute for paint. Three blazes in a triangle indicate the beginning or the end of a trail, and major turns are indicated by two blazes with the turn direction indicated by the upper blaze. A trail is a dynamic entity and rerouting takes place frequently; the original paint blazes are then painted out, but are often still visible for some years.

Ideally, markers are spaced so that you can easily see the next as you move along the trail. At times, markers become obscured by new growth or blowdowns, and their clarity also varies from time to time. The hikes described in this book are mostly on marked trails, and we have noted where markers are indistinct or missing. Markers tend to be prolific where you need to be alert.

Ticks and Chiggers

During the hot summer, in grassy areas with damp soils, hikers may come into contact with chiggers. Chiggers are a species of mite and are parasitic on humans only in the juvenile stage of their life cycle. They are extremely small and are only noticed by the itchy red spots that appear after the mite has attached itself to the skin. Welts may appear for several days after exposure as the mites move around the body. Immersion of the affected areas with alcohol is recommended as a treatment.

Ticks are a problem in New Jersey and other nearby states. Lyme disease is not to be trifled with. The deer tick *(Ixodes scapularis)* that carries Lyme disease is very small (the size of a period in this text). Do not confuse it with the common wood tick, which is the size of a match head, or—when engorged with blood—the size of a pea. Deer ticks are more abundant in shore areas where deer are common. A bite from an infected deer tick will result in a rash (sometimes, but not always, in the shape of a bull's-eye), which should be immediately treated by a doctor. Learn to look for and remove ticks after hiking in an infested area. Long-sleeved shirts and pants with the legs tucked into socks are a must in these areas. Spray your feet and legs with a tick repellent containing DEET. A flier on Lyme disease is available from the New Jersey State Department of Health, PO Box 360, Trenton, NJ 08625; call 609-292-7837. Or check the Web site of the New York–New Jersey Trail Conference at www.nynjtc.org.

Wildlife

The black bear is the largest animal in New Jersey, and is native to the Garden State. In recent years, the bear population has increased, particularly in areas close to Pennsylvania, and near areas in New Jersey where new homes are invading the territory once exclusively the domain of these animals.

Food smells attract bears, and in many cases they learn that where there are campsites there will be food. When camping, it is advisable to use a commercial bear-proof box (available from outdoors stores) to store all foods, as well as such items as soap, deodorant, and toothpaste. Never store anything edible in the tent or shelter, and prepare meals at least 100 feet away from your tent. Do not take the clothing worn for cooking into the tent, because food odors and food spatters cling to fabric.

The next best protection for food is to string it high in odor-proof bundles from a tree branch, making sure that the packages hang at least 10 feet off the ground, and well away from the tree's trunk. Bears are smart animals and have been known to retrieve these caches, so it is advisable to use a tree branch well away from your tent. There is a trend among parks to supply metal bear-proof lockers to campers, and you should use these if they are available.

If a bear should come into camp, banging pots will sometimes scare the animal away. Remember, though, that a human is smaller than a bear—males usually weigh between 135 and 350 pounds.

Information and advice on black bears is available on the New Jersey Division of Fish and Wildlife Web site at www.njfishand wildlife.com. Click on the Black Bear link in the Education pane.

Because rodents have sharp teeth and are good climbers, they can cause much damage to packs and tents if they detect food smells, so similar precautions should be taken to store food items away from camp.

Mountain bikes

When this book was first published in 1987, there were no bicycles on New Jersey trails. But modern technology has produced a rugged bicycle that can withstand trail use, and today's mountain bikes can traverse terrain once reserved for the hiker alone. The popularity of these new bicycles has been phenomenal, and by the early 1990s many New Jersey trails had experienced sharp increases in use. User conflicts soon arose, and continue to be a problem in many places. Mountain bike riders assumed that the trails made and maintained by hikers were there for them to share. Hikers resented the encroachment and trail destruction mountain bikes can cause—though mountain-biking proponents often deny these problems—and fought to have them banned or limited in parks and forests, because mountain bikes create

many erosion problems and intrude on the natural setting many hikers seek. Equestrians resented the speed at which some bikers travel along trails, scaring their horses. These problems are still with us, and policies are constantly being shaped and reshaped. If mountain biking is of concern to you, you may wish to contact the park or forest in which you will be hiking for information on policies and complaints, or to express your opinion.

Parking fees

Many state parks and forests charge moderate fees for parking, normally between Memorial Day weekend and Labor Day weekend. Weekday rates are lower than weekend rates, and Tuesdays are free. A New Jersey State Park pass is available that provides free entry to all parks for one year. State residents older than 62 can obtain a free parking pass, good at any time. Apply at any park or forest office.

Hunting

New Jersey has a short deer hunting season, usually in December. A short bear hunting season was established recently, though it may not become a permanent feature. Avoid hiking in hunting areas during firearms season. Check with the local park office, the New Jersey Department of Environmental Protection, or the New York–New Jersey Trail Conference for specific dates. As of this writing, there is no hunting in New Jersey on Sundays.

TRAIL ETIQUETTE

There is a certain etiquette to hiking. Two of the most important phrases to remember are the familiar "take only photographs, leave only footprints" and "carry out what you carry in." If every user of our woods followed these guidelines, litter would not be a problem. Many concerned hikers carry empty garbage bags in their packs and toward the end of the hike pick up litter and carry it out.

Some trails border or actually cross private property. NO TRESPASSING signs should be honored and care taken to respect private landowners by not damaging fences or trees and by not littering. A few thoughtless walkers can damage good relations built up over the years with trail neighbors.

On the trail, give way to the person walking uphill. If there are trail registers, carefully fill out the first register on your hike, and sign out at the last.

On overnights at existing shelters, remember that lean-tos should be available for all who need to use them. On those wet and windy nights, make room cheerfully for latecomers. Pack away all evidence that you have been there, and leave the shelter exactly as you would wish to find it on arrival.

Before beginning your backpacking hike, check whether fires are permitted in the area. Rules are changing, mostly in the direction of banning them. When fires are permitted, no live trees should be cut for firewood, and the fire should be contained in the fireplace provided at many shelters. It is courteous to gather enough dead wood so that the next occupant can at least get another fire started. Wood is in short supply in frequently camped areas. Whether you build them for atmosphere or for smudge (keeping mosquitoes away), keep fires small and safe. A small, lightweight backpacking stove is preferable for cooking. These are inexpensive, cook quickly, and keep pots unblackened.

There are certain areas in the United States—on the beaches of the Colorado River in the Grand Canyon, for instance—where human body waste has become such a problem that now it is required that all human excrement be carried out. With the increasing number of people using New Jersey trails, it is not unthinkable that in the future we might all be required to carry out our personal waste. To avoid this inconvenience, use the outhouse where one is provided, and otherwise be a "copy cat"–act as a feline does. Choose a spot far away from any water and the trail, remove the layer of leaves and twigs, dig a hole at least 3 inches deep in the soil with either a rock or a sturdy stick (some hikers carry a special trowel for this purpose), take care of your business, cover the whole mess over so that no disturbance is apparent, and take out the used toilet paper. Double Baggies work well.

HIKING ORGANIZATIONS

The umbrella organization for hiking in New Jersey is the New York–New Jersey Trail Conference (NYNJTC), a nonprofit federation of 10,000 individuals and 85 hiking and environmental organizations working to build and maintain trails and to preserve open space. Its trail network includes more than 1,600 miles of foot trails. Formed in 1920, the Conference built the first section of the Appalachian Trail in 1923.

The Conference is supported by dues, publication sales, and donations–along with thousands of hours of volunteer time. Members receive the bimonthly *Trail Walker,* and can purchase maps and guides at a significant discount, avail themselves of the Conference library, and obtain a 10 percent discount on purchases at many outdoors stores. At present, dues are $25 for individuasl, $18 for students and retirees, and $31 for families. A single life membership is $500; a couple or family membership is $750.

We encourage you to support the people who maintain the trails. The NYNJTC office is located on US 202 just north of its junction with NJ 17. Reach the Conference by mail at 156 Ramapo Valley Road, Mahwah, NJ 07430-1199, call 201-512-9348, or find them on the Web at www.nynjtc.org.

There are also many fine hiking clubs in New Jersey, catering to all grades of hikers in many areas of the state. These clubs are an excellent way to meet people who share your love of the outdoors. The clubs are your ticket to the special natural sections of your area and will help you learn the ins and outs of hiking in the Northeast. For a listing, send a self-addressed, stamped envelope to the New York–New Jersey Trail Conference at the address above or at www.nynjtc.org.

Volunteers maintain many of the trails described in this book. Respect their work and their tender loving care, and do not cut corners on switchbacks or otherwise erode the trail unnecessarily. If you'd like to help maintain a trail, contact the New York–New Jersey Trail Conference.

MAP KEY

USGS

Topographic quadrangle maps are available for all parts of the United States. For a New Jersey index, write to the United States Geological Survey, Branch of Information Services, Box 25286, Denver Federal Center, Denver, CO 80225. You can call USGS at 303-202-4700 or find them on the Web at www.usgs.gov. The USGS maps mentioned in this guidebook are all 7.5' quads. They were not designed with hikers in mind and often do not show the trails—or show them incorrectly. The exception to this generalization is the Pinelands, where USGS topos clearly show nearly all the sand roads in the area. Despite their drawbacks, USGS maps depict general topography superbly, which is why we have used them as the base maps for the hikes in this book. The New Jersey index also lists retail stores throughout the state that sell these maps over the counter. USGS maps are also available from the New Jersey Geological Survey, Bureau of Revenue, New Jersey Department of Environmental Protection, PO Box 438, Trenton, NJ 08625-0417; phone 609-777-1038. A catalog is available.

NYNJTC

The *New York–New Jersey Trail Conference* publishes and sells waterproof, color topographic maps, usually in sets. Contact them at 156 Ramapo Valley Road, Mahwah, NJ 07430-1199. Call 201-512-9348, or find them on the Web at www.nynjtc.org.

NJWB

Topographic color maps printed in the rear of the *New Jersey Walk Book,* 2nd edition, by the New York–New Jersey Trail Conference, are available in many bookstores or directly from the Conference. This book, together with the *New York Walk Book,* 7th edition, is regarded by many as the hiker's bible.

DEP

These are sketch maps, usually free, from the various state park and forest offices. Or, write to the New Jersey Department of Environmental Protection, Division of Parks and Forestry, PO Box 402, Trenton, NJ 08625; call 1-800-843-6420.

NPS

National Park maps, usually free, are available from individual park offices. Addresses are in the hike text.

Ridge and Valley

1

South of High Point

Total distance: 6 miles

Hiking time: 4 hours

Vertical rise: 300 feet

Rating: Moderate to strenuous

Maps: USGS Port Jervis South; NYNJTC North Kittatinny Trails #18; NJWB #18; DEP High Point State Park map

South of High Point Monument and the popular Lake Marcia is a section of High Point State Park (1480 State Route 23, Sussex, NJ 07461; 973-875-4800, www .njparksandforests.org) that is wild, expansive, scenic, and lightly used. In contrast, the portion of the park that is north of NJ 23 is heavily used. The Appalachian Trail (AT) passes through this southern section, and the Rutherford shelter, one of the few New Jersey AT trail shelters, is also found here. A warning is in order. If you have not had any experience with this section of the AT, or if your feet are particularly sensitive, be prepared for a rocky path that will test your boots. The first 2 miles of this hike will be demanding on your feet and on your balance. Most people prefer to do the hike in the direction described below, because the second leg of the hike is on a flat woods road. You'll get the worst done first.

HOW TO GET THERE

The trailhead is just east of the High Point State Park Visitor Contact Station in Sussex County. Take NJ 23 to the Visitor Contact Station at the top of Kittatinny Ridge on the south side of the highway. Stop in at the office for a map or a permit if you are camping and leaving your car overnight. Park at the AT parking area, which you can reach via a driveway found about 200 feet east of the office on the same side of NJ 23. The trailhead is found here.

THE TRAIL

From the back of the parking area near the directory, enter the woods on a path marked

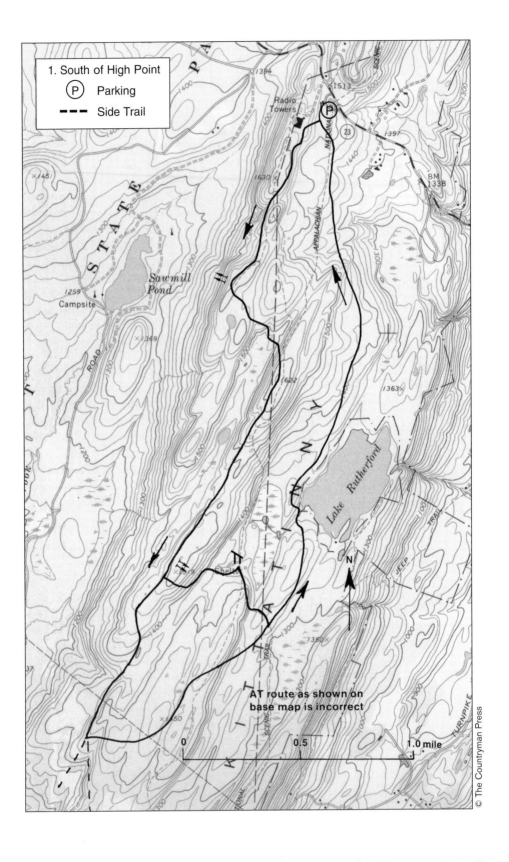

1. South of High Point

Ⓟ Parking

- - - Side Trail

AT route as shown on
base map is incorrect

0   0.5   1.0 mile

© The Countryman Press

by two large granite blocks. This trail, marked with both the white markers of the AT and the yellow markers of the Mashipacong Trail, quickly turns left and heads south. In another 200 yards you will arrive at a trail junction that is marked by signs and a strange, vertically placed drainpipe. At this four-way junction, where the yellow trail turns right and the Iris Trail starts on your left, walk straight ahead, now following only the white markers of the AT.

After only a short distance, the AT begins to climb. There will be a large cliff (more like a wall) on your right as you ascend along a man-made embankment. The next section of the AT passes through a beautiful stretch of trail and forest. In places pine needles cover the rocky trail, which winds through huge fern fields under oak, maple, and large white pines. The trail follows the eastern side of a ridge for a while, then swings over to the western side. Your feet will notice that the rocks are particularly jagged in this section, a characteristic of the AT in Pennsylvania and New Jersey. You'll pass a junction with the Blue Dot Trail, which descends steeply and reaches Sawmill Lake below in about 0.5 mile. Vistas along the trail in this section offer good views of this lake and beyond—including the Delaware River and Pennsylvania. The AT next turns away from this ridge and descends steeply over rocks into a valley.

After climbing a parallel ridge to the east, the AT again turns south, reaching a series of rocky outcrops vegetated only sparsely with pitch pines and scrub oaks. For the next mile the trail is quite rugged and very rocky in places as it passes through first this ragged forest and then an oak and maple woods. After a long and gradual descent, the trail arrives at a series of openings offering some of the best views on this hike.

Here is Dutch Shoe Rock, a long, glacially polished rock slab of Silurian sandstone that offers a tremendous vista to the east. Lake Rutherford and a large marsh are just to your left. In the distance are Pochuck Mountain and Wawayanda Mountain, both traversed by the AT farther north. As you walk south on the AT, the vistas over the enormous slab continue. The best viewpoint is located about 150 feet north of a trail junction, where a blue-blazed trail leads down the slope to the Rutherford AT shelter.

You have two options at this point. The first, which is all on good trail but will add about 0.5 mile to your hike, is to continue following the AT south for another 0.8 mile to its junction with the red-blazed Iris Trail. Turn left here and follow the red markers through a deep woods. The Iris Trail utilizes an old woods road that will feel positively soft after those first few miles on the jagged rocks of the AT. Keep left at a junction, staying with the red markers, and soon you will arrive at the west shore of Lake Rutherford. The trail description from there follows below.

Your other choice is somewhat more adventurous but definitely worth considering if you are backpacking. You can take the blue trail down to the shelter, then pick up an old woods road that leads east out to the Iris Trail. From the AT, follow the blue markers down the steep slope and onto the eastward-trending footpath to the shelter. You'll cross over a small stream and pass a rock-lined spring that feeds a small brook along the way. The Rutherford shelter is one of the more remote AT shelters in New Jersey. The presence of large lilac bushes around it reveals that it was built on land that was once farmed. In back of the shelter are a number of attractive campsites at the edge of the marsh you saw earlier. This remote area is a good place for lunch or a snack, and of

Dutch Shoe Rock

Trail in about 0.5 mile. Turn left here and walk another 0.5 mile or so to the west shore of Lake Rutherford. On the way you will cross over one of the small brooks that feed the lake. Here the bright red cardinal flower, a type of *Lobelia,* blooms during the summer.

Regardless of which option you chose, you are now on the west shore of Lake Rutherford, a reservoir that meets the water needs of the town of Sussex. Where the Iris Trail comes closest to the lake, look for a side trail that will take you to a rocky overlook near the shore of the lake. Lake Rutherford is quite large and, except for one distant building, is uninhabited and quite wild. Unfortunately, swimming is not permitted.

On leaving the lake, continue northward on the Iris Trail through a dark and dense forest. The trail, now covered with fine gravel, gradually widens in this section and is used in the winter by snowmobiles and cross-country skiers. Low rock outcroppings line the trail in places. Forest birds, such as the rufous-sided towhee, are often seen hopping in the bushes. The seldom seen Swainson's thrush, with its ethereal call, also inhabits these woods. The trail gradually rises through a more open forest that is filled with lowbush blueberry bushes, then descends through a mixed oak forest with an understory of ferns. After crossing a small brook on a footbridge, the trail heads uphill and eventually arrives at the junction where you began the loop. Turn right here and follow the white markers back to your car.

course for primitive camping—except during times when insects are biting.

To continue with this option, leave the shelter, following a path that exits the small clearing in front of the shelter. This path, actually an old woods road, is not heavily used, nor is it maintained. Parts of it are grassy and mossy, parts are quite wet, and there may be a few blowdowns blocking the path. For a ways, off to your left, you will see the large marsh in back of the shelter. This marsh is the remnant of a lake shown on older maps. The path rises gradually, crests a small ridge, descends, and then meets the red-blazed Iris

BCS

2

Rattlesnake Swamp to Catfish Pond

Total distance: 5 miles

Hiking time: 3.5 hours

Vertical rise: 500 feet

Rating: Moderate

Maps: USGS Flatbrookville; NYNJTC South Kittatinny Trails #16; NJWB #16; NPS Millbrook Area Trails map

This loop hike in the heart of the Kittatinnies skirts the edge of a swamp, passes a lake, and then climbs to an excellent overlook from the ridge. The area is still not heavily used, and if you are hiking during the week, your chance of encountering others is minimal. Though you probably will not see any rattlesnakes (which are on the endangered species list and very rare), prepare for a very rocky trail by wearing sturdy boots with good ankle support. An overnight option is possible by making arrangements to stay at the AMC's Mohican Outdoor Center.

The Appalachian Mountain Club (AMC) is a Boston-based hiking club that has a strong presence in the White Mountains of New Hampshire and several other areas in New England. The club was founded in 1876 and was a model for the Sierra Club, founded in 1892. The AMC's Mohican Outdoor Center (formerly Camp Mohican) might be called a guide center: it is part nature center, part hotel, and part conference center. Workshops are held on weekends, covering topics such as backpacking, canoeing, and birding. Hikers may stay overnight for a fee in one of their cabins or at a walk-in campsite. Since the AMC has been at Camp Mohican, the trails in the area have been well maintained. On the second weekend of each summer month, volunteers do trail work in exchange for lodging. The Mohican Outdoor Center is at 50 Camp Road, Blairstown, NJ 07825-9655. Call 908-362-5670, or check the Web site at www.mohicanoutdoorcenter .com. Call ahead for rates and availability if you plan to stay overnight.

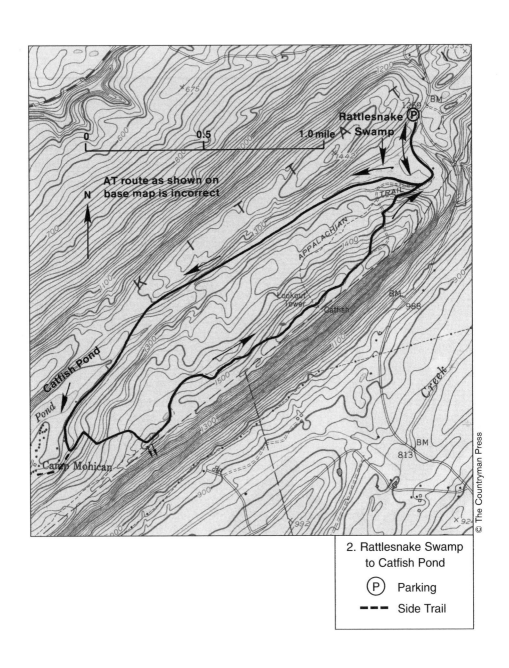

AT route as shown on
base map is incorrect

N

Rattlesnake
Swamp

1.0 mile

Catfish Pond

Pond

Camp Mohican

APPALACHIAN TRAIL

Lookout
Tower

Catfish

BM
988

Creek

BM
813

© The Countryman Press

2. Rattlesnake Swamp
to Catfish Pond

Ⓟ Parking

— — — Side Trail

HOW TO GET THERE

From exit 12 on I-80, take County Road 521 north to Blairstown. After about 5 miles, you'll come to a junction with NJ 94. Make a left here and, after another 0.2 mile, turn right at the light. Drive through part of Blairstown on Bridge Street. Do *not* make the sharp right on CR 521. When you come to the end of Bridge Street at the top of a sharp rise, bear right and then make the next left. This road, Millbrook-Blairstown Road (CR 602), will take you 6.2 miles to the top of the ridge where the Appalachian Trail (AT) crosses the road. You'll see the ridge and the fire tower looming in front of you a mile before you approach the area. Parking for a few cars can be found near the gate on the left side of the road (don't block the gate). Additional parking is located on the right about 150 yards west in a small area just off the road, and also on the left farther ahead.

THE TRAIL

Begin hiking south from the gate on a gravel road, following the white markers of the AT. Pass an AT trail sign then cross a small brook. In an area with several clearings (no camping allowed), the gravel road veers to the right, entering a corridor through a jungle of immense rhododendrons. Rattlesnake Swamp appears on your right with its hemlock, ferns, mosses, and skunk cabbage. Take note where the AT turns left off the gravel road, heading uphill through the rhododendron. Continue straight ahead past this junction and Rattlesnake Springs (50 feet ahead on the left) and then look for the orange markers of the Rattlesnake Swamp Trail. At a signed junction, the orange markers will lead you to the right, off the gravel road and onto a cut footpath. The footing, typical of trails on the Kittatinny Ridge, becomes extremely rocky almost immediately.

Amanita *toadstool*

The Rattlesnake Swamp Trail continues to the left of and slightly above Rattlesnake Swamp. Some sections are deep and dark, dominated by hemlock and other shade plants, while other areas, with dead trees and high ostrich ferns, are open to the sun. As you leave the swamp, the trail, now traversing a thick growth of mountain laurel, enters a deep hemlock grove. Farther along the footing becomes mossy and in places quite wet. Cross over a small brook and begin to climb toward higher ground and more open forest.

Don't be surprised if you startle a deer in this section, sending it crashing through the brush. After a stretch of much drier woods, the trail descends and crosses a small brook twice. Immediately after the second crossing, notice a large swamp (part of the drainage that feeds Catfish Pond) to your right. About 45 minutes to an hour into the hike, Catfish Pond appears through the trees on your right.

As you walk past the northern end of the pond, enjoy the views of lily-covered water against the steep western banks, some of which are bare of foliage because of rockslides. The sounds of frogs fill the air in spring and summer. The trail follows a rocky old road lined with both low- and highbush blueberries. The highbush blueberries, ripe in late July and early August, are delicious. Catfish Pond is the centerpiece of Camp Mohican, which includes several buildings and is leased from the federal government by the Appalachian Mountain Club.

The Rattlesnake Swamp Trail will gradually veer away from the pond and soon come to a junction—just past a concrete slab—where a sign indicates a turn to the left. (A right turn here leads to the Mohican Outdoor Center and views of Catfish Pond.) To continue the hike, turn left and after only a few hundred feet, the orange markers will direct you to turn left again onto a road leading uphill. Just after the road swings to the right, the trail turns off the road onto a footpath and begins to climb the Kittatinny Ridge in earnest. The ascent is quite steep and takes you over large rocks and through clumps of laurel. After a few minutes of work, there is a temporary respite where the trail levels off before it resumes climbing, this time not so steeply. After meandering through another level section, the trail climbs once more, leading to the flat, level summit of the Kittatinny Ridge.

Here, among dense huckleberry bushes, a vast vista of forest and farmland opens up through the trees. Just a few steps ahead is a junction with the AT and a magnificent view over cliffs to the east and south.

After resting from the climb and enjoying the spectacular view, return to the junction and head north, following the white markers of the AT. The trail twists and winds along the broad summit through a parklike, open area of trees and grass. To the right are vistas out to the eastern horizon. After about a half hour of walking, arrive at the Catfish Pond fire tower, which is operational and manned during the fire season. Climb the tower for views in all directions. On a clear day even the distant Catskills to the north are visible.

Continue straight ahead on the AT, which now follows the utility road allowing access to the fire tower and passes several campsites. Watch where the AT veers off to the left from this service road and begins to descend the ridge through an open area covered with blueberry bushes and ferns. The AT joins the service road again, now gravel, for a few hundred feet before turning right, back into the woods on a cut trail. After a descent through dark woods on a rocky trail under a power line, bear right. After another 200 yards, the AT joins the gravel road once again, this time near Rattlesnake Springs, which you passed early in the hike. A right turn here will lead via the AT to the gate and your car.

BCS

3

Mount Tammany

Total distance: 4 miles

Hiking time: 3 hours

Vertical rise: 1,200 feet

Rating: Moderately strenuous

Maps: USGS Portland, Bushkill; NYNJTC South Kittatinny Trails #15; NJWB #15; NPS Kittatinny Point Area Trails map; NY–NJ Appalachian Trail Guide map #6

Overlooking the Delaware River on the New Jersey side of the Delaware Water Gap stands Mount Tammany. This mountain, a portion of the Kittatinny Ridge and located within Worthington State Forest and the Delaware Water Gap National Recreation Area (Bushkill, PA 18324; 908-496-4458, www.nps.gov/delua), offers one of the steepest climbs in all of New Jersey as well as spectacular views from its summit. Because of its easy access from I-80, the trail to the summit is heavily used year-round, especially in summer. Also in the area are Dunnfield Creek with its many falls and cascades, the Appalachian Trail (AT), and Sunfish Pond, making this location a major natural area in the state.

The Delaware Water Gap, certainly one of the scenic wonders of New Jersey, is a 1,200-foot-deep gorge carved by the waters of the Delaware River through the long, wall-like Kittatinny Ridge. Back in Cretaceous times, roughly 100 million years ago, the Water Gap did not exist. The entire area, which was once very mountainous, had been worn down by erosion to a flat plain that sloped gently toward the Atlantic Ocean some 40 miles away. The streams that drained the land meandered through this landscape on their way to the sea. In the late Cretaceous Period the land began to rise, and the streams began cutting deeper channels.

As the land rose, the ancestral Delaware River found itself confronted with a major barrier—the relatively resistant rock that makes up the Kittatinny Ridge. This rock,

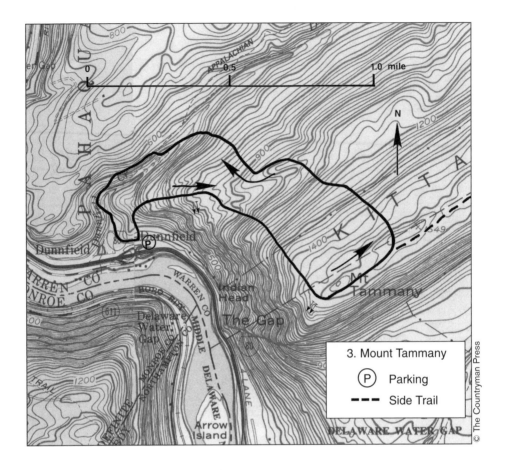

made of the tough sandstone and conglomerate of the Shawangunk Formation, dips to the north at the entrance to the gap. These rocks and the red rocks that overlie them are warped into many folds. The cross section of the ridge exposed by the gap is a geology lesson in itself. Right at the gap, the Kittatinny Ridge is fractured, its long continuity broken. Because of this structural weakness, the Delaware River has successfully maintained its course through this section of the Kittatinny Ridge. Today, the river continues to cut and remove rock as the land continues to rise slowly.

HOW TO GET THERE

Take I-80 west to the Delaware Water Gap. As the highway enters the gap itself, turn off to the right, following signs to a rest area. Pass the rest area parking, pass the underpass beneath I-80 on the left, and turn right into a second parking area. A sign here reads DUNNFIELD CREEK NATURAL AREA.

If you miss the turnoff to the rest area, take the next exit off the highway—the last exit in New Jersey—and follow signs to the Delaware Water Gap National Recreation Area Kittatinny Point Information Center. You will be able to find the parking area by passing the visitor center, crossing back under I-80, and bearing left. The trailhead is in the parking area for the AT and Sunfish Pond.

THE TRAIL

Begin the hike on the River Ridge (or Red Dot) Trail, which leaves the parking area near its entrance. The trail, marked with red-on-white markers painted on trees, follows some steps and heads back toward the rest area parking. It soon merges with a branch of the trail leading up from the rest area parking and then begins to climb, a foreshadowing of things to come. After this brief elevation gain, the trail levels off, temporarily paralleling Dunnfield Creek, well below on the left. Where the trail turns sharply right, it begins a steady climb on a well-used, rocky path lined with evergreens, hemlocks, and rhododendrons. The sounds of the falls on Dunnfield Creek, even farther below now, are still in the distance. Watch for where the trail turns right, climbing over tilted but parallel beds of sedimentary rock.

After this last climb, you'll arrive at the first of several overlooks. Here, at the edge of a steep cliff and exposed to the elements, cedar trees struggle for survival. Below, looking south, the Delaware Water Gap opens in front of you. Mount Minsi on the Pennsylvania side is to the right and Mount Tammany to the left. Mount Minsi, which rises 1,463 feet above sea level, is named after the Native Americans who lived in the area. Mount Tammany, at 1,527 feet, is named after the Lenni-Lenape chief Tamenund.

After skirting a few more viewpoints, the trail crosses a brook and then passes a reliable spring on the left. After this brief respite, it once again begins seriously climbing the mountain ridge. Because of the rocky terrain, climbing this section is difficult in any season, but it can be particularly challenging and

Lady's Slipper

even dangerous in icy conditions. First you cross a boulder field; then, through a beautiful forest of hemlock and rhododendron, you must navigate a steep rock slab. Use both your feet and your hands when you need to, while still paying attention to the markers so as not to lose the trail. After leveling off temporarily through a more open forest, the trail begins climbing again on a rocky footpath high on the ridge. From here to the summit, the forest is sparse, offering little protection from the winds. Along the way, you will find a cedar-lined viewpoint on the right.

Just before you reach the summit, notice that the forest to the left is more open; a fire burned over this area some years ago. The former oak forest is being replaced by thick laurel growth. Finally you reach the summit. Here the oak forest stops at the edge of a 1,200-foot cliff overlooking the Delaware River. Only scrub oak and pitch pine survive in this rocky, exposed environment. At the summit area, walk to the right and down

Mount Tammany

over the exposed rocks, which offer you an expansive view west to Mount Minsi and the Blue Mountain Ridge behind it. The Pocono Plateau of Pennsylvania stretches out to the horizon in the north; in the south the plains of the Great Valley, and beyond it the Reading Prong section of the Highlands, extend to the horizon. If you walk down the exposed rocks of the summit you will see the Indian Head profile—located on a portion of the cliff below and to the north (upriver) of the viewpoint—staring out over the river.

From the summit follow the trail, now marked with blue, away from the overlook area. Heading northeast, the trail meanders along the summit ridge for about 0.25 mile, then bears sharply left near a viewpoint through the trees to the east. Do *not* continue straight ahead or follow the gray markers. A sign indicates that you are on the Blue Dot Trail.

After a long, steady descent from the ridge over rocks, the trail swings to the left toward the river, following a nearly level walkway. Finally, after a long walk, the Blue Dot Trail arrives at Dunnfield Creek near one of its many falls. The trail, now concurrent with the green-blazed Dunnfield Creek Trail, bears left and then right, crossing the creek on a wooden bridge. Here in this dark hemlock gorge are numerous cascades and plunge pools, the white water creating a sharp contrast to the dark rock it glides over. Along with some spectacular rock, water, and plant scenery, you may encounter many people, including families with small children, men wearing ties, and women wearing high heels, who have stopped in their travels along I-80 to look at the ravine. For some, this may be their first experience with a natural area.

After following the right bank of the creek for a short distance, the Blue Dot Trail reaches its terminus as shown by three markers on a tree. From here, follow the white markers of the AT downhill along the stream, and cross the creek again on a wooden bridge. Leave the AT here—it bears to the right—and follow the pathway out to the parking area.

BCS

4

Appalachian Trail Backpack

Total distance: 28.2 miles

Hiking time: 17 hours—allow 3 days, 2 nights

Vertical rise: 2,750 feet

Rating: Strenuous

Maps: USGS Portland, Bushkill, Flatbrook-ville, Culvers Gap; NYNJTC North and South Kittatinny Trails, #15, #16, and #17; NJWB #15, #16, and #17; NY–NJ Appalachian Trail Guide maps #5 and #6

Most hikers know that the Appalachian Trail (AT) is a marked footpath extending 2,000 miles from Springer Mountain, Georgia, to Mount Katahdin, Maine. The first stretch of trail was built in the 1920s in Bear Mountain–Harriman State Parks in New York State. A crew from the Civilian Conservation Corps cut the last section on a remote ridgeline in Maine between Spaulding and Sugarloaf Mountains in the summer of 1937. Trail markers are white rectangles; side trails to water, viewpoints, and shelters are marked in blue.

The AT is often rerouted, so if you find a discrepancy between the markers and the guide or map, follow the markers. This backpacking trip begins at the Delaware Water Gap and follows the ridge of the Kittatinny Mountains generally north through Worthington State Forest and the Delaware Water Gap National Recreation Area. The terrain is rocky, and we recommend that you wear sturdy hiking boots instead of sneakers. The hike is rated as strenuous because of the need for a backpack.

Squirrels and chipmunks are numerous and are always attracted to campsites where food scraps are available. Their sharp teeth can do a tremendous amount of damage to tents and packs. You must protect your food from bears as well as from smaller animals. The numbers of black bears in New Jersey have escalated in recent years, making it essential to use proper bear-resistant hanging procedures. Please read the section on bears in the introduction to this book.

Most natural water sources along the trail are liable to be contaminated, so you should purify all water by boiling, filtering, chemical treatment, or a combination. Open ground fires are not permitted in the Delaware Water Gap National Recreation Area, so a portable camp stove is essential. Camping is permitted along the trail with certain restrictions, and you should check on regulations with the ranger at the Delaware Water Gap Visitor Center before setting out.

Because the term "rattlesnake" is used frequently in these parts, hikers often assume that timber rattlesnakes are numerous. In fact, this snake is on the New Jersey list of endangered and rare wildlife species. Do not meddle with any snakes you encounter. However, most retreat quickly unless interfered with.

This hike requires transportation at each end. The best arrangement is to leave the majority of cars at the end point, using as few cars as possible to transport all the hikers back to the other trailhead. If you are willing to do some investigation on where cars should be placed, you could walk the three following sections of the AT as day hikes.

HOW TO GET THERE

Leave one car at Culvers Gap—the end point of this hike—at the parking lot on Sunrise Mountain Road. To reach this lot from US 206, turn east onto Upper North Shore Road just north of Culvers Lake, 3.4 miles northwest of Branchville, then immediately turn left onto Sunrise Mountain Road. The lot is at the first bend on the left (west) side of the road.

Drive to the Delaware Water Gap. You can park either at the Delaware Water Gap National Recreation Area Information Center south of I-80 at the gap; or at the Dunn-

field Creek Natural Area. The latter lot, which is east of the information center, is often crowded. It can be reached by turning left at the underpass under I-80, then making another left onto a paved road. Go to the parking lot on the right with the sign DUNNFIELD CREEK NATURAL AREA. For more information, write to the Delaware Water Gap National Recreation Area Information Center, Bushkill, PA 18324; call 570-588-2451; or check the Web site at www.nps.gov/dewa.

THE TRAIL

First Day
Delaware Water Gap to
Catfish Fire Tower
Total distance first day: 12.6 miles
Hiking time: 7 hours
Vertical rise: 1,000 feet

Hoist your backpack and enter the woods at the far end of the Dunnfield Creek Natural Area parking lot. Follow the stream's right bank until the trail crosses a substantial wooden bridge and parallels the stream on the opposite side. The trail leads steadily upward, away from the stream, through a mixture of deciduous and coniferous trees and ferns. Look to the right: you can see distinct layers of rock on the opposite bank. Look down as you climb high above the stream to see numerous pools and waterfalls and enjoy this delightfully cool section.

Back on the main trail, 0.5 mile from the start of the hike, the woods road forks. There is a metal sign with a painted map at this junction, and the blue trail to Mount Tammany leads away to the right. Follow the left trail through small sweet chestnut trees, which will probably never reach maturity because of blight; the disease practically destroyed these trees in the 1930s. The blue trail and Dunnfield Creek are visible below.

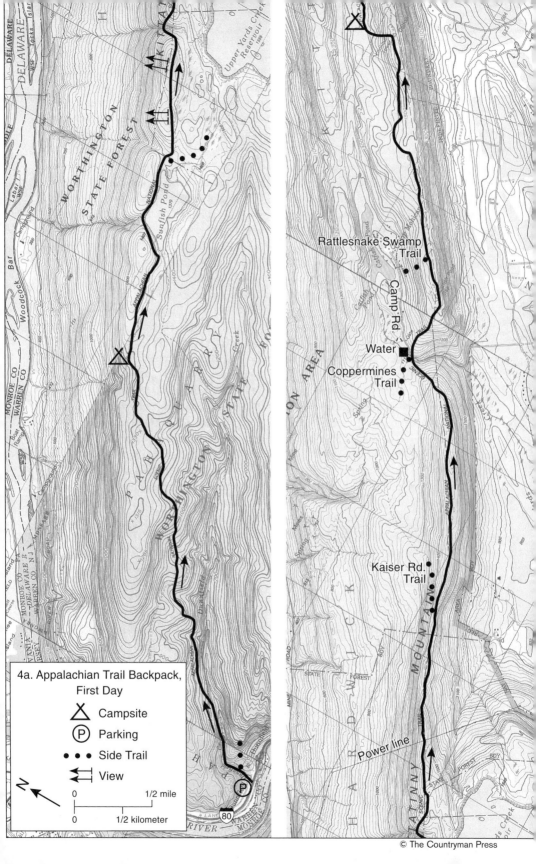

4a. Appalachian Trail Backpack,
First Day

△ Campsite

Ⓟ Parking

●●● Side Trail

◄═ View

0   1/2 mile

0   1/2 kilometer

N

Rattlesnake Swamp
Trail

Camp Rd.

Water

Coppermines
Trail

Kaiser Rd.
Trail

Power line

© The Countryman Press

Still climbing, the woods road changes dramatically into a rocky trail, and at 1.5 miles reaches an intersection with the Beulahland Trail. Your route climbs still farther before leveling out, paralleling the ridge of the Kittatinny Mountains to the right. By now you have been on the trail for about an hour, and after another 30 minutes through an open area on a rocky trail with tall mountain laurel, you will reach the intersection for the Backpacker Campsite. No fires are permitted and a stay of only one night is allowed but, because this site tends to be overcrowded, it has not been used as an overnight stop on this backpack. Another 40 minutes brings you to the southern tip of Sunfish Pond. The center of much environmental controversy, this glacial lake is 1,380 feet above sea level and is considered a natural geological oddity. Just to the left of the trail here is a stone monument dated 1970. Walk straight ahead to the shore of Sunfish Pond, then turn left to follow the trail around the western shore. The no-camping regulation is strictly enforced at Sunfish Pond.

The trail is now rocky and narrow. It soon crosses a small outlet from the pond, climbs, turns right, and descends again to the water's edge. Many rocky areas on the shore of the pond invite the traveler to rest. In one area, we came across a stony beach where industrious folk had built many Stonehenge-like edifices. This nondestructive graffiti must have kept someone busy for many hours.

At the end of Sunfish Pond, the trail moves back deeper into the woods, and you can find a spring 600 feet to the left of the trail, though the water supply is dependable only in the springtime. In this section, a blue-marked trail enters from the right and a turquoise-marked trail from the left.

The trail levels out after a short climb, turns left, and descends again through magnificent mountain laurel. Two and a half hours into the hike, at about the 4.5-mile point, cross a small brook. After climbing a short way, it is possible to make a detour to the left of the trail to see the Delaware River and the Pennsylvania Mountains. Within 30 minutes, a power line crosses the trail; slightly farther ahead, where the trail reaches the crest of the ridge, there are views in both directions. Walking slightly to the left improves the view of the river and Pennsylvania. Directly ahead is the Catfish fire tower, and to the right the Yards Creek pumped water-storage ponds can be seen.

The Yards Creek Pumped Storage Electric Generating Station began operation in 1965. The upper reservoir was created from two small swampy areas on the mountaintop, and the lower, about a mile east and approximately 700 feet below, is located on Yards Creek. An auxiliary reservoir, now part of a Boy Scout camping area, is just to the north of the lower Yards Creek reservoir.

The trail remains high on this slabby terrain for a short distance. From here you can see the bow in the Delaware River, which is not visible from other places. On a clear day the Catskills are also visible. Just as the trail begins to drop, there is a large AT sign on the boundary between Worthington State Forest and the Delaware Water Gap National Recreation Area.

The trail continues downhill on the ridge—called Mount Mohican—with glimpses of the views seen previously, until it reaches a sign for a spring 0.3 mile down the Kaiser Road Trail. Continue ahead until the Kaiser Road Trail turns to the left and the AT continues straight ahead, bearing slightly to the right. The Kaiser Road Trail at present is marked in blue, but the blazing will shortly be changed to blue on white. In another mile, the trail becomes rockier, descending steeply through mountain laurel. The Coppermine Trail soon enters from the left, and the AT then reaches a stream crossing at Camp Road, once called Mohican Road. This stream is a dependable water source. Fifty yards to the left on Camp Road is the Appalachian Mountain Club's Mohican Outdoor Center, where there are cabins and tent sites available for rent. For information call 908-362-5670. You have now walked about 9 miles, and as it will soon be time to make camp, you should collect water here for overnight use.

New Jersey claims the first copper mine opened in America, around 1640. The miners were Dutch settlers in the Kittatinny Mountains. The Coppermine Trail leads to a number of mines that can still be entered and explored by flashlight.

Cross Mohican Road and immediately enter the opposite woods. It will take about 10 or 15 minutes until the trail emerges onto a ridge with a view of an agricultural valley to the right. This section of the trail is spectacular—it travels along the side of the ridge through cedar and scrub pines. There is a sharp drop-off, and if you look back, Yards Creek Reservoir is visible in the distance. A short way along this ridge is a sign to the left for Rattlesnake Swamp Trail and another for Catfish Pond, only 0.5 mile distant. The trail turns away from the ridge and climbs slightly left, then descends and passes through a more open area with many dead trees.

After the trail leaves the ledges, it passes areas that could be used for camping, but we recommend you proceed just beyond Catfish fire tower. This tower, built in 1922, is 60 feet high, and it is well worth climbing the stairs for the splendid 360-degree view if the tower is open. The elevation here is 1,565 feet, and it is possible to see the Catskills in the distance and, closer in, Sand Pond.

From Catfish fire tower, the trail descends on an old woods road toward Millbrook–Blairstown Road. There are some ideal campsites just past the fire tower, both left and right of the woods road. It is your responsibility to comply with camping regulations.

Second Day
Catfish Fire Tower to Junction with Trail to Buttermilk Falls
Total distance second day: 7.8 miles
Hiking time: 5 hours
Vertical rise: 1,000 feet

Still heading north, the trail leaves the old woods road, turns left, and descends slightly on a rocky path overlooking a different valley until it rejoins the woods road. Then it once again leaves the old road, veering left and reentering the woods to the right through a lush section. At the foot of a steep descent on a narrow, rocky trail winding through tall mountain laurel, turn right at the power line and proceed through an extensive rhododendron thicket onto a gravel road. Turn left on the gravel road and look for Rattlesnake Spring in the left bank at the side of the road. This spring is delightful and is a dependable source of water—after purification, of course—for today's hike. The next water is approximately 5 miles ahead.

Walk back to where the AT joins the wide gravel road and continue on the AT until it shortly makes a sharp turn to the left. You will reach paved Millbrook–Blairstown Road within approximately 35 minutes of leaving your campsite.

Turn left on the paved road and, after a very short walk, enter the woods again on the right where there is a register. After signing in, take the left fork. At the beginning of this section, the trail is wide and passes a beaver pond on the left. The path is high on a ridge above this wet area, with glimpses of an even higher ridge on the right. After about 10 minutes of walking,

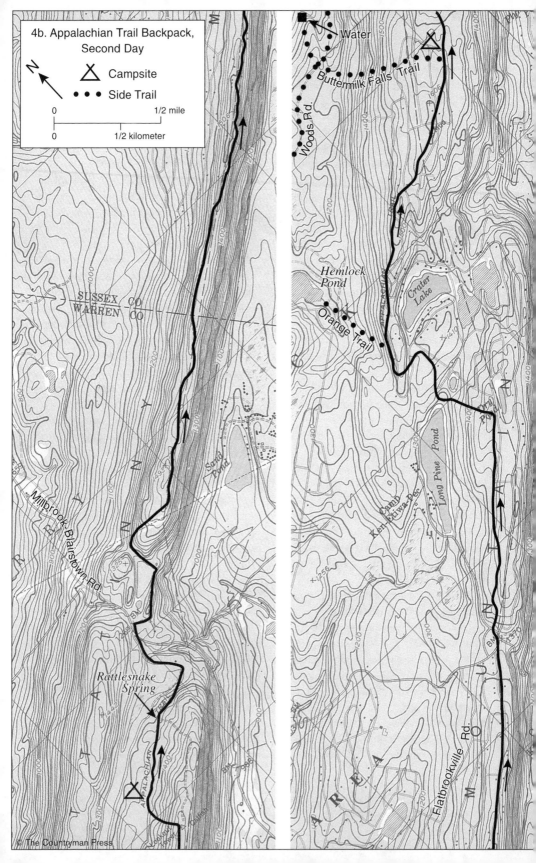

4b. Appalachian Trail Backpack,
Second Day

N

△ Campsite
• • • Side Trail

0   1/2 mile

0   1/2 kilometer

Water

Buttermilk Falls Trail

Woods Rd.

1500

Hemlock
Pond

Crater
Lake

Orange Trail

SUSSEX CO
WARREN CO

Sand Pond

Long Pine Pond

Camp
Ken-Etiwa-Pec

Millbrook-Blairstown Rd.

Rattlesnake
Spring

Flatbrookville Rd.

APPALACHIAN

© The Countryman Press

watch for a sharp turn to the left that detours around the northern end of the pond, away from the road. The trail becomes narrower, then opens out at the top of a short climb. There is a rocky bank on the left, and you must watch carefully for a sharp right turn leading steeply uphill. The Wallkill Valley and Pocono Plateaus are visible from the clearing at the top of the hill. Several small cedars are scattered around this viewpoint, and the power lines march down the hill past Sand Pond. The view to the east continues as you follow the ridge. The main trail is soon joined from the right by one marked with a mix of rectangular red and white metal emblems. The AT intersects the Boy Scout Trail (red on white) ending or beginning here and leading to BSA Camp No-Be-Bos-Co, which is private property. Fairview Lake is visible through the trees to the right. The wide, rocky road is high on a ridge, and it very shortly passes a large boulder on the left from which views of the valley to the west are available. There is another register at this point.

After about 5 miles and just before reaching paved Flatbrookville Road, look for a water pump on the left. If you miss it, there is also a spring contained in a metal pipe about 0.1 mile down the hill on Flatbrookville Road on the right (east) side of the road. After emerging onto the road, turn right, walk a few steps down the road, and turn left into an area of small white pines. Just a few minutes later, cross a woods road. Walk straight ahead and register on the left.

The trail traverses a pretty area here, and is narrower and cut through mountain laurel. It is clearly marked and descends steeply through rock slabs until it reaches a rock-strewn bog on the right. If you look back and to the left through the trees, you can see Long Pine Pond. Various lakes and ponds in the vicinity are all potential sources of water, though all water should be treated before drinking. Cross a gravel road by bearing slightly to the right, and reenter the woods on the left. Observe the outcrop of rock to the left–the trail is routed over this. At the top of this escarpment, you cross another gravel road and are rewarded by a good view to the west. Within a few minutes, you can get a view of Crater Lake (or Lake Success) by taking a blue-blazed trail to the right. A metal post is embedded in the rock at this viewpoint.

The walking is very easy on a wide, grassy trail that soon makes a sharp left turn. Notice the pipe to the left of this turn; there may have been a spring here at one time. There are beautiful views of Hemlock Pond at this point, and the orange trail to Hemlock Pond is marked practically at the crest of the rise.

This attractive section is still on a slightly uphill gradient, with more views of Crater Lake to the right. The trail is on a ledge, with the ground dropping down to the left and rising to the right–a rock-slab slope dotted with white pines. Two other trails join the main path here from the right and the left, and soon there is a marked left turn onto a gravel road, followed within 100 yards by the blue-blazed trail to Buttermilk Falls on the left. This trail is marked by a wooden sign.

Choose one of the many secluded and attractive campsites in this location for the night. You can find a prime site by proceeding down the AT approximately 100 yards from the Buttermilk Falls sign and turning left onto a wide, grassy woods road. Within a minute you will find a delightful, flat, grassy opening with a beautiful white pine at each end. After setting up camp, water and a refreshing wash are available by taking a side trip (1.75 miles) to Buttermilk

Asters along the Appalachian Trail

however, might make the extra effort to get water very worthwhile.

Third Day
Buttermilk Falls Trail to NJ 206 at Culvers Gap

Total distance third day: 7.8 miles
Hiking time: 5 hours
Vertical rise: 800 feet

After you leave camp, the gravel road bends to the right, departing from the AT, which turns left on a narrow footpath into the woods. Follow the AT. Two good views west to the Poconos are available here (one of them via a blue-blazed trail on the left) before the trail descends steeply through a rocky section. At the next fork, turn right and cross a stream (the alternate camping spot past the Buttermilk Falls area).

The trail now goes through a mature hemlock and sheep laurel grove. A few minutes after the stream crossing, it makes a sharp left turn to begin the climb up Rattlesnake Mountain. This section has been burned out and consequently is quite open. Rattlesnake Mountain (1,492 feet) was once called Columbus Mountain. As you approach it, the route up through the boulders and white pines becomes clearer, and during the ascent, good views become more and more apparent to the left until the entire panorama is visible from the summit. This vista includes the Normanook fire tower and High Point. Walk slightly to the right to reach the highest point.

Continue northward, gently descending on a narrow, rocky trail through many small pine trees toward a short swampy section, which is easily crossed by rock-hopping. This swamp is approximately 2 miles from the Buttermilk Falls area. Within 0.5 mile, the trail has climbed to a rocky area where it turns right onto an old dirt road and begins to descend again. This section affords

Falls. The trail to the falls is very steep, but—except in dry weather—it is not necessary to go all the way to the falls for water. Ten minutes down the trail, you cross a woods road; in another few minutes, you hear the sound of water. Where the trail goes downhill and makes a sharp left turn, go straight ahead a few more yards to a group of two or three pools of water. If these pools should be dry, follow the streambed down to find a suitable water-gathering spot. On the way down, the trail passes through several open blueberry patches, which in season might provide a snack.

If you prefer not to add this side trip for water to the day's walk and want to camp closer to a water supply, continue for approximately another mile until the trail descends to a stream crossing. Water is also available farther along, about 200 feet down a blue-blazed trail to a dependable spring. The beautiful campsite at the head of the Buttermilk Falls Trail (described above),

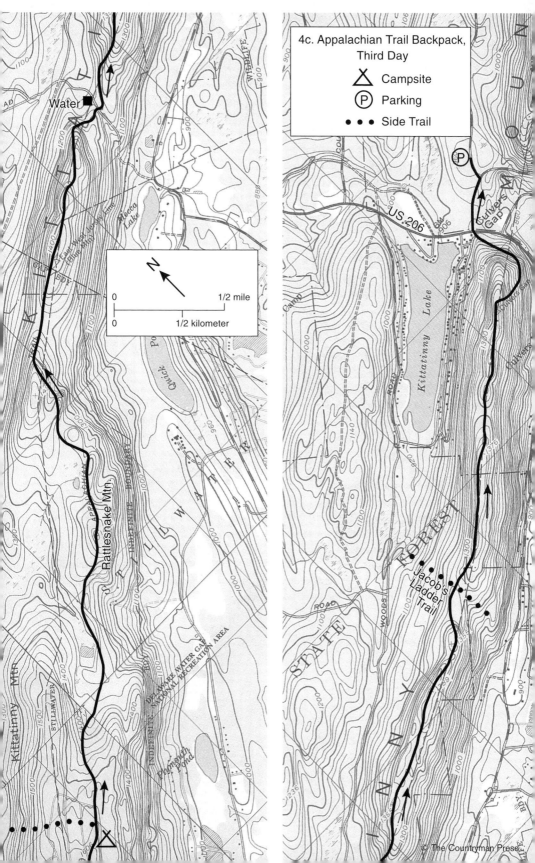

4c. Appalachian Trail Backpack, Third Day

△ Campsite

Ⓟ Parking

••• Side Trail

N

0   1/2 mile
0   1/2 kilometer

Water

Mecca Lake

Rattlesnake Mtn.

APPALACHIAN TRAIL

KITTATINNY

Quick Pond

STILLWATER

DELAWARE WATER GAP NATIONAL RECREATION AREA

INDEFINITE BOUNDARY

Plymouth Pond

Kittatinny Mtr.

US 206

Culvers Gap

Kittatinny Lake

FOREST

STATE

KITTATINNY

Jacob's Ladder Trail

WOODS ROAD

CAMP ROAD

Culvers

© The Countryman Press

views of Quick Pond and Mecca Lake. This road is wide and obviously used by four-wheel-drive vehicles.

Just to the left of the road are cages and blinds in disrepair. This banding facility was once operated by members of the New Jersey Raptor Association and the Raptor Trust in cooperation with state and federal agencies. Raptors migrate during the fall in great numbers along the Kittatinny Ridge and were banded at this site.

When the road bears left, the trail turns right and begins to climb through white pines. There are views to the left from the rock ledges and, at the top of the ridge, extensive views of the Wallpack Valley and the Poconos, before the trail moves back into the woods on rocky terrain. This high area is commonly known as Blue Mountain, and the larger area of water you glimpse through the trees is Lake Owassa. You will see this lake more clearly later. The general trend is now downhill, becoming more steep as you approach Brinks Road. As the trail leaves the wooded section, you can see the next ascent ahead.

Brinks Road is 4 miles from the Buttermilk Falls camping area. There is a shelter here with a spring, accessible by a blue-blazed trail to the left. Uphill from Brinks Road is a pretty area with tall mountain laurel, white pines, massive rhododendrons, and hemlock. The climb is short, lasting only about 10 minutes, and the trail follows the crest of the ridge for a similar amount of time. Just before a rocky, wet area on the right of the main trail, watch for the first unmarked side trail leading to an overlook and, after about another 0.5 mile, for a second unmarked trail leading to an observation point above Lake Owassa. The trail now alternately rises and falls until the final drop to US 206. You'll reach the Jacob's Ladder Trail, with blue-silver markings, another 0.5 mile from the Lake Owassa viewpoint. The first view of Culvers Lake, through the trees to the right, is usually not available in summer when the trees are in full leaf. Near the end of the trip is a large cleared area. From this vantage point, the Culvers fire tower, Culvers Lake, and US 206 are apparent straight ahead, and Lake Owassa is behind you. The trail turns back into the woods, reaches another clearing with US 206 visible on the right, and emerges onto a gravel road. Traverse the side of a hill, and be careful not to miss the turn to the right. Continuing on the gravel road would lead to US 206, but also would involve crossing private property. Instead, use the AT on the north side of Route 206 to reach the parking lot on Sunrise Mountain Road. Walking a little farther on US 206 brings you to the site of Worthington's Bakery, now closed. A delicatessen is slated to open in its place in the fall of 2005. Maybe you will be able to find a treat to reward you for your backpacking efforts.

SJG

Highlands

5

Schuber Trail, End to End

Total Distance: 7.2 miles

Hiking time: 5 hours

Vertical rise: 800 feet

Rating: Strenuous

Maps: USGS Wanaque, Ramsey; NYNJTC North Jersey Trails #22. (The Schuber Trail is not shown on the 2002 edition of this map, but is included on the 2005 edition.) Maps for the ending section of the hike in Ramapo Valley County Reservation are usually available in a box outside the rest rooms. A revised version showing the entire trail is being prepared.

The new Schuber Trail traverses the rugged Ramapo Mountains from Skyline Drive to US 202, crossing streams, paralleling rivers, climbing to viewpoints, and using parts of older trails and woods roads. Its trend is gradually downhill, though this tendency is not obvious because of the many uphill sections. The Schuber Trail is named after William "Pat" Schuber, the recently retired Bergen County Executive, who was mainly responsible for purchasing some of the tracts of land through which the trail passes. The trail was dedicated during a National Trails Day ceremony in Ramapo Valley County Reservation on June 1, 2002.

Beginning in Ramapo Mountain State Forest, the trail ends in the Ramapo Valley County Reservation. The Schuber Trail passes through Camp Glen Gray and Camp Tamarack, both former Boy Scout camps acquired by Bergen County in 1998. Camp Glen Gray was originally developed in 1917, and is now managed by the Friends of Glen Gray. Overnight camping is still available. For reservations call 201-327-7234 or submit a form at their Web site, www.glengray.org.

For more information on Ramapo Mountain State Forest, contact Passaic and Bergen Counties, c/o Ringwood State Park, 1304 Sloatsburg Road, Ringwood, NJ 07456; call 973-962-7031. For more information on Ramapo Valley County Reservation, contact Bergen County Parks, One Bergen County Plaza, Hackensack, NJ 07601; call 201-336-7275 or call the park

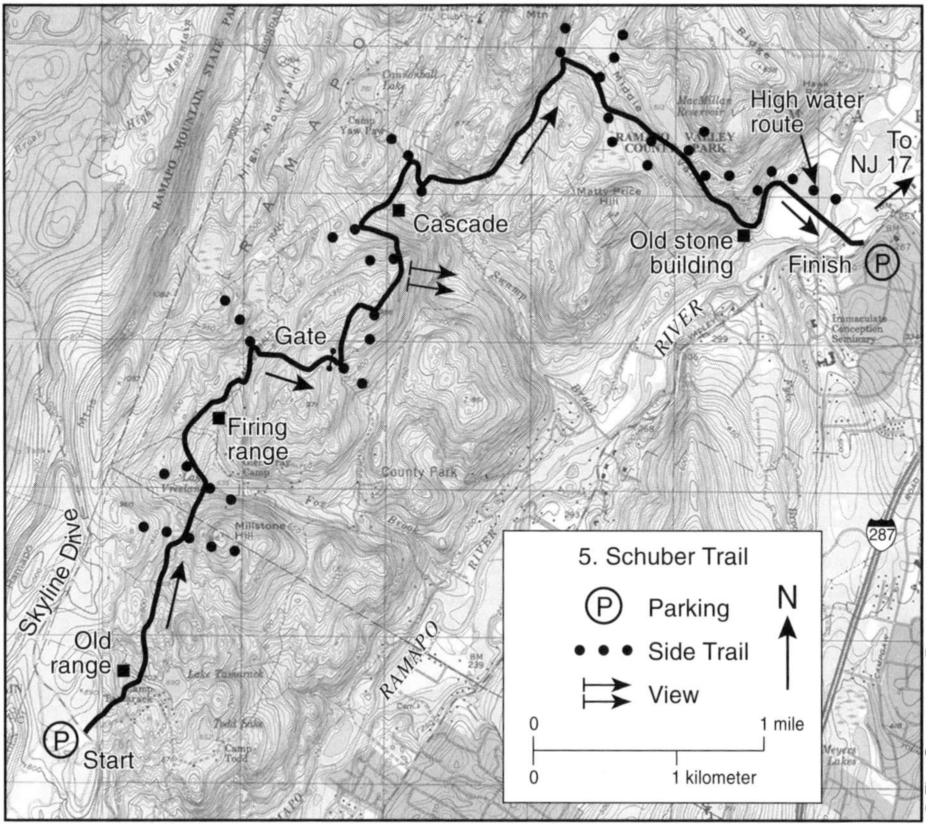
High water route
To NJ 17
Cascade
Old stone building
Finish
Gate
Firing range
Skyline Drive
Old range
Start
RIVER
RAMAPO
287
5. Schuber Trail
Parking
Side Trail
View
N
0
1 mile
0
1 kilometer
© The Countryman Press

office at 201-327-3500. Or check the Bergen County Parks Web site at www.co.bergen.nj.us/parks.

The state acquired Ramapo Mountain State Forest through the use of Green Acres and federal funds in 1976. The land that eventually became Ramapo Valley County Reservation was purchased from the Native Americans in 1720 by Samuel Laroe. Though the principal use of the land was farming, in addition it housed a gristmill, a sawmill, and later a bronze foundry. The land changed hands several times until its 1872 purchase by Alfred Burbank Darling, a native of Burke, Vermont and owner of many other properties, including the Fifth Avenue Hotel in Manhattan. It was his country estate, and the area became known as Darlington. The name Ramapo means "round ponds."

HOW TO GET THERE

The hike requires transportation at both ends. Leave one car at the Ramapo Valley County Reservation. Reach the large parking lot on the right-hand side of US 202 north by driving 1.9 miles south from NJ 17.

To place the second car and to begin hiking, turn right out of the Ramapo Valley County Reservation and drive 4.5 miles to a traffic light. Go straight across, and at Courthouse Place (the second light), turn right after 0.1 mile onto I-287. Within 0.5 mile take Exit 57 and proceed uphill on Skyline Drive for 1.4 miles to the crest. Park on the left at the roadside parking area.

THE TRAIL

Walk straight across Skyline Drive toward the Camp Tamarack sign. There is a plethora of markers on a tree to the left of the sign. The trailheads indicated are the Schuber (orange), the Todd (white), and the crossing of the Hoeferlin Memorial Trail (yellow). The beginning of the Schuber Trail is marked in orange with three traditional blazes, and this color is the one to follow for the rest of your hike. Almost immediately, turn left into the woods on a rocky, narrow path that goes steadily downhill, entering Bergen County Parks property. Signs indicate that the trail is for hiking only. Look to your left approximately 0.5 mile along the trail where it bears right to see the remnants of a Camp Tamarack archery range, demolished during the summer of 2004. Bergen County plans to remove the remaining rubble. Quite soon the trail crosses two streams about 500 yards from one another, the first one on breeze blocks, and the second in a rocky area. The white-blazed Millstone Trail crosses the Schuber Trail just over a mile into the hike. The footway then becomes wider and rockier, with glimpses of Lake Vreeland ahead. Just 1.5 miles from the start, the trail descends to the lake in the vicinity of Camp Glen Gray. Turn left. A shelter on the shore of Lake Vreeland offers a tempting excuse to take a short break, though officially hikers must stay on the trail because the camp buildings are off-limits to non-campers. The trail briefly parallels the water before beginning the climb on a wide gravel road. In this section there are numerous other gravel roads, old trail names, some beaten-up picnic benches, Camp Glen Gray buildings, and campsites. Lega-

cies from the previous trail system are visible, one—with blazes in the shape of a coffeepot marking the route of the Mary Post Trail—circling the main part of the camp. The newer, small circular orange ones added by the Bergen County Department of Parks are property markers, not trail markers.

The Matapan Rock Trail—marked by three red squares on white tags—veers off to the left five minutes from the lake, and the Schuber Trail continues ahead to cross a major stream on a wooden plank bridge. The trail soon approaches the archery range, which it bypasses through the woods to the left. The shelter here appears to be another attractive place to take a break, but again, non-campers are not permitted to use the camp buildings, and you should follow the trail route to the other side of the open space.

North Brook on the right-hand side parallels the Schuber Trail before a sturdy bridge permits the footway to cross over that substantial watercourse. The markers of the Old Guard Trail—a green tulip tree leaf on white—follow the same route as the Schuber Trail for about 0.5 mile before leaving to the left.

After crossing the bridge, the Schuber Trail becomes more traditional, at times close to the stream to the left of the path, and sometimes a distance away. The Schuber Trail turns to the right when the Old Guard Trail swings away to the left, climbs away from the stream, and within a few minutes crosses over a wide woods road, the historical route of the Cannonball Road. Here the old rock walls are reminders that the area was once farmed.

The Schuber Trail continues ahead on a wide gravel road, which eventually becomes grassier and begins to descend to a gated road and a wooden bridge crossing a culvert that carries the outlet from Sanders Pond to

McMillan Brook, Ramapo Valley County Reservation

the left. Within a few minutes, and 2 miles into the hike, the traditional blazes of the Yellow/Silver Trail are seen to the right, while the Schuber Trail makes a left turn and begins climbing to an excellent viewpoint. The vista encompasses the high ridges of the Ramapo Valley County Reservation, suburban Bergen County, and on a clear day, the Manhattan skyline on the horizon to the right. A wooden sign, HT2, (a remnant from the de-blazed History of the Glen Trail, though a pamphlet is still available) can be seen on the approach to the crest. The Yellow Trail joins the Schuber Trail here from the right to co-mingle with the orange blazes.

The Yellow Trail/Schuber Trail is grassy and narrow, and heads downhill with super views to the right. In this section it is interesting to see the unique concept used for trail marking on the open stretches. The Old Guard Trail starts to the left off the Schuber Trail within a few minutes from the overlook, just before the trail descends steeply away from the ridge through deep woods. Twenty minutes from the viewpoint, the Yellow Trail continues ahead and the Schuber Trail makes a sharp right turn. Watch carefully for this turn, after which the footway crosses a seasonal stream, and passes a derelict lean-to on the right, a former Camp Yaw Paw outpost, and continues to cross a larger watercourse on large rocks. We suggest taking a break here to enjoy the beautiful cascades at this crossing.

The Schuber Trail now follows along the bank of Bear Swamp Brook, a large river to your right, and it is tempting to stop to admire its cascades and canyons. You are now about halfway through the hike as the trail descends to emerge onto paved Camp Yaw Paw Road.

Turn right, cross over the water on a wide wooden-planked bridge, and turn right again onto Bear Swamp Road with the wild trout stream now cascading down on your right. The trail makes a sharp left turn back into the woods within a couple of minutes walking on the paved road, climbs, and veers left.

Just short of 5.5 miles, a stream crossing ahead indicates the beginning of the Red/Silver Trail, marked as its name suggests, and the Schuber Trail bears right, entering the Ramapo Valley County Reservation core trail system. In fact, you've been using this system for some time now because the Ramapo Valley County Reservation now includes Camp Glen Gray. The Schuber Trail is now wide, rocky, and slightly downhill, and within five minutes passes the Ridge Trail (blue) coming in from the left, and in another few minutes the Marsh Loop (red) and the Yellow/Silver Trails from the right. The MacMillan Reservoir and its outlet can be glimpsed down to the left. It is always interesting to pause a few minutes at the reservoir and to enjoy the exuberance of the dogs relishing their outing. You will encounter more walkers here than you have probably seen all day.

The Schuber Trail turns right, away from the Silver Trail, which begins here and uses the park road. This turn is just before the second bridge with stone abutments, and proceeds down a more traditional, though very rugged, trail. The outlet from the reservoir with its great waterfall, pools, and cascades is visible down into the gorge on the left of the trail. After 15 minutes downhill on the trail, the ruins of a large, old camp cabin built of stone with a substantial fireplace can be seen to the right, and the trail bears left, still descending, to cross a narrow wooden plank bridge, beyond which the green-over-white Halifax Trail begins to the left. Follow the orange blazes of the Schuber Trail, bearing right and then left, to follow a shoreline footpath close to the Ramapo River. This section is often muddy, and tangled with vines, because it is in the floodplain of the river, but trail maintainers use weed whackers to keep the trail itself clear.* The footway soon crosses a grassy area to emerge onto the Silver Trail, which follows a gravel road bordering Scarlet Oak Pond. Turn right, cross the steel truss bridge over the Ramapo River, and climb the short distance to the end of the Schuber Trail and back to your car.

If you find that the Schuber Trail is impassible because of flooding, use the following high-water route. From the abandoned stone shelter and after crossing the small wooden bridge, turn left onto the green-over-white Halifax Trail for 0.2 mile, then turn right onto the Silver Trail for 0.1 mile, and thence back to your car.

SJG

6

Ramapo Lake, Ramapo Mountain State Forest

Total distance: 5.5 miles

Hiking time: 3.5 hours

Vertical rise: 700 feet

Rating: Moderate

Maps: USGS Wanaque; NYNJTC North Jersey Trails #21; NJWB #20

Covering more than 2,200 acres, Ramapo Mountain State Forest is part of a rugged ridge straddling the Bergen–Passaic County boundary. Added to New Jersey's public lands in the mid-1970s, much of it had been the estate of the late William McEvoy, a wealthy public works contractor. The centerpiece of the forest is the attractive Ramapo Lake, formerly know as Lake LeGrande, and before that Rotten Pond. Swimming is not permitted, but fishing is a popular pastime. A few privately owned inholdings remain, with their owners using several one-lane access roads not available to the public except by foot or bike. These and other former estate roads have made this a popular area for mountain bikers, especially on weekends.

Miles of marked hiking trails lace the forest and lead to viewpoints and rock outcroppings. This hike loops to one of the best of these outcroppings and adds an out-and-back to the interesting remains of one of the more prominent estates. Parking areas can fill up early on weekend days. However, on weekdays the area is often an island of tranquility just a stone's throw from busy I-287. Ramapo Mountain State Forest is administered by Ringwood State Park (1304 Sloatsburg Road, Ringwood NJ 07456; 973-962-7031).

HOW TO GET THERE

To get to the parking area on Skyline Drive, take I-287 to Exit 57. If you are coming from the north (heading south), the exit ramp will take you directly onto Skyline Drive. If traveling up from the south, make a

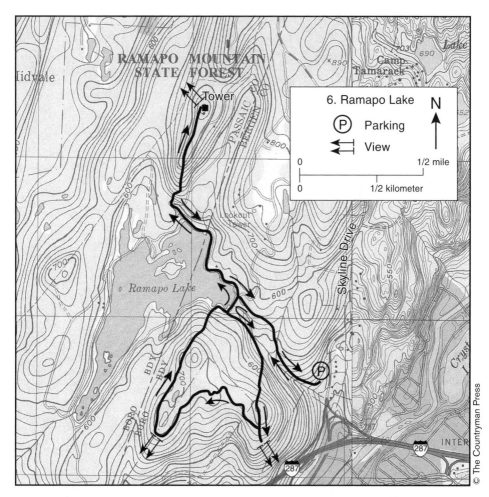

left after the exit ramp, proceeding under I-287 directly onto Skyline Drive. The well-signed parking area comes up quickly, on the left at milepost 0.3. Skyline Drive is a busy road. Take extra care when making the left into the parking area.

THE TRAIL

The blue-marked McEvoy Trail, which will take you up to the lake, starts from the corner of the parking area, near a bulletin board and several portable toilets. This pathway travels along a wide woods road with a stream down along the left. The grade is moderate with an occasional short, steep pitch. About three-fourths of the way up to Ramapo Lake, you will pass by the white-marked Todd Trail, which begins to the right. Stay on the blue McEvoy and it will soon bring you up to the lake, some 15 minutes into the hike. Now leave the blue trail, turn left, and cross the wide road above the concrete dam and spillway. You may notice some yellow markers on this, a part of the Hoeferlin Trail. Only 20 yards after the dam, the red-marked Lookout Trail begins on the left.

Take the Lookout Trail (the three red markers denote its start) as it travels away

STELLA GREEN

Ramapo Water Tower at Castle Point, Ramapo Mountain State Forest

from the lake. Sometimes this marked trail may diverge from a more obvious footway. As you travel along, remember you are following the red paint markers, not the footway. For example, a few minutes in from start, there is a sharp left turn—well marked, but not the more obvious route.

Parts of the trail are narrow and rocky as it meanders up and down on a bank above a stream—the same one that you saw along the McEvoy Trail. It is well marked with a combination of red plastic and paint blazes. As you climb up the ridge, the trees get shorter and you'll encounter some grassy areas. The trail levels off as you reach the ridge and then passes a large rock and begins to descend a little.

At a sharp right, you will notice an unmarked trail straight ahead. Here you should proceed ahead (instead of right) about 100 yards to an expansive viewpoint, which looks over Oakland and beyond to High Mountain. On a clear day, you can see the New York City skyline in the distance. I-287 is visible to the left, and unfortunately the sounds of its traffic are always intrusive.

Return to the red trail and continue left along the marked trail as it meanders up and down, sometimes steeply, for less than a mile to a T-junction with the yellow-blazed Hoeferlin Trail. Important: this hike continues by turning right and following the jointly marked Lookout/Hoeferlin Trail, (yellow and red blazes). However, before continuing take a moment to wander over to the left of the junction. Here is an especially scenic place to rest, a large rock ledge with a splendid pitch pine and a nice view across the Wyanokies.

Back on the trail, following both yellow and red blazes, you'll now travel across the ridge and begin the descent back down to the lake. You'll pass several more viewpoints, with Ramapo Lake getting closer and looking more serene as you reach each spot.

After reaching the lake, turn right along the road and walk back across the dam. If you should want to shorten the hike, turn right and follow the blue markers back to your car. Otherwise, turn left and follow the blue McEvoy blazes along the lakeshore.

The houses to your right are some of the private inholdings previously mentioned.

Some 10 minutes along the lakeshore will bring you to a nice waterfall, and another 5 minutes to a major trail junction. Here you turn right, uphill, continuing to follow blue markers and passing between two concrete posts. After a few minutes the blue trail will turn left off the road you've been following. Continue straight ahead on the Cannonball Trail—marked with a white C in a red field—but only for a very short stretch.

As the road/trail bends to the right, look to your left for the three white blazes denoting the start of the Castle Point Trail. Proceed left onto that trail. It is a rough, steep trail, but short. As you begin to reach the top of the ridge, the trail passes directly over a cement wall. There is a nice view behind you.

Now the white trail winds through and past the remains of the Foxcroft Estate (it's on Fox Mountain), also known as Van Slyke Castle. The first ruin you'll encounter is the mansion itself, built in the early 1900s by William Porter, a stockbroker. He died soon after it was finished, but his widow occupied the house until her death around 1940. Sadly, it fell into ruin and was burned by vandals in the 1950s. Continuing up the trail, you will pass the remains of an in-ground swimming pool. A bit later, you'll spot a massive stone tower. This most attractive water tower served the estate. A detailed history, including pictures, awaits you at www.users.nac.net/axtell.

After you finish enjoying the view from the tower, retrace your steps back to your car. Follow the white trail down past the mansion and down to the lake, then follow the blue trail along the lakeshore and to the left down to your car.

HNZ

7

Ringwood Manor Circular

Total distance: 3 miles

Hiking time: 2 hours

Vertical rise: 250 feet

Rating: Easy

Maps: USGS Greenwood Lake (NY/NJ); NYNJTC North Jersey Trails #22; NJWB #20; DEP Ringwood State Park

Ringwood Manor, part of the larger Ringwood State Park (1304 Sloatsburg Rd., Ringwood, NJ 07456; 973-962-7031), is located in northeast Passaic County. The history of the area is closely tied to the local iron industry, which started at Ringwood in 1740. The products of the forges and furnaces were of much importance to the colonies during the Revolutionary War. Troops were stationed here, and George Washington made Ringwood his headquarters on several occasions. Robert Erskine, manager of the mines, served General Washington as surveyor general and prepared many of the maps for the campaign against the British.

Peter Cooper purchased the property in 1853. Cooper, a New York philanthropist, is best known as the founder of Cooper Union for the Advancement of Science and Art. The property later passed to Abram Hewitt, a famous ironmaster. He had become a family friend of the Coopers and later of their daughter Amelia. The greater part of the present mansion was built from about 1810 to 1930. It was always a summer house; the family spent winters in New York City. Abram Hewitt and Peter Cooper were relatives as well as business partners in Cooper-Hewitt & Co. Mr. Hewitt married Amelia Cooper, Peter Cooper's daughter. The house passed to the Hewitts during Peter Cooper's lifetime, and they were the primary summer residents of the estate.

The greatest part of the present manor house was built between 1854 and 1910, during the Hewitt period. However, the earliest part of the house dates to 1807 from the Ryerson family.

In 1936, Erskine Hewitt donated the manor house and 95 acres to the State of New Jersey. His nephew, Norvin Green (namesake of nearby Norvin Green State Forest), made an additional gift to bring the total to 579 acres. Later purchases, using Green Acres funds, continued until as recently as 1978. The park now extends east into Bergen County, connecting with Ramapo Mountain State Forest and a Bergen County reservation to form a large network of public lands. Volunteers coordinated by the New York–New Jersey Trail Conference developed an extensive network of trails in the area in the 1970s.

In recent years, Ringwood State Park—especially on the eastern side of Sloatsburg Road—has become a very popular mountain biking area. The bikers are supposed to stay off the marked hiking trails, but many are either unaware of or ignore the rule. The trails you'll follow on this hike are not open to bikes.

HOW TO GET THERE

Ringwood Manor is on Sloatsburg Road, just south of the New York–New Jersey border. Access to this road is from County Road 511 (1.8 miles north from Skyline Drive) or from NY 17, just south of the village of Sloatsburg, New York via CR 72. From NY 17 it's a 4.5-mile drive to the park. The area has many roadside directional signs for this park and the adjacent Skylands Botanical Gardens (see Hike 8, Skylands Manor). As in many state parks, there is a fee for parking from Memorial Day to Labor Day. New Jersey residents older than 61 can get a pass that allows free parking at all state parks and forests (see the Introduction).

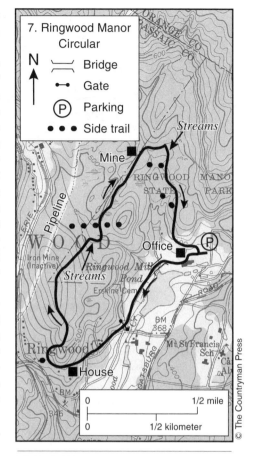

THE TRAIL

History is everywhere at Ringwood Manor, and it is a fine idea to combine your hike with a tour of the manor house. Call ahead (973-962-7031) to determine the house tour schedule, usually Wednesday through Sunday year round. The hike commences at the park office, where maps and brochures are usually available. Heading out toward the clearly visible Sally's Pond (a local name; the USGS and NYNJTC maps show this as Ringwood Mill Pond, which is really one of the smaller ponds, closer to the manor house), go to the end of the manor house by the porch. Follow the new yellow-marked

Gardens at Ringwood Manor

STELLA GREEN

trail through the wrought-iron gates—standing by themselves on the lawn—and continue to the far side of the pond. Pass a row of large oak trees and come to a dirt road. Bear left and watch for the first sign of a blue-marked trail on a telephone pole. This is the Manor Trail, and you will follow its blue markers throughout the hike. The pond is stocked with bass and pickerel, but fishing is, of course, subject to the various New Jersey laws. If interested, inquire at the park office.

Continue along the shore, with the pond on your left. As you cross a small stream on a bridge, note the rust-colored rocks, indicative of the iron ore present throughout the area. Along the shore, the route passes several small graveyards. Pause and browse. Names such as Morris, Paterson, Erskine, and Hewitt are central to regional history. Many of the graves are those of small children, who died often in the 18th

and 19th centuries. Some cedar trees add to the tranquility of the area—unless you made the mistake of coming late on a summer weekend! The large building visible across the pond is the sanctuary of the Order of Saint Francis. This estate was originally the summer home of the Hewitts' daughter, Amelia Hewitt Green, and her husband, Dr. James O. Green, and their family. It was built for them as a wedding present from the Hewitts.

Pass the end of Sally's Pond and proceed through a gate. Make a right on the gravel road going uphill, and, as always, follow the blue markers. The house you'll pass was acquired when the area became parkland, and now houses various state agencies.

Ignore the dirt road on the left and continue uphill, following the main road, now more dirt than gravel. As the route crests and then begins a gentle drop, watch the blazes carefully. Two blazes together indicate a sharp right turn onto a smaller woods road, which you will take. (If you go too far, you'll soon see a paved highway, Margaret King Avenue.) The woods road continues uphill and is generally level, with short pitches up and down. This place is good for observing the surrounding woodlands. In spring, flowers abound: jack-in-the-pulpit, rue anemone, spring beauty, and trout lily, to name just a few. Note the rusted cables half buried in the trailbed. Park historians surmise that they may have been used as part of the transportation system for iron-ore carts, but they don't know for sure.

Watch also for a large rock to the left of the trail, with a green metal marker on top. Called benchmarks, these have been placed—many on the summits of mountains—by the United States Geological Survey throughout the country. They generally identify key spots in the government's mapping work. This one, however, is a remnant of the Cooper Union Camp.

About 45 minutes into the hike, you'll see a power line ahead. The marked trail turns right *before* reaching the line, but you might want to take the short jog out to the power line for this hike's only view. The trail is narrower now, and the woods are deeper. Soon you reach a lovely stream. Note the rusty red rocks—some of the region's abundant iron ore. This spot is a good place for a break. Pull up a rock and have a snack.

The trail follows the stream for a short distance and then crosses it on some stones. Watch your footing here! The path again heads into the woods. Note the large stumps, evidence of past logging activities. Beech, oak, maple, and dogwood abound in this area. Soon, off to the left, is a large water-filled rectangle. This depression is an old mine pit. Note again the rust-colored rocks.

A few more minutes brings you to a clearly marked junction with the yellow-marked Hasenclever Iron Trail. You have hiked just under 2 miles. A right turn onto this new yellow-marked trail would take you quickly back to the manor house and shorten your hike. However, the Manor Trail continues straight ahead, crossing a few small streams. Beware of poison ivy here. If you are not yet sure what to watch out for, avoid all three-leafed plants and vines.

The trail turns right, following an old woods road downstream. There may be some muddy stretches here—just walk to either side into the woods to avoid them. The trail passes under a canopy of 12-foot trees, forming a lovely arch. More flowers are here, as well as some false hellebore and skunk cabbage.

Upon reaching an intersection with a wide road, follow the blue markings that indicate a right turn, downhill. The white-blazed trail, which follows the road to the left, makes an interesting, if somewhat longer, alternate return route. Should you decide to take the longer route, just follow the white markings carefully. There is one sudden turn right off the road that you could miss.

Although the white trail is well marked, it is easy to lose concentration when walking along such a wide and obvious footway. The white trail, which adds about 0.7 mile to this hike, will return you to Ringwood Creek just upstream from the manor house section of the park.

To be back in sight of the Manor House within a few minutes, though, continue to follow the blue blazes. Perhaps you have time now for a Manor House tour?

HNZ

8

Skylands Manor

Total distance: 6.25 miles

Hiking time: 3 hours

Vertical rise: 1,000 feet

Rating: Easy to moderate

Maps: USGS Ramsey; NYNJTC North Jersey Trails, #22; NJWB #20; New Jersey DEP, Division of Parks and Forestry: Ringwood State Park; Skylands Association Self-Guiding Tour map of the gardens available from the register at Parking Lot A.

This hike is located in Ringwood State Park (PO Box 1304, Ringwood, NJ 07456-1799; 973-962-7031) in the northernmost part of New Jersey. Trails used are the Ringwood-Ramapo (red), Halifax (green), Crossover (white), Cooper Union (yellow), and Cupsaw Brook (blue). The itinerary affords an opportunity to linger in Skylands Botanical Gardens and to walk past Skylands Manor House. The peacefulness of the hike is somewhat spoiled by the noise of shooting—Thunder Mountain is a shooting range—but the sound is less obtrusive along certain sections of the hike and at certain times of day. Pay careful attention to the blazes as you walk, and to every trail junction, because the many trail changes can be confusing. For this hike it is almost imperative to carry and to understand a good trail map of the area. Multi-use trails have recently been established in the park, and at most trailheads there are signs indicating the trail's designated use.

HOW TO GET THERE

From Sloatsburg Road, turn onto Morris Drive just south of the New York–New Jersey border. Access to Sloatsburg Road is from County Road 511 (1.8 miles north of Skyline Drive) or from NY 17, just south of the village of Sloatsburg, New York (3.6 miles north of the New York–New Jersey border). Approaching on Sloatsburg Road from the northeast, pass Ringwood Manor and Sally's Pond on the right, and turn left into Morris Road about 0.75 mile farther at the sign for Thunder Mountain and the Holy

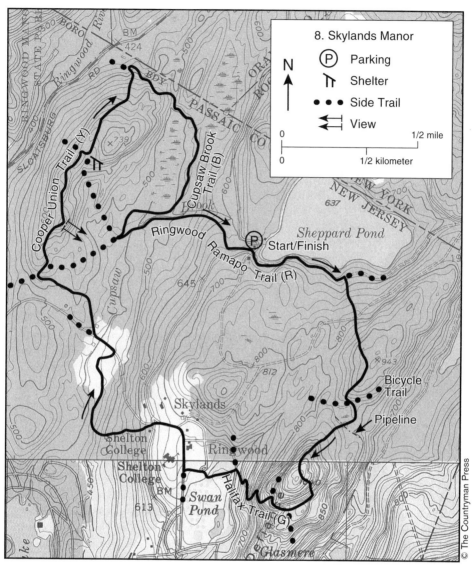

Name Friary. From the southwest, Morris Road is approximately 0.5 mile past Margaret King Avenue. Park at Shepherd Lake. (There appear to be alternative spellings to the lake's name; USGS maps and the *New York Walk Book* spell it "Sheppard.") To reach the lake, turn left as you approach the two stone eagles, pass through a pair of iron gates, and drive past the gatehouse.

There is no charge for parking out of season. As this book goes to press, fees during the swimming season are $5 on weekdays and $10 on weekends, and the parking lots often fill up early.

THE TRAIL

Shepherd Lake is approximately 1,000 feet above sea level, and the water remains cool because it is spring-fed. St. Luke's Chapel stands on a knoll behind the parking area, and the lake is immediately in front with the bathhouse on the left and the boathouse on the right. With the lake in front of you, walk to the right—toward the boathouse and past the DO NOT ENTER sign—to the first red marker. Proceed, at first on gravel, then on a substantial woods road that hugs the lakeshore. The first footpath used for this hike, the Ringwood–Ramapo Trail, is marked in red and soon passes between two stone pillars past the remnants of a gate. Only a portion of this trail, which extends from Ringwood Manor to the Ramapo Mountain State Forest, is presently in use.

After about seven minutes walking along the woods road, and just after passing a leaning tree and a bend in the road, watch the right side closely for a wooden post and the red turn signal that indicates the trail leaving the road and entering the woods. This narrow foot trail parallels an old, eroded woods road and emerges onto it after five minutes of steady climbing. Follow the red markers across another woods road, climbing a little more steeply until the trail flattens out. In winter, you can see the long ridge and the high point of Mount Defiance through the trees, and in spring you may hear spring peepers at this point.

The trail now moves slightly downhill and, about a mile into the hike, crosses an official bicycle trail, marked with a post but not blazed. Shortly thereafter the trail crosses a pipeline, continues straight to reenter the woods, and almost immediately climbs through boulders. Bear to the right if you find the next marker difficult to spot. Farther along, a large isolated boulder stands to the right of the trail. After a short flat section, the trail begins to climb again to

an excellent viewpoint to the north, and a view of Cupsaw Lake to the left.

After leaving the viewpoint, walk uphill again for another couple of minutes, then begin to descend—at first gently and then more steeply—through boulders. The trail bears to the right along the base of some interesting cliffs and provides a view of Pierson Ridge through the trees to the left.

Approximately 2 miles into the hike, look for the cairn that marks the intersection of the Halifax and the Ringwood–Ramapo Trails, and turn right onto the Halifax Trail, blazed with a green square on a white background. Here the footway is smooth and slopes gently upward, with those remarkable cliffs still on the right. Soon the cliffs come to an end and the trail begins to switchback downhill.

Within a few minutes you arrive at a fork. This hike follows the green trail to the left, but it is well worth taking the short side trip on the path to the right, which leads to an excellent view of Skylands Manor and Cupsaw Lake. This viewpoint is also home to an especially beautiful cedar tree that will be visible when you walk past the manor house later.

Return to the Halifax Trail, which now descends quite steeply in a series of switchbacks, probably because it was constructed as a bridle path many years ago. Notice the impressive stonework supporting the downhill side of the path. Half a mile farther on, watch for the combination of three green markers indicating the end of the Halifax Trail and the white blazes indicating a junction with the Crossover Trail.

There is a decision to be made at this point. To shorten the hike drastically, turn right and follow the white markers of the Crossover Trail until you reach Parking Lot A and the paved road back to your car.

Gatehouse at Skylands Manor

STELLA GREEN

However, we suggest that you make the right turn on the white trail, and almost immediately turn left onto a woods road between two large stones. Walk past a large stand of evergreens, take the right fork, and proceed through the gate ahead into the cultivated, peaceful Skylands Botanical Garden.

The New Jersey State Botanical Garden was originally a working farm assembled from pioneer farmsteads by Francis Lynde Stetson, a prominent New York lawyer. In addition to outbuildings and gardens, it included a vast lawn used as a nine-hole golf course, and many famous people—including President Grover Cleveland, actress Ethel Barrymore, and industrialist J. P. Morgan— were guests at Skylands Farms. The estate was sold in 1922 to Clarence McKenzie Lewis, an investment banker and a trustee of the New York Botanical Garden, who demolished the Stetson farmhouse and replaced it with the Tudor mansion now on the site.

Once through the gate and past the small stream, bear right on the grass toward a wooden seat dated 1991 and dedicated to Humbert "Al" Cincotti, a Skylands volunteer. Turn right; when you reach another gate, turn left and admire the stone birdbath; continue toward a curved wooden bench on the grass to the right. After walking through another gate into an open field, the manor house is visible to the right. The fences and gates are necessary to keep the deer from eating the ornamental shrubbery. The peaceful gardens are extensive, and marked with informative signs, and it is probably more sensible to explore these gardens later on.

Walk straight ahead toward Maple Avenue, the paved auto road. Cross Crab Apple Vista, pass underneath an arbor, and turn right when you reach the road, about 15 minutes from the end of the Halifax Trail. Look up to the right as you walk to see the cedar tree and rocky outcrop at the viewpoint you just left.

Maple Avenue takes you past Skylands Manor House on the left. This house was designed by John Russell Pope and built from stone quarried from Pierson Ridge. The building's weathered facade and the sags and ripples in its slate were deliberately introduced to make it appear older. Clarence Lewis collected plants from all over the world—including New Jersey roadsides—resulting in the fine collection now in the botanical gardens. He also planted most of the trees framing the house. The state of New Jersey bought Skylands Gardens in 1966. This property was the first purchased under the Green Acres program, and was later designated the state's official botanical garden.

Although the manor house is usually closed to the public, it is open, and often decorated, on certain days during the year, such as Mother's Day and during the Christmas season. Sixty gardeners worked here during Mr. Lewis's ownership, but volunteers now help out. For information on volunteering and for minimal-cost membership in the New Jersey Botanical Gardens Skylands Association, call 973-962-7527 or 973-962-1553. The Skylands Association is a nonprofit organization founded in 1976 to assist with the preservation and restoration of the gardens and manor house.

Continue down Maple Avenue, past the rest rooms and visitor center on the right, until you reach Parking Lot A. This lot is the one at which you would have arrived if you had followed the Crossover Trail instead of walking through the ornamental gardens. Stay on the paved road outside Parking Lot A until you see the large boulder with two white blazes, indicating a left turn at a fork in the paved road. The two stone statues you passed in the car on the way in are on either side of this road. If you need to curtail the hike at this point, turn right and walk down the road to the Shepherd Lake parking lot and your car.

Continue by returning to the woods at the wooden trail sign on the left, passing a large entry signboard on the right. Follow the white markers of the Crossover Trail downhill, ignoring two unmarked trails coming in from the left. This section tends to be muddy, especially in spring. Confirm that you are still on the white trail by looking for the wooden post to the left of the trail, with two white markers indicating a right turn. At this point the route nears a fenced-in water treatment facility and almost immediately reaches a pipeline. The trail turns right—confirmed by a white marker on a wooden post to the right at the top of a short rise—and follows the pipeline to Morris Road. Approximately 45 minutes will have elapsed since you entered the gardens.

Turn left down the road, cross the stone bridge labeled 235 PASSAIC COUNTY over Cupsaw Brook, and within 20 yards turn right between two large evergreens, back into the woods, climbing slightly. Some of the markers are now paint blazes, but some are white metal rectangles affixed with nails.

The trail continues to climb gradually, crosses over the ruins of a stone wall, and quite soon reaches the junction of the Cooper Union Trail, marked in yellow, where you need to turn right, uphill. A junction with the Cupsaw Brook Trail, marked with three blue blazes, is at the top of the rise a little way ahead. You may shorten the hike here by taking the Cupsaw Brook Trail to the Ringwood–Ramapo Trail, and thence to your car. The route of this hike, however, continues easily uphill on the Cooper Union Trail, and in about 10 minutes reaches an excellent viewpoint, elevation 680 feet, facing Mount Defiance.

Beyond the viewpoint the trail descends slightly along a ridge, with a shallow drop-off to the left and a steeper one to the right. After another 10 minutes of walking, you can see the Cooper Union Shelter downhill to the right. At this point the Ringwood–Ramapo Trail (red) comes in from the left and joins the yellow Cooper Union Trail for a short distance. Just a few yards ahead, the Ringwood–Ramapo Trail leaves to the right. Follow the red markers down to the shelter for a short break if you wish, then backtrack to resume easy walking downhill on the now much wider Cooper Union Trail.

Within 10 minutes after leaving the shelter, the trail moves more steeply downhill. Almost at the end of the downhill stretch, watch carefully on the right for the three blue markers indicating a right turn into the woods on the Cupsaw Brook Trail (blue). If you miss these markers you will find yourself at the bottom of the hill on a pipeline and will need to retrace your steps. The trail begins to climb, but because the footway is not as well established here as on the other trails, be sure to follow the blue markers. Walk down through boulders scattered among the with evergreens and, after another few minutes, emerge onto another woods road with a pipeline going uphill immediately ahead. Turn right, still following the blue blazes, bearing first left and then right to follow a tributary of the Cupsaw Brook for a short distance before the trail moves away from the stream. If the leaves are off the trees, Cupsaw Mountain can be seen to the right.

Within approximately 15 minutes, the trail again moves closer to the stream, which is now considerably bigger. After another 10 minutes, turn left at the junction with the Ringwood–Ramapo Trail (red). Red and blue markers follow the same route here for a short distance, and almost immediately Cupsaw Brook comes into view. Turn left, cross a watercourse and then the main flow on large boulders. Exercise caution, because the boulders are often slippery. Plans are in the works for a trail rerouting here to avoid the wet sections, and to make the Cupsaw Brook crossing easier. The trail markers are a combination of red paint blazes and painted round metal disks. Cupsaw Brook is now to the left of the trail. About 15 minutes after the stream crossing, the trail climbs up through large boulders and—if the water is high enough—you may see cascades on the left. After another 15 minutes, the terrain flattens out again and walking becomes easier. Turn left when the trail emerges onto a wide woods road, and glance to the right to see an abandoned bulldozer. Almost immediately you reach the parking lot and your car.

SJG

9

Governor Mountain

Total distance: 5.5 miles or 2.0 miles

Hiking time: 3.5 hours or 1.25 hours

Vertical rise: 430 feet

Rating: Easy

Maps: USGS Wanaque, Greenwood Lake (NJ/NY), Sloatsburg (NJ/NY); NYNJTC North Jersey Trails, #22; NJWB #20; DEP Ringwood State Park

This hike leads to a peninsula of state-owned land in the southwestern portion of Ringwood Manor State Park (PO Box 1304, Ringwood, NJ 07456; 973-962-7031). In 1936, Erskine Hewitt deeded his manor house and 95 acres to the state for preservation. His nephew, Norvin Green, gave New Jersey considerable lands. Additional purchases in the 1960s and as late as 1978 brought the park to its present size. Because the boundaries of Ringwood join those of Ramapo Valley State Forest and Ramapo Valley (Bergen) County Reservation, an extensive and varied trail network now exists. Volunteers coordinated by the New York–New Jersey Trail Conference maintain most of the hiking trails in this area. In recent years, mountain biking has become very popular here. The bikers are supposed to stay off the marked hiking trails, but many are either unaware of or ignore the rule. Clear "uses-allowed" signage is now in place.

HOW TO GET THERE

Drive along Sloatsburg Road to Morris Avenue, the entrance road to the Skylands section of Ringwood State Park. Access Sloatsburg Road from NY 17 just south of the town of Sloatsburg, New York (3.6 miles from the New York–New Jersey border), or by driving north 1.8 miles on County Route 511 from its junction with Skyline Drive. The area has many roadside directional signs for Ringwood and Skylands.

Proceed east on Morris Avenue for 1 mile, past the wooden entrance posts (0.4 mile) and across a small bridge at the end

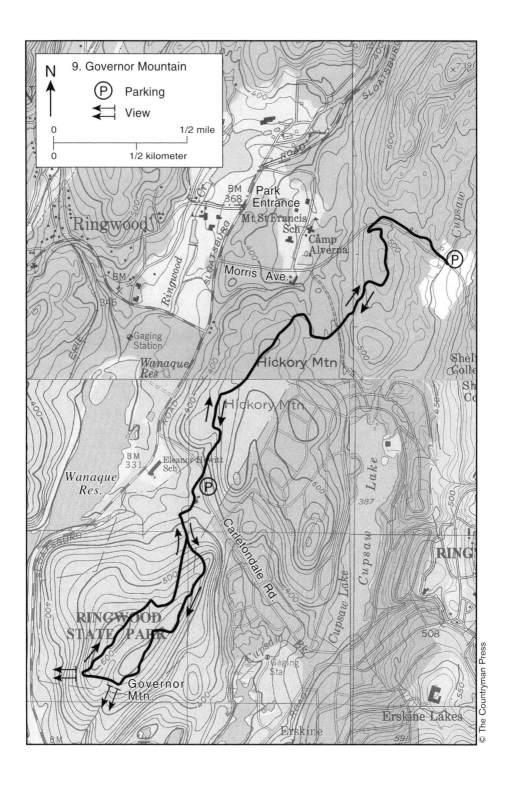

of a downhill section. The bridge has rock-faced sidewalls. Just past this bridge on the left is a wide dirt- and gravel-surfaced parking area (unsigned). Unfortunately, this parking spot is closed on weekends and holidays from Memorial Day to Labor Day. An alternative is the main parking area farther up the road, but this will add a mile of road walking to the full hike. Another possibility is to park near the trail crossing on Carltondale Road. To do this, return to Sloatsburg Road and turn left. After 0.7 mile, turn left onto Carltondale Road for 0.2 mile where there is very limited road shoulder parking. A little farther down is a large church and school parking area where you can ask permission to leave your car. This alternative reduces the hike to 2 miles.

THE TRAIL

The Cooper Union Trail, which starts near the New York–New Jersey border, crosses Morris Avenue back at the top of the hill you just drove down. Cross the bridge and walk up the road for 5 or 10 minutes till just short of the crest. Avoid the white-blazed trail you may notice going off to the right. Keep to the roadway: The sides are resplendent with poison ivy! Take a well-marked yellow-blazed trail to the left (south). It enters the woods on a wide path through a deep cut in the embankment. The trail wanders through open hardwoods for less than 10 minutes before coming to a pipeline. Follow the blazes right along the pipeline down through a wet muddy area. As the pipeline right-of-way again begins to rise, the trail will leave the pipeline, heading left. For the next half hour or so, the trail continues south until it reaches Carltondale Road. There are several well-defined but unmarked trails branching off, but only one turn. Stay with the blazes.

The trail crosses Carltondale Road and almost immediately levels out and heads into deep woods. There is some evidence of illegal mountain biking, but for the most part the trail is in good shape. The wide path passes through tall woods with lush undergrowth. Indian pipe, as well as some poison ivy, is evident. In spring, wildflowers are abundant. Pass by a faint, dirt path going left to a school building yard and continue straight ahead.

In little more than 5 minutes, the trail splits, and a loop begins. Both forks are marked yellow. Take the left one–a 90-degree turn. Note the large hemlock tree in this particularly dense forest. The trail begins an uphill course here, gently at first and then more steeply. The steep parts of this hike are, however, always short-lived. At the top of the rise, the woodland thins out and gives way to more grasslands and open areas. The cedar trees here are especially lovely, large specimens with their typical symmetrical shapes. This stretch also has patches of poison ivy, so stay on the trail and be attentive, especially if you have children along.

The footpath narrows with gentle ups and downs as you traverse a plateau of the mountain, interspersed with some dense underbrush. There are small outcrops of rocks, blackberry bushes, more cedar groves, and moss patches. Though there is some evidence of illegal camping in this area, the moss on the trail is indicative of the generally light use. The walking is pleasant, and the ground is soft underfoot. Most people go in and out to the upcoming vista, using only the exit route of this hike. They see the fine view at the summit but miss this peaceful section.

After crossing a wet area on some stepping-stones, the trail swings steeply up to-

View from Governor Mountain

ward a panoramic viewpoint known locally as Suicide Ledge, just below the true summit of Governor Mountain. At a 600-foot elevation and some 300 feet above the water, the view is extensive. Below and ahead is the Wanaque Reservoir. Across the water, Board and Windbeam Mountains are prominent, the territory of the popular Stonetown Circular hike. Farther south are the hills of Norvin Green State Forest (see Hikes 10, 11, and 12).

Unfortunately, this area also attracts people who leave considerable litter. Each spring, the New York–New Jersey Trail Conference sponsors a Litter Day, when volunteers clean up many of the trails in the area of the New Jersey–New York metropolitan area. Governor Mountain has received special attention over the last several years and is much cleaner, at times, than it used to be. Each time we take this pleasant walk, we bring along a litter bag and spend 10 min-

utes cleaning up. It seems that litter attracts more litter, so if we leave it clean, we hope it stays that way longer—at least, that's the theory.

According to Ringwood Borough historian Bert Prol, the name Governor Mountain is probably a corruption of Gouvernour, the family name of the early owners (until 1764) of the Ringwood Ironworks. There was a beacon here during the Revolutionary War, part of a system linking Ramapo Torne Mountain near Suffern, New York and Federal Hill in Pompton Lakes. For more on the history of this area, see Hike 7, Ringwood Manor.

Leaving the viewpoint, turn right—uphill— to the actual summit of the mountain and follow the yellow blazes straight ahead. Ignore the white paint-marks here. You will soon pass a large glacial erratic on the left side of the trail. These boulders, quite common in New Jersey, were left behind as the

Governor Mountain

Ice Age glaciers retreated and melted. The large ones attest to the awesome power of nature's force.

Passing through a conifer grove and descending a little more steeply, the trail bends right, crosses another wet area on rock steps, and swings back to its original northward course. In a few minutes, you'll be back at the trail fork, having completed the loop. Continue over the same route upon which you entered, following the yellow markers. Be careful to take the one well-marked turn shortly before the pipeline.

The best time to journey forth is early on a weekend morning when you may be alone on the mountain and have the trail and viewpoint to yourself—your own personal "wilderness."

HNZ

10

Wyanokie Circular

Total distance: 7.3 miles

Hiking time: 6 hours

Vertical rise: 1,200 feet

Rating: Moderately strenuous

Maps: USGS Wanaque; NYNJTC North Jersey Trails, #21; NJWB #20

The Wyanokie Ridge, which forms part of the New Jersey Highlands, dates back to the Precambrian Period, and many of the rocks in the area are more than 600 million years old. These hills were here long before there was a Wanaque Reservoir or a New York skyline to be seen from the viewpoints on this hike. Blue iron ore was abundant, and villages grew up around the iron mining operations and charcoal furnaces scattered throughout the area. Construction of the Wanaque Reservoir, which is visible from several high points in the area, was started in 1920, and the reservoir was filled by 1949. Many Native American names remain in these parts. Wanaque and Wyanokie mean "sassafras"; other Native American words will be noted in the text of this hike.

This hike offers spectacular views, pleasant walking in the woods, some rock scrambling, waterfalls on Blue Mine Brook, and two mines in rugged territory. Partially on private land but mostly in the Norvin Green State Forest (c/o Ringwood Park, RD Box 1304, Ringwood, NJ 07456; 973-962-7031), the hike uses one of the largest concentrations of trails in New Jersey. Only a few trail junctions need your attention, because the hike's route mainly follows the red-marked Wyanokie Circular Trail (WCI), though portions of the Otter Hole (OH) (green); the recently blazed Will Monroe Trail (rhododendron, aka pink); and the Mine Trail (M) (yellow) are used as well. Several options are offered if the described hike needs to be shortened. Pets must be leashed. In season, one attractive possibility

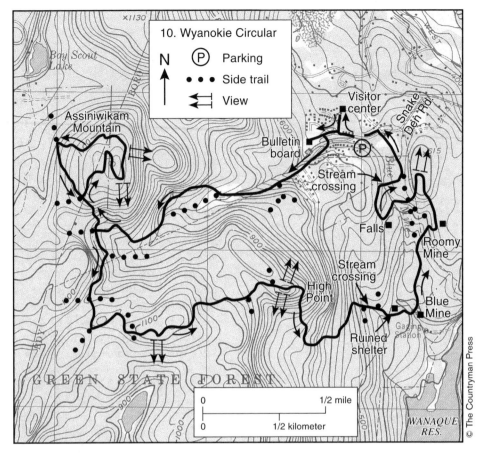

is to swim after your hike in the freshwater Highlands Natural Pool, adjacent to the Weis Ecology Center. A provisional membership is available permitting visitors to swim on three separate days. For updated information, call 973-835-2160 or visit the Web site at www.geocities.com/highlands_pool.

HOW TO GET THERE

Norvin Green State Forest is accessible from County Route 511, reached from the north by way of Skyline Drive or from the south by NJ 23. Turn west on West Brook Road about halfway along the Wanaque Reservoir. The road soon crosses the reser-

voir on a causeway, then parallels the water on the left. Shortly beyond the end of this reservoir inlet is a junction with Stonetown Road to the north. Bear left on West Brook Road, and after about 0.5 mile look for Snake Den Road on the left. Drive uphill, bearing left, past private homes to the main gate into the Weis Ecology Center.

The hike starts at the Weis Ecology Center (973-835-2160), now operated by the New Jersey Audubon Society. Two parking lots are available. The Center's parking lot is on the left just inside the gate, and the other outside the gate. The hike returns to the parking lot from a different direction than the starting point, so it is probably best to use the lot on Snake Den Road outside the gate. Also, the gate is locked during the winter months, when the office is closed. Overnight accommodations are available at moderate charges. The visitor center is small but worth a visit to pick up the trail map and information on the Weis Ecology Center's programs and workshops.

THE TRAIL

Walk to the western end of the parking lot to find the green triple blazes indicating the beginning of the Otter Hole Trail, which you will follow for the first part of this hike. Other blazes belonging to trails offered by the Weis Ecology Center appear from time to time, and the first one to be seen, on a tree to the right, is the outline of a bird on a beige and blue background. The Otter Hole Trail turns left just before the ball field, opposite the trail to the visitor center and then, almost immediately, turns right. This particularly pleasant entryway parallels the Blue Mine Brook on the left, and a row of large Norway spruce trees on the right. Wooden bridges to the left across the brook lead to the interior parking lot. Bear right, still following green blazes. The lower end of the Highlands Pool can be seen on the left, and a bulletin board on the right. The green W and the orange L blazes mark the routes of trails in the Weis Ecology Center system, and the Otter Hole Trail co-mingles with them in this section.

Climbing now, bear left at a fork in the road, and quickly make another left to walk by the side of the cement-bordered weir that regulates the supply of water to the pool. After crossing on a wooden bridge over the brook, proceed on the rocky trail to emerge on Snake Den Road. The rerouted Hewitt–Butler Trail, the yellow markers of the Mine Trail, and a bulletin board recently constructed as an Eagle Scout project are immediately opposite. Turn right to follow the continuation of Snake Den Road, which soon dips down to cross Blue Mine Brook at an old bridge abutment. The next 2.5 miles are mostly a steady climb until the summit of Assiniwikam Mountain is achieved.

Just as the woods road bends to the left, watch carefully for a turn to the right on the Otter Hole Trail. The narrower, rocky footway enters this new terrain at a gap in a rock wall, but eventually descends to join the same woods road farther along. About 1.5 miles into the hike, watch carefully on a tree to the left for a green turn signal indicating that the Otter Hole Trail turns left. There is a faint red paint arrow, and a sign for the Glenwild Fire Road opposite that tree. A badly eroded fire road, occasionally marked with white paint blazes, also joins here from the right, and this gullied and rocky track is the one to take. It is often easier to walk on one of the sides of the ditch rather than in the center. (Should you fail to spot this intersection and turn left on the Otter Hole Trail, continue until it intersects the WCI, then turn right.)

Partway up the ascent of this rocky road, turn right where it crossed the WCI, blazed with a red dot on a white background. A partly demolished cairn on the right might also alert you to the turn. (If you should miss it, and continue ahead on the road, a right turn on the yellow-blazed Wyanokie Crest Trail also leads to the junction with the pink trail, and little harm would be done.)

After the turn and an initial rocky climb, the trail flattens out, and approximately 2 miles from the start, reaches another major junction. The WCI continues ahead to Boy Scout Lake, the yellow-blazed Wyanokie Crest Trail begins (or ends) here to the left, and the Will Monroe Loop begins on the right, marked with three pink blazes on a tree and some on a boulder. This loop to the summit of Assiniwikam Mountain is one of the highlights of the hike, not to be missed.

Professor Will S. Monroe was the original Wyanokie trailblazer during the 1920s. This recently opened 1-mile loop was created from the segment of the Wyanokie Crest Trail that the landowner had closed to hikers. The trail is now entirely on state land, and incorporates great views to the southwest and the east, which would otherwise have been lost. It also includes some interesting ups and downs on rock slabs, and passes by some outstanding rock formations. Unfortunately, some stands of trees have been killed by recent droughts and by gypsy moth caterpillar infestations, but in spring, the blooming shadbush–also called downy serviceberry–makes a wondrous sight. Tradition claims that these trees bloom at the same time that shad ascend the rivers to spawn.

A favorite spot to take a break and take in one of the many views is at the large boulder perched on other, smaller rocks on an open slab. Over to the right is the Wanaque Reservoir, and straight out are the Pine Paddies, an alluring place now unfortunately closed to hikers.

After completing the Will Monroe loop, turn left on the WCI, soon retracing your previous route, and continue to follow the red markers, crossing that familiar eroded road, and the OH Trail, heading toward High Point. (The hike can be cut short here by turning left on the OH Trail and walking the 1.3 miles out to the Weis Ecology Center.) After a short climb, the WCI arrives at a large boulder and the junction with the end of an orange-blazed trail. Turn left here, cross an unmarked woods road, and perhaps take another break in 0.75 mile at the viewpoint where the WCI makes a sharp turn to the left. The WCI now descends for about a mile to a junction with the blue-blazed Hewitt–Butler Trail, where the red, blue, and turquoise markers of the Highlands Trail co-mingle, and there are wooden signs for High Point and the OH Trail. The WCI crosses a streambed, sometimes only a wet area, and begins the short, sharp climb to the summit of High Point. The Hewitt–Butler Trail leaves to the left at the base of the final climb, and can serve as an escape route back to your car. The trip of 1.2 miles, steeply downhill, emerges on the OH Trail, where a right turn leads back to the Weis Ecology Center.

Follow the red markers past an enormous boulder (with HIGH POINT painted on it in white) until you reach the large slabs of rock that form High Point. Views appear during the climb, first on the right, then on the left, until at the top is a magnificent 360-degree vista. The Manhattan skyline and the Wanaque Reservoir are visible, and be sure to turn your back to the reservoir and look for two power lines on the horizon. If you follow the left one with your eyes to the second ridge, you can see the Pine Paddies mentioned previously.

When the time comes to leave this superb viewpoint, seek the trail in the direction of the reservoir. The trail switchbacks steeply downward for 500 feet, at first on rock slabs, then later through woodlands. The terminus of the Lower Trail (white) enters from the right, while the WCI proceeds straight ahead to cross a stream on large boulders to meet the almost T-junction with the Mine Trail (yellow). Bear right, following both the yellow and red blazes of the joined trails.

The trail continues to drop until it reaches a grassy clearing with the Green Mountain Club shelter on the left. This lean-to is situated in an attractive open area but is in exceptionally poor repair, because for some time now it has been reduced only to rocky walls. Pass the ruined shelter and

Wyanokie glacial erratic (and hiker)

STELLA GREEN

continue on the trail, which leaves the open area, and after a few minutes bears left, leading to a bridge over Blue Mine Brook. Eagle Scouts built the sturdy bridge in 2002, together with volunteers from the New York–New Jersey Trail Conference.

Cross the bridge and turn right to see one of the entrances to the Blue Mine, so called because of the dark blue color of the local ore. Currently filled with water, it is also known as the Iron Hill, London, or Whynockie Mine. Until 1855, most of the ore was processed at a hot-blast charcoal furnace called the Freedom Furnace. For a short period after the Blue Mine's reopening in 1886, the mine produced about 300 tons of ore per month. Water in the mine was obviously a problem, and the mine was "dewatered" several times. This operation was quite difficult. Mine workers stood on a raft that sank lower as the water was pumped out. Their job was to remove the debris left clinging to the walls of the mine and to

shore up the timbers in the sides of the shaft, while keeping their balance on the raft. After another de-watering operation in 1905, the mine was not worked again. The concrete pad in front of the mine was once used as a base for steam-operated equipment, and by exploring the surroundings you can detect other evidence of mining operations.

Go back to the bridge and continue along the rocky, eroded route of the old mine road, following the co-mingled Mine and WCI Trails, noting the sign indicating that you are on the way to the Weis Ecology Center. In less than another mile, turn right where the yellow blazes of the Mine Trail leave the red ones of the WCI, and follow the Mine Trail to visit Roomy Mine. If by now you have had enough hiking, then the two loops of the Mine Trail can be avoided by walking straight ahead on the WCI, back to the parking lot on Snake Den Road. The Mine Trail loops are attractive, and if you decide to eliminate them

today, a shorter, most enjoyable walk is recommended for another day.

Five minutes of climbing will bring you to
the entrance of Roomy Mine, also called
Laurel or Red Mine, and probably opened
shortly after 1840. This mine is said to have
been named for Benjamin Roome, a local
19th-century land surveyor. Extensive mining
was carried on here through an entrance in
the side of the hill above water level as well
as from the surface. The ore was compact
and mostly free of rock. The vein was about
4 feet thick with a pitch of 58 degrees, dip-
ping sharply to the southeast.

Roomy Mine's passage can still be entered. With a flashlight—and maybe a hard
hat—crawl through the mine entrance into
an open-air section; the passageway itself
lies straight ahead. Even in dry seasons
there is water underfoot, but the passageway can be walked for a distance of about
50 feet until it forks and dead-ends. Round
dynamite holes are visible in the roof. Exploring Roomy Mine takes about 30 minutes, but is not recommended in winter
conditions. Again the hike can be shortened
by using the orange-blazed Connection Trail
across the front of the mine. This shortcut

takes five minutes downhill to reach the
WCI, turning right to reach paved Snake
Den Road and the parking lot in another ten
minutes.

The Mine Trail climbs above Roomy Mine
on a steep and rocky path, passing several
exploratory mine holes on the way, but once
on top, the trail levels out and offers views
from the summit of Ball Mountain across the
valley to High Point, before descending
steeply to cross the WCI. Walk straight
across past a massive boulder and continue
on the Mine Trail to rock-hop over the top of
the falls on Blue Mine Brook, before descending to another stream crossing and a
short climb and descending to the WCI on
the old mine road. The loop to the falls and
back is about 0.5 mile. Turn left on the WCI,
and walk the 0.25 mile through an area of
spruce trees and the backyard of a private
home to emerge on Snake Den Road. Take
a moment to appreciate the graciousness of
the homeowners, who permit hikers to walk
across their property. Be aware that if hikers
become a nuisance here, permission to use
this route could easily be rescinded. Turn left
at the road and walk a minute or so back to
the parking lot of the Weis Ecology Center.

SJG

11

Carris Hill

Total distance: 5 miles

Hiking time: 4 hours

Vertical rise: 580 feet

Rating: Moderately strenuous

Maps: USGS Wanaque; NYNJTC North Jersey Trails, #21; NJWB #21

Although this hike is only 5 miles long, the rugged terrain and possibly difficult water crossings make for an exciting and challenging day hike. Carris Hill is not the highest point in Norvin Green State Forest (c/o Ringwood State Park, 1304 Sloatsburg Rd., Ringwood, NJ 07456-1799; 973-962-7031) but it includes a strenuous climb and an arduous descent. Good footwear is necessary, and take special care if you attempt this hike in winter—certain sections are on steep slopes of bare rock that could be difficult to navigate when covered with snow and ice. Posts Brook, which you will cross four times, is normally on the dry side and easily crossed on rocks. After a snowmelt or heavy rain, however, it becomes a raging torrent and can present serious problems.

HOW TO GET THERE

From NJ 23, follow County Route 511 north to Butler. After a series of turns, bear right at the railroad tracks on Main Street, then make a left turn at the T-intersection with Riverdale Avenue. From NJ 23 to here is 1.3 miles. Just 0.1 mile after this left turn, bear right onto Glenwild Avenue (sometimes called Glenwild—or Glen Wild—Road).

From I-287, Exit 53, take the Hamburg Turnpike east to Bloomingdale. In just less than 2 miles, bear right onto Riverdale Avenue, then right onto Glenwild.

Proceed another 3.3 miles on Glenwild and park at the Otter Hole parking area on the right-hand side of the road. There is space here for about 10 cars.

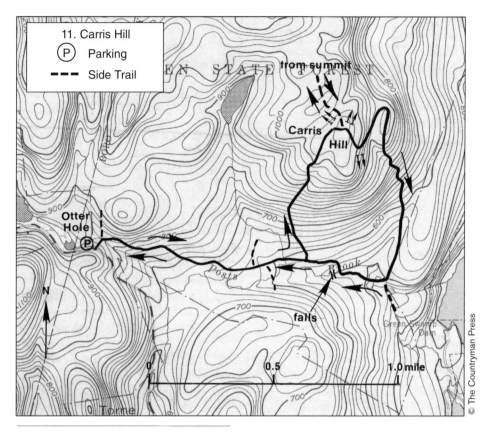

Otter Hole

Carris Hill

falls

0   0.5   1.0 mile

N

© The Countryman Press

THE TRAIL

For the first part of this hike, you will be following the blue-marked Hewitt–Butler Trail, an 18-mile hiking trail that traverses the entire Wyanokie Range. You will find blue markers heading north into the woods just before the parking area. Soon you will arrive at Otter Hole, a small cascade and falls on Posts Brook, popular with local young people. It is normally possible to cross the brook on rocks, but if this is impractical or dangerous, you should abort this hike and try another one. (Just across the road the Hewitt–Butler Trail ascends the Torne, a summit with several fine views.)

After you leave Otter Hole, follow the blue markers to an intersection with the green-marked Otter Hole Trail. Stay right on

the blue-marked Hewitt–Butler Trail, heading uphill and roughly parallel to Posts Brook. From here to the summit of Carris Hill, your route will be concurrent with that of the new 150-mile Highlands Trail (see the Introduction) marked with green and blue diamond blazes. After a short distance, the trail begins a long, steady decline. Be alert for a left turn—the markers direct you away from the woods road and onto a narrower footpath. The trail is now a little more rugged in places. About 15 to 20 minutes from the start of the hike, you will reach a junction with the yellow-marked Wyanokie Crest Trail. Bear left. For a short distance the two trails share the same path; after only 75 feet, though, the Crest Trail swings away to the left. Continue straight ahead, following blue markers along an old road that can be wet in places. Logs laid crosswise like railroad ties help keep your feet dry. To the right, catch glimpses and hear the sounds of falls and cascades as Posts Brook now splits temporarily into two streams. Just ahead the trail goes to the edge of the brook and crosses another, smaller stream coming in from the left. You are at a junction of running waters, a place where streams merge. Immediately after this potentially difficult stream crossing, the Hewitt–Butler Trail turns left. Straight ahead is the Lower Trail. You will reach this point again on the return trip. The steady uphill climb to the summit of Carris Hill begins here.

At first the trail gains elevation very slowly as it snakes its way through the woods. Soon the footing gets rockier, although there is a temporary reprieve along the bed of an abandoned woods road. The trail then bears to the right and the climb begins in earnest. The Hewitt–Butler Trail now follows what appears to be a man-made path up the side of the mountain, possibly used for lumbering in the past. Eventually the slope lessens and the footpath meanders through an area characterized by blueberry bushes, moss, occasional glacial erratics, and numerous exposures of bedrock. This terrain is typical of the Precambrian gneiss and granite of the New Jersey Highlands. A slight descent into an area that is sometimes wet brings needed relief, but almost immediately the climb resumes.

Now gaining elevation, the trail passes through laurel and traverses the first of a series of bare rock outcrops contoured with green moss and tall grasses. The first evergreens (hemlocks) are encountered here, and pitch pines appear, often heavily laden with clumps of pine cones. The trail descends slightly into a dense heath forest before it continues, now fairly gradually, up to

Mushrooms

bare rock and the first of a few small false summits. Look behind you. The views of the Torne, Osio Rock, and beyond are steadily improving. After another slight descent into a laurel depression, the trail winds through scrub pine to the true summit with views to the south, west, and north. There is a real feeling of accomplishment from reaching this heavily glaciated summit. Wyanokie High Point is to the north, and from this vantage point it looks like a small cluster of bare rocks. Beyond it and to the right is Windbeam Mountain. To the immediate west are Assiniwikam Mountain, Buck Mountain, and the Torne.

At the summit look for the yellow markers of the Carris Hill Trail, which begins here and heads east. Follow this trail for a few minutes out over the broad, flat summit of Carris Hill to other viewpoints. Here you'll find pines on bare rock outcrops and a large glacial erratic. The expansive views are to the south and southeast. To the left of the large boulder, follow yellow markers downhill, off the summit. After only 100 yards you will reach yet another viewpoint, this one overlooking the Wanaque Reservoir, nearby Green Swamp Dam, and the more distant Raymond Dam. From here the trail begins a steeper descent. The footing can be difficult until you reach a rock formation not unlike a wall. The trail turns right, following to the right of the wall. If you scramble up the ledge on your left you'll find an even broader view of the reservoir and beyond. Then head south and down, rather steeply in places. A few cedars line the trail, which winds around a deep and jagged cliff. In some sections you have to be very careful, and you'll need careful planning and proper equipment (crampons) in icy or slippery conditions.

Once off the main part of the hill, the going is much more manageable, though still quite steep. Continue following yellow markers steadily downhill over rocky ground. Eventually you will reach a small brook; crossing might be difficult in times of high water. (If this is a problem, keep to the west of the brook and bushwhack downstream to Posts Brook, about 0.1 mile from here.) Soon the yellow-marked Carris Hill Trail terminates at a junction with the Lower Trail, marked in white. Turn right here, following white markers, with the Wanaque Reservoir fence to your left.

At a rock outcropping near the fence corner, find a trail junction and turn right, now following the white markers of the Posts Brook Trail; do not follow the white markers of another trail that lead straight ahead. Soon you'll need to cross Posts Brook; if this presents a problem, one option is to follow the brook upstream to a rocky area where there is a large fallen tree that you can use as a bridge. If you find this too difficult, you may have to wade across the brook.

A short distance ahead is Chickahoki Falls—a 25-foot sluiceway of water, split in two as the water tumbles into a huge plunge pool. These falls are impressive in spring or after a rain. Just below the falls, the trail once again crosses Posts Brook and climbs the bank—bearing left and following Posts Brook closely—revealing other cascades farther upstream. In just a few minutes you will reach the junction with the blue-marked Hewitt–Butler and the green- and blue-marked Highlands Trails that you encountered earlier, where the climb to Carris Hill began. Follow the blue markers straight ahead, the way you came. Most of the way back is a gradual uphill climb and can be tiring. After about a half hour, turn left, cross over Otter Hole, and return to your car.

BCS

12

Torne Mountain–Osio Rock

Total distance: 2.2 or 3.7 miles

Hiking time: 2+ or 3.5 hours

Vertical rise: 525 to 850 feet

Rating: Easy to Moderate

Maps: USGS Wanaque; NYNJTC North Jersey Trails, #21; NJWB, #21

Although this hike starts at a popular trailhead, most hikers head north into the main section of Norvin Green State Forest. The climbs can be steep but most are very short. Views abound and you are likely to find solitude for most of the day. This hike includes a visit to the Stone Living Room, which is featured on the Web site www.weirdnj.com. The main section of this hike (2.25 miles) is a loop while the optional extension is an out-and-back climb to a yet another fine viewpoint. While the hike utilizes a number of different trails, the main one is a segment of the blue-blazed Hewitt–Bulter Trail, one of the area's longest at 14 miles.

Members of the local chapter of the Green Mountain Club planned and constructed many of the trails in Norvin Green in the 1920s, and later the trails were maintained by the Nature Friends. Their former camp is now the Weis Ecology Center a few miles to the north (see Hike 10, Norvin Green State Forest, and Hike 11, Carris Hill). This area must have seemed pretty remote 90 years ago.

HOW TO GET THERE

To get to the trailhead, take I-287 to Exit 53. Follow the Hamburg Turnpike 1.4 miles east into and through Bloomingdale and bear right at a fork. Very shortly after the fork (careful or you'll miss it), go right onto Glenwild Avenue for another 3.2 miles to a dirt parking area on the right. If this lot is full, there is space for more cars a little farther down the road.

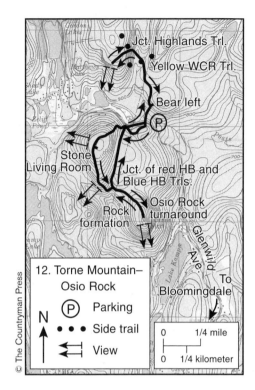

12. Torne Mountain–
Osio Rock

N

(P) Parking

●●● Side trail

⇄ View

0   1/4 mile

0   1/4 kilometer

© The Countryman Press

THE TRAIL

Cross the highway and begin heading south along the blue blazes of the Hewitt–Butler Trail. A wooden post hosts the first blaze as well as a blue reflector. You begin climbing a narrow rocky trail and quickly seem to leave civilization behind—well, except for some road noise! After a small dip the climb resumes and then a descent begins into a ravine and you'll notice how close you are to Glenwild Avenue again, but not for long. Make a mental note of this spot, because this is where this loop hike closes.

Pass by the junction with the start of the red-blazed Torne Trail and continue ahead (slightly left) following the blue blazes, climbing steeply at times. After 15 minutes or so you'll reach a large rock ledge with an extensive vista to the north. Most of what you see is Norvin Green State Forest land.

Note the rock outcropping just across the valley. This is the extension hike destination.

Continue ahead following blue blazes—there are some unmarked paths in this area—as the trail contours around the edge of Torne Mountain (1,120 feet). A minute's hike through woods brings you to a second open area, this time with a view to the west over a sea of trees. Soon you'll reach yet a third open area. Here you should be able to see three blue blazes: one on a dead tree, one on a rock, and the third on the surface rock. Look to your left and you'll see the open area through a small patch of brush. Note where you are (you'll need to return here) and bushwhack about 30 yards over to the open area. The large man-made circle of rocks is called the Stone Living Room.

A large circle of rock chairs, tables, and sofas around a fireplace (fires are illegal), the Stone Living Room was built, according to at least one local, by a cult. Reportedly you could hear the cult members chanting at night as they got close to the stars. In any case, whoever built it was certainly energetic, because some of the stones must weight hundreds of pounds. This is not a good place to stick fingers into crevasses—we have seen snakes every time we have been here. Regrettably, vandalism in 2005 has marred the site. There is talk of restoring it, so we hope your visit will be as rewarding as ours.

Return to the trail and continue circling the mountain, which offers many fabulous views to the south and east if the sky is clear, including the New York City skyline. Here you'll notice that many of the larger trees are dead. It turns out not to be from an old fire, as we first thought, but a combination of a series of dry summers and heavy gypsy moth infestations, one of the less attractive parts of the forest's life cycle. Follow the blazes carefully in this brushy area and take your

Torne Mountain glacial rocks

time, especially when descending. There are good views over toward Osio Rock.

The trail now descends to a low point between Torne Mountain and Osio Rock, where you should spot the three red blazes that denote the start of the Torne Trail, our route back. You'll be returning here, but for now continue following blue blazes (the trail bends to the right) as the trail begins to climb Osio Rock, passing one very large glacial boulder.

The view at the top of Osio, some 15 minutes from the low point, is a fabulous, 360-degree vista and it's a great place for lunch. The large body of water is the Wanaque Reservoir, and the curving elevated roadway in the distance is I-287. The little lake below is Lake Kempfe, which is privately owned. Some pathetic graffiti mars the summit itself.

Return to the low point and now switch to the red-blazed Torne Trail as it climbs steeply up a (hopefully dry) streamed to a

pass, levels for a while, and then gently descends back to the blue/red junction near Glenwild Road—the same one you passed early in the hike. From here you can walk out to the road shoulder, turn right, and return to your car in about a minute.

You've hiked 2.2 miles and climbed (and descended) 520 feet. Ready for more?

On the same side of the road as the parking area (at the eastern edge), follow the blue-blazed Hewitt–Butler trail north. Soon you'll be rock-hopping across a wide part of Posts Brook. If the water is high or the rocks icy, leave this part of the hike for another day.

This section is known as Otter Hole. Sorry, there are no otters (anymore?) but there is a lovely series of pools and cascades.

Shortly after the crossing is a major trail junction. Note the three green blazes that begin the Otter Hole Trail, occasionally marked as well with the blue diamonds of the Highlands Trail. Follow the green blazes to the left on a rocky woods roads for 10 or 15 minutes. Watch for a yellow blaze that will alert you to an upcoming junction where the Wyanokie Crest Trail crosses. Here you turn left onto the yellow trail, now and then also marked with blue diamond blazes.

After a short descent crossing a wet area, the steady and sometimes steep 300-foot climb up Buck Mountain begins. Follow the blazes carefully, because the route can be unclear in the brushy areas of the slope. At one point the path makes a left instead of climbing straight up. There are some nice views behind you.

At last the slope gets gentler and you'll emerge at a viewpoint rock guarded by a wonderfully sculptured pine tree, one of my favorite spots. The view across the valley is of Torne Mountain and Osio Rock.

Retrace your steps to the parking area. It should take about a half hour.

HNZ

13

Terrace Pond

Total distance: 4.5 miles

Hiking time: 3.5 hours

Vertical rise: 350 feet

Rating: Moderate

Maps: USGS Wawayanda, Newfoundland; NYNJTC North Jersey Trails #21; NJWB #21.

This hike in Wawayanda State Park (Box 198, Highland Lakes, NJ 07422; 973-853-4462) is on land once called the Sussex Woodlands when it was owned by Fred Ferber, a Depression-era immigrant from Austria. Ferber was not a lover of state parks; he objected to hunting and to such facilities as restaurants, toilets, and campsites, normally found in state parks. His ambition was to keep his property as wilderness, untouched by such facilities. But gradually, as he ran into debt over the years, he sold portions of his land to the state. Bearfort Mountain Ridge, which contains Terrace Pond, was one of the last tracts sold, in 1973.

This hike uses the Terrace Pond South Trail (marked in yellow); the Terrace Pond Red trail; the White Trail circling Terrace Pond; and the Terrace Pond North Trail (marked in blue). The terrain is varied, and all sections are superb. At first the hike is gentle, but the approach to Terrace Pond—the climax of the hike—is reminiscent of a roller coaster. You must also negotiate some wet areas.

HOW TO GET THERE

The trailhead is on the east side of Clinton Road, which runs north from NJ 23 to Warwick Turnpike. Look for it 1.7 miles south of the junction with Warwick Turnpike, or 7.3 miles north of NJ 23. There is a parking area just north of the entrance to the Wildcat Environmental Center. This marking is designated as P7 on some New York–New Jersey Trail Conference maps.

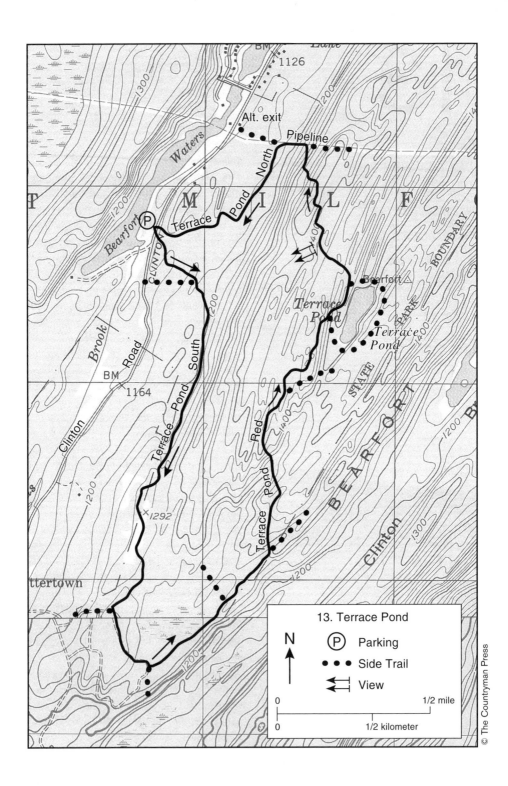

BM
1126

Alt. exit

Pipeline

Waters

1300

1200

T   M   I   L   F

Bearfort

P

Terrace Pond North

1200

1164

Brook

Road

BM

Clinton

Terrace Pond South

×1292

ttertown

CLINTON

1200

1200

Bearfort △

Terrace Pond

Terrace Pond

PARK

BOUNDARY

1400

1400

STATE

Red

Terrace Pond

B E A R F O R T

1400

1200

Clinton

1300

1200 B

13. Terrace Pond

N

P   Parking

• • •   Side Trail

◄—   View

0   1/2 mile

0   1/2 kilometer

© The Countryman Press

THE TRAIL

Cross the road and enter the woods on a steep uphill gradient, following yellow markers. Ignore the blue trail on the left. Instead follow the mossy, yellow-marked trail up and over a small hill through mountain laurel and white pine. Trail markers are mixed; some are painted blazes, some are can tops painted yellow, and others are premade and nailed to trees. Large signs have been placed at some trail intersections indicating the trail name, color, and usage. Volunteers from the New York–New Jersey Con- ference continue their work to improve the trail through wet sections. Very soon the trail winds around a swampy area to the left over bog bridges, then parallels a small stream. You soon move away from the stream to the right and, still climbing, proceed through a piney area and across an interesting rock.

A ridge appears ahead, and eventually the trail meanders along the valley on its right side, winding through white pine and mountain laurel. The trail here is sometimes wet, and there are some blowdowns. Within 30 minutes from the beginning of the hike, you turn left to climb this same ridge. This section of the trail is spectacular. It becomes rockier, travels along the side of the hill with a drop to the right, and follows substantial cliffs on the left that are scattered with huge boulders. A magnificent grove of tall rhododendrons arches completely over the trail. Red paint marks appear on the trees to your right, probably indicating the state park boundary.

Pick your way through boulders and blowdowns until you reach the top of the ridge, where the trail levels out through a more open area until it reaches a whale-shaped rock formation on the left. Look straight ahead for a yellow marker on a tree, and walk out to very open terrain through oak trees. Within two minutes from the whale-shaped rock, the trail leads to the right, near the rubble of an old farm wall. Before the wall, there is a pleasant place to take a break on a large rock to the left. This rock looks down over a tiny, elongated lake. At times this area is probably just a marsh, but the rocks to the left make a natural dam to hold back the water.

Back on the trail, walk through larches and remnants of old rock walls and turn left onto an old woods road. There are many woods roads and old walls in this spot. Within a very short time, the trail makes another left onto a woods road, and you'll see evidence of another ruined wall. Though trail markers are infrequent, the woods road is very wide at this point, and the route is obvious. After another wall crossing, be sure to turn right through an area of deciduous trees and mountain laurel.

Another 10 minutes brings you to a T-junction. Turn left, descending through a swampy area, then climb back up until you reach another woods road junction. Turn left again. The swampy area on the left here drains to the valley on the right through two concrete conduits that cross the road. The trail here is often flooded because of the blocked culverts and diverts occasionally to avoid standing water. Shortly, the trail turns left off this woods road. By climbing to the top of the rocks to the right of this junction, you can see the Lookout Tower in the Newark watershed.

Two miles into the hike, the yellow Terrace Pond South Trail leaves to the left and three blazes resembling fried eggs (a yellow circle on a white background) indicate the beginning of the Yellow Dot Trail. Walk straight ahead on this wide woods road for 0.2 mile. Leave the Yellow Dot Trail here—it continues straight ahead—and turn left onto the Terrace Pond Red Trail, which is now a

Autumn tree

more traditional trail. When we last walked here we found the blazes to be infrequent and sometimes indistinct.

The trail flattens out briefly, but then climbs through more rugged terrain before descending into an attractive valley with a stream crossing. Your route now crosses several low ridges before the trail continues along the base of a large slab of pudding-stone rock, which it then climbs to continue across the top. After approximately 45 minutes walking on the Terrace Pond Red Trail, the footway descends to a junction with the Terrace Pond South Trail, the trail originally used for this hike. For a short distance you'll see both red and yellow markers, until the yellow blazes leave to the right almost immediately. Bear left for less than 0.5 mile, continuing to follow the red blazes of the Terrace Pond Red Trail, which traverses large rocky scrambles, sometimes interspersed with traditional trail sections, until it descends to a junction with the white-marked Terrace Pond Circular Trail.

Turn left. The Terrace Pond Circular Trail encircles Terrace Pond, but making a right turn leads farther from Terrace Pond, and the outlet of the pond is sometimes difficult to negotiate. Your route is north along the west side of Terrace Pond, with many beautiful rock slabs overlooking the water to tempt you to rest awhile and enjoy the wonderful sight of this glacial lake. In less than 0.25 mile this section of the trail ends at a T-junction with the blue-marked Terrace Pond North Trail, which goes both left and right. Turn left.

The blue-marked Terrace Pond North Trail will take you consecutively over ridges and through wet areas, sometimes on puncheons. Stay on the trail until it leads you to a high ridge, which you should climb for a stupendous view of the Wawayanda Plateau.

After refreshing your spirit with the beautiful panorama, continue on the blue trail, which passes alternately through woody, wet areas and rock outcrops. Some of the descents, although short, are steep and slippery. The main direction is downhill, until quite suddenly the trail comes upon the ugly slash of a pipeline. You are now about 20 minutes away from your car.

Turn left and follow the pipeline down for approximately 0.5 mile, keeping to the left of the gash on the hill and looking for the blue arrows to confirm that you are still on the trail. Ignore the several woods roads to the left. Just as the pipeline levels off, you will reach a very distinct, blue-marked woods road. If you miss it, follow the pipeline to Clinton Road, turn left, and walk 0.3 mile along the road to the parking lot. Consider taking this alternate route in wet weather.

The blue-marked road is wide, but somewhat damp. Stay with the blue blazes where the woods road bears right and the trail continues straight ahead. The trail is very low-lying, and as you walk, you will notice the ridge to the left, down which you have just walked. This section is very pretty, passing through white pine, thick mountain laurel, and a dense hemlock grove with large trees. There are several streams to cross, however, and the trail bends left and right. The path somewhat parallels the paved road, finally turning right and climbing, then descending, to the road immediately opposite the parking area.

SJG

14

Bearfort Ridge

Total distance: 7 miles

Hiking time: 5.5 hours

Vertical rise: 1,200 feet

Rating: Moderately strenuous

*Maps: USGS Greenwood Lake (NY/NJ);
NYNJTC North Jersey Trails, #21;
NJWB #19; DEP Hewitt State Forest map*

This hike is in Abram S. Hewitt State Forest, administered by the superintendent of Wawayanda State Park (885 Warwick Turnpike, Hewitt, NJ; 973-853-4462) as a day-use area; no camping or swimming is permitted. Bearfort Mountain, which this hike traverses, may still even have a few bears—they have been seen in nearby Wawayanda—and it is assumed that this is the derivation of the name. This is a balloon hike with a very short in-and-out tail to your car.

HOW TO GET THERE

From the large shopping center—which contains a post office and an A&P superstore—in Browns, on the southwestern shore of Greenwood Lake where County Route 511 meets CR 513, continue west 0.1 mile on CR 513 to a fork in the road. Take the right fork (Warwick Turnpike) going uphill. Cross a small concrete bridge marked #446 and park on the right side of the road just after the bridge. If you go too far, you'll immediately come to another junction, White Road going off to the left.

THE TRAIL

The pathway leaves the north side of the road, just to the left (north) of the bridge. Three white paint blazes—the typical start-of-trail marking—clearly indicate the beginning of the Bearfort Ridge (BR) Trail. It has also been newly signed as the Jeremy Glick Trail, to honor a local hero of 9/11. Glick was one of the passengers who tried to regain control of Flight 93, which crashed in Pennsylvania.

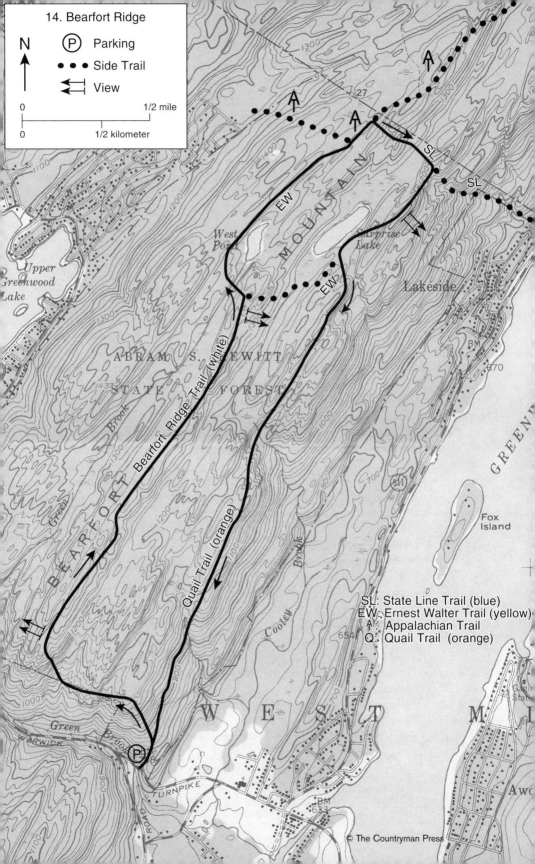

14. Bearfort Ridge

Ⓟ Parking
••• Side Trail
⇄ View

N

0   1/2 mile
0   1/2 kilometer

SL: State Line Trail (blue)
EW: Ernest Walter Trail (yellow)
A: Appalachian Trail
Q: Quail Trail (orange)

© The Countryman Press

Starting uphill through a pretty grove of hemlocks and rhododendrons, the trail traverses the slope for a short time before heading gently up and joining a woods road. Following the white markers, proceed left along the woods road and, after a short distance, turn left again, uphill and off the road. The main woods road, marked with orange paint blazes, continues northward to Surprise Lake. Note this spot, as it will be your route back.

The BR Trail is well marked with white paint rectangles. It climbs moderately uphill, with some steep pitches, through a mixed hardwood forest consisting of red, black, and white oak, and some maple, ash, beech, and birch. The forests here were heavily timbered for charcoal production during the area's iron-producing period. This forest is therefore the second—or even third—growth of trees.

After crossing a boggy section in a small hollow, the trail continues ahead along the side of a slope. Except for some road noise from nearby Warwick Turnpike, there is a feeling of isolation in deep woods. You may or may not notice a side trail to the left, which is a short link to Warwick Turnpike and the Terrace Pond North trailhead. As you proceed, gaining elevation, the road noise quickly fades, and the real beauty of this area becomes evident. Passing through some tall and lush rhododendrons—magnificent in June when they bloom—the climb begins to steepen. After you ascend through some rocks and along the base of a ledge, there is a worthwhile, south-facing viewpoint off the trail to the right. The steep, bare-faced peak across the road is another part of this same mountain. Continuing ahead and upward, you soon reach the first of the pitch pines that dominate the main part of the hike.

As the trail turns right onto the ledge, a scramble up the large rock on the left of the trail yields another fine view. The water in the distance is a small section of Upper Greenwood Lake. This viewpoint is also a good place to take note of the rock formation that composes much of Bearfort Ridge. A collection of white quartz pebbles imbedded in a red puddingstone, it is considered similar to the Shawangunk conglomerate of the Kittatinny Mountains. These rocks generally make for secure footing, but, as usual, take extra care when they are wet or icy.

Now a little more than a half hour into the hike, continue on the trail as it climbs up onto the ledges. The BR Trail now begins a several-mile course along the outcroppings, with several dips back into the woods to cross small hollows and streambeds. There are some sudden but well-marked turns; if you lose the white blazes, retrace a short way back and pick up the turn. The elevation is generally 1,300 feet or more, and the climb up has been more than 600 feet. The views from this section of the BR Trail are not as sweeping as those behind you or to come, but the charm of the landscape surrounds you. Note the fine array of mosses along—and occasionally even in—the footway, indicative of the surprisingly light use this tract receives. The boulders strewn along the way have been moved to these spots by glaciers, remaining from the ancient ice sheets as they melted and retreated north. Striations on the rock surface can also be attributed to this period. I've always had a special fondness for the pitch pines with their distinctive, thick shingle bark. To me they are like large Japanese bonsai trees. I admire their intricate shapes and the way they cling to life on the otherwise barren rocks.

One of the nicest spots in all of New Jersey is about a half-hour hike along this ridgetop. Here, a large section of rock has split away from the base, leaving a deep

Hiking on Bearfort Ridge

STELLA GREEN

crevice just to the left of the footway. On the far side of the split is an attractive swamp. This spot has long been a favorite of ours for lunch or "elevenses" (our traditional, mid-morning snack break around 11 AM). The separation of rock here possibly commenced as water seeped into cracks and then expanded with repeated freezings. Time and erosion have widened it to more dramatic dimensions. At first we named this spot the knife edge, but when one companion suggested it was more like a butter knife, we dropped the name and have been looking for a more appropriate appellation ever since.

Continuing ahead, pass a rather large boulder. After a while, cross a stream, then climb up through a rock notch. The ridge soon becomes less pronounced, with fewer rock outcroppings and rhododendron and mountain laurel reappearing. As the trail gently rises out of the woods, a symmetrical

cedar tree dominates the skyline. Another 40 yards ahead are three white paint blazes on the top of a small rock bump, indicating the end of the BR Trail, about 2.5 miles (and about 2 hours) from the hike's start.

From this spot you discern your first good view of Surprise Lake. You will pass this lake later, and the hike's route will return to this spot. The view is extensive, with only small traces of civilization. Off to the right in the distance is a section of the new Wanaque Reservoir. From here, the hike begins a loop that starts and ends on the yellow-blazed Ernest Walter Trail (EW Trail), named for a dedicated hiker and trailblazer.

This trail, like the others in the area, is normally well marked. However, in the late 1980s, a vandal systematically and repeatedly painted out the blazes on this trail and portions of many others. Volunteers with the New York–New Jersey Trail Conference made extra efforts to keep the trail well marked, and the vandal now seems to have stopped his mischief. The loop you now begin, past West Pond and Surprise Lake, is worth the small extra effort involved.

The yellow blazes lead both right and left. Proceed left, walking the loop in a clockwise direction. The trail descends 20 feet down a rock face and onto a narrow footpath. Because it crosses "against the grain" on the ridge, the route undulates pleasantly through the woods and outcroppings, soon crossing Green Brook, the outlet stream of West Pond. Shortly afterward, you will see your first view of the pond. You may see a yellow arrow for a short trail to a viewpoint or take a few minutes to bushwhack down to the shore to appreciate its backcountry charm. The trail wanders above the shore but does not actually go down to the pond's edge

The EW Trail continues along the ridge, then crosses the small outlet of a swamp. The trail bends to the right and leaves the ridge, heading down to a hollow where it ends at a T-junction with the white-blazed Appalachian Trail (AT). See Hike 4, Appalachian Trail Backpack, for background information on this National Scenic Trail.

Follow the white blazes of the AT, climbing to the top of a 20-foot rock outcropping where the trail veers to the right. Not long after, you will catch another glimpse of Surprise Lake before the AT descends to a junction. Here the State Line Trail, a blue dot (or square) in a white field, departs to the right. Follow the blue blazes downhill off the ridge.

After about 15 or 20 minutes going generally downhill on the State Line Trail, you will encounter another junction. This spot is the other end of the U-shaped EW Trail. Some of the yellow markings may be visible through the woods to the right before you reach the junction itself. Make a sharp right turn onto

the EW Trail and climb steeply up to a promontory overlooking Greenwood Lake.

Surprise Lake is now about 20 minutes away, but the journey may take longer—the views on this rise are super and invite lingering. Much of the two-state area of Greenwood Lake is visible. The large island in the middle is Fox Island, and across the lake are the mountains of the new Sterling Forest State Park (NY) and Wanaque Wildlife Management Area (NJ). Area hikers were a major (arguably *the* major) supporting force in a successful campaign to bring these lands into the park systems of the two states.

Leave the ridge and turn right into the woods, passing a pile of shale ruins. The origin of the ruins is unknown to us. (Any ideas?) Just before the shore of Surprise Lake, there are a few unmarked side trails, so keep a close watch on those yellow markers. Your impressions of this graceful lake may be determined by how many people are there or by what litter and debris they have left. It sees heavy warm-weather use.

Here you have a choice. You can continue following the yellow EW blazes for a half-mile climb to its end at the previously encountered junction with the BR trail then retracing your steps on the BR trail back to your car. This adds about a mile to the hike, but you'll be pleasantly surprised at how different the trail looks when you're traveling in the opposite direction.

If you want to make more of a loop, look for the orange-blazed Quail Trail (QT). The orange and yellow trails split about 100 feet from the beach, the yellow EW trail turning sharply right and the orange QT going straight ahead.

The Quail Trail is an old woods road that was marked about a decade ago to make the road easier to follow, creating a marked loop route. It is not often maintained, shows signs of illegal all-terrain vehicle (ATV) use, and at times can be wet underfoot. However, it is mostly easy walking and passes by some lovely rock and cliff formations on both sides of the trail. Its length is just under 2.5 miles.

Less than 2 miles from the lake, the trail heads steeply downhill for a short stretch, then passes a major woods road heading sharply off to the left.

Two or three minutes farther along, you'll see the last orange blaze at the previously encountered junction with the Bearfort Ridge Trail. Continue ahead, now following the white blazes back to your car, just a minute or so away.

HNZ

15

Pequannock Watershed

Total distance: 8 miles (9.5 without car shuttle)

Hiking time: 6 hours

Vertical rise: 400 feet

Rating: Moderately strenuous

Maps: USGS Newfoundland; NYNJTC North Jersey Trails #21; NJWB #21; Pequannock Watershed trails map

This outstanding hiking area is named for the Pequannock River. Pequannock is an Algonquin word said to mean "battlefield." The river is fed by the streams, lakes, and reservoirs of this mountainous and particularly scenic section of western Passaic County. Owned by the city of Newark, this natural area just south of Wawayanda State Park supplies much of Newark's drinking water. The Newark Watershed Conservation and Development Corporation (NWCDC), a nonprofit organization, has cut and blazed about 30 miles of excellent hiking trails in this largely uninhabited area, and the land is open for recreational use by permit only. You must apply in person at the NWCDC headquarters on Echo Lake Road, on the left about 1 mile north of NJ 23. At the time of this writing, the fee is $8 per year and well worth it. Contact the NWCDC at PO Box 319, Newfoundland, NJ 07435, or call 973-697-2850.

Originally, all the trails in the watershed were blazed in white, but when the New York–New Jersey Trail Conference took over the task of trail maintenance, they were color-coded. Markings are standard: Three blazes indicates the beginning or the end of a trail, two blazes indicates a turn, and one blaze simply shows the route of the trail.

This hike takes you on a grand tour of some of the watershed's more scenic and interesting features. Though it is long, the walking is not difficult, and much of it is along the shores of ponds and reservoirs. You will traverse some deep hemlock forests typical of this area, and there are a

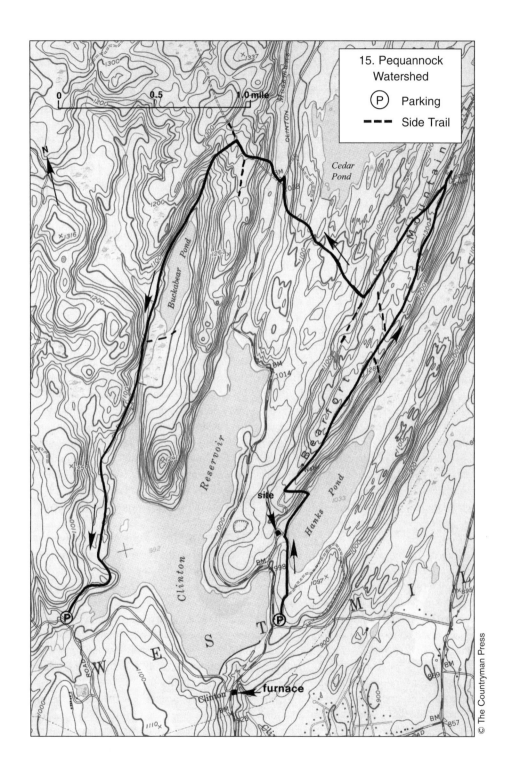

few overlooks as well as the Bearfort fire tower, from which you can survey the area. Part of the hike is on the Bearfort Mountain ridge, with its pink to purple sandstones and conglomerates. This ridge, composed of Paleozoic (Silurian and Devonian) sedimentary rock, occurs in the midst of the much older Precambrian Highlands formation. Apparently, Bearfort Mountain is the remains of the sand and silt deposits of a long, narrow inland sea or sound that penetrated the older Highlands. Notice the distinct change of bedrock as you hike from Bearfort Mountain to Buckabear Pond, the latter being entirely in the Highlands with its typical gray Precambrian gneiss.

Of interest on this hike is the site of the former Cross Castle or Bearfort House, a large mountain estate built by Richard James Cross about 80 years ago. Cross, a native of England, made a fortune in banking and later erected a fantastic but short-lived mansion. The entire 365-acre estate featured a three-story castle with views in all directions, hot and cold running water, numerous fireplaces, stables, carriage houses, guest cottages, and a boathouse on Hank's Pond. The foundations and walls of stone—which survived the dismantling of the mansion by the city of Newark when it acquired the property in 1919—were demolished in the late 1980s.

Also of interest is the Clinton Furnace, one of the very few surviving furnaces used during the region's iron-making era. The furnace, located just off Clinton Road near its intersection with Schoolhouse Road, is still in fairly good shape. Iron-smelting furnaces were always built near running water, necessary for the waterwheel-driven bellows. As you would expect, a substantial series of waterfalls is located immediately to the side of Clinton Furnace. Once the furnace was fired up and loaded with iron, it would burn for months at a time. Its location at the base of a sharp drop facilitated the loading of iron from the top of the furnace.

HOW TO GET THERE

The hike can be done as a circuit, which would include an additional 1.5 miles of road walking, or cars can be parked and a shuttle arranged. The walk along the road is not at all unpleasant and will only add about a half hour to your hike. If you choose to do the extra walking, park at Parking Area 9 (P9) and walk to P1. If you don't, leave one car at P9 and drive another to P1 to begin the hike.

To find P9 from NJ 23, take Clinton Road north for 1.2 miles and turn left on Schoolhouse Road, a gravel road with good views of Clinton Reservoir. After 1 mile, make a right turn onto Paradise Road; you will find the small parking area on the right in 0.1 mile. After parking, walk or drive down Schoolhouse Road the way you came to Clinton Road. At this intersection, directly in front of you—though it may be obscured by foliage in the summer—are the Clinton Furnace and the falls described earlier. Turn left at the intersection, and walk or drive 0.3 mile north on paved Clinton Road to where Van Orden Road (gravel) comes in on the right. This is P1, and you will begin your hike from here.

THE TRAIL

Walk north on the dirt road, which is marked white, heading into the woods. After several minutes, turn left onto a blue-blazed trail. This connector trail leads past some old foundations, crosses the Hanks Pond outlet, and meets the Fire Tower Ridge Trail. Turn right here, now following red/white markers that lead uphill to the former site of the Cross Castle.

After inspecting the site, continue by walking north on the Fire Tower Ridge Trail. Follow the red/white markers, passing the stone water-storage tower that supplied water for the castle, and bear right, following the markers where the trail forks. The footing becomes rockier now, and, after a short rise, the trail swings to the right on what is now a footpath over exposed bedrock. White pines, mountain laurels, and an occasional cedar make this section of trail especially scenic. Continue following the red/white markers (a trail comes in on the right in a rocky area) over slabs of glaciated, conglomerate bedrock and downhill over a small stream and into deeper woods. At another trail junction, bear to the right and slightly uphill among hemlock and laurel.

As you rise to the broad summit area of Bearfort Mountain, which contains oaks, laurels, and patches of grass, you'll see that the mountaintop is actually a series of parallel, narrow ridges separated by swamps and wet areas. Some of these ridges are well worth exploring. After less than an hour of walking from the Cross Castle site (and about 2.5 miles from the start of the hike), you'll come to a clearing, picnic tables, and the fire tower—a good place for a snack or lunch. Take the time to climb the five flights of steps to the top of the fire tower. You will be rewarded by views of the entire watershed.

From the picnic table area, near a stone fireplace, head west for 100 feet and turn left and south on a yellow-blazed footpath, the Fire Tower West Trail. You are now heading south through hemlock and laurel and will soon come out to a viewpoint near a large glacial erratic. Cedar Pond, a natural glacial lake, is below to the north. Continuing, the trail traverses some beautiful woodland with large puddingstone rock outcrops framed with white pine. Soon you will see a trail on the left, and soon after you will reach another, more critical—and possibly obscure—trail junction. Stay to the right here,

the way the trail naturally seems to go, and head downhill off the mountain on the white-blazed Two Brooks Trail.

Soon you will come to a small clearing; follow the white markers through ferns and deep hemlocks and then out to a brook, crossing on a bridge. If you look around, you may find beaver-gnawed trees in this area. After crossing the brook, the trail turns sharply to the right through tall and dense hemlocks. Continue over rocks and pine needles and then out to another brook with a log bridge. After crossing, watch for the trail to turn left and uphill. After a rise, the trail descends slightly through moss, pine, beech, maple, and especially hemlock, which gets thicker as the trail approaches Mossman's Brook. After a pleasant walk on hemlock needles through a primeval forest along the brook, the trail comes out to Clinton Road at P4. This area is quiet and still. Standing to listen, it is sometimes possible to hear needles falling from the hemlock trees like a light rain.

Make a left on Clinton Road and look for white blazes on the right side of the road. After only 100 yards of road walking, follow the blazes as they turn right onto a woods road. Another right turn comes up almost immediately as the trail heads temporarily north. In a short distance, it swings left and heads steeply uphill. This climb is the longest of the hike (250 feet at most). Notice that the rock in this area is different from that on which you have been walking. Here is Precambrian gneiss, a much older rock than the purple sedimentary sandstones and puddingstone conglomerates that make up Bearfort Mountain. When you reach the top of the rise, you will arrive at a junction. The white markers of the Clinton West Trail turn left here, but you'll continue straight ahead, now following blue markers. Almost immediately you'll come to another junction. Turn left here, following yellow markers south from the main crest of the rise. You should now be heading down toward Buckabear Pond.

This trail, the yellow-blazed Bearfort Waters/Clinton Trail, heads gradually downhill through blueberry bushes growing abundantly below some dead oak trees decimated by gypsy moths. As the trail descends, more ferns appear, and the land gets wetter. You may need to climb over blowdowns in this remote and little-used section of the watershed. Soon the hemlocks begin to predominate again, until you reach the north shore of Buckabear Pond in a swampy area. Cross a little stream and follow the trail, now an old stone and dirt road that runs parallel to and above the west shore of the lake. At about the midpoint of the pond, the trail makes a slight jog to the left where it meets a dirt road used by four-wheelers, but then continues heading south in laurel and rhododendron along the west shore of the pond and also higher up the slope to avoid wet or flooded sections near the pond. At the trail junction at the south end of the pond, bear to the right, still heading southward, on the white-blazed Clinton West Trail, formerly a horseback trail built by the Civilian Conservation Corps (CCC) in the 1930s.

Soon you will see Clinton Reservoir on the left, the largest body of water on this hike. As the trail veers away from the reservoir, it will turn left off the woods road it has been following and then head back toward the reservoir on a footpath. It now hugs the shoreline with good views of water, islands, and hills and again turns left and downhill where a rocky woods road comes in. In this vicinity, on the right and uphill, you will find a number of plaques set in boulders and outcroppings commemorating the lives of hikers and trail builders of the past. Still following the shoreline, the trail passes a cove popular with Canada geese, which frequently forage there. Just a short walk ahead you will emerge from the woods at Parking Area 9 and your car.

Note: Shorter explorations of this scenic but vast area are possible. Consider the following options: Park at P9 and walk along the shore of Clinton Reservoir for a mile or two and then turn back. Park at P1 and explore the shoreline of Hanks Pond. A good 4.5-mile hike starts at P2 and follows the yellow Fire Tower West Trail to the fire tower. You can return the same way or via the red/white Fire Tower Ridge Trail to the Cross Castle site, then turn right, following the blue markers to the yellow trail. A left turn here will lead to your car.

BCS

16

Wawayanda State Park

Total distance: 7.5 miles

Hiking time: 4 hours

Vertical rise: 530 feet

Rating: Easy

Maps: USGS Wawayanda; NYNJTC #21; NJWB, #19; DEP Wawayanda State Park

Wawayanda State Park (885 Warwick Turnpike, Hewitt, NJ 07421; 973-853-4462), which covers almost 10,000 acres of forest and water, is located along the Passaic and Sussex County boundary and the border of New York State. The park opened to the public in 1963. According to one source, the name Wawayanda is the phonetic rendition of a Lenape word meaning "water on the mountain." Another source claims it is a Munsee word meaning "winding, winding, water."

Despite urban development, the feeling in Wawayanda is that of wilderness, and this hike is delightful in any season. In summer, you are protected from the heat of the sun by the leafy canopy of mature trees and able to cool off in the lake after hiking; in fall, the same trees are a riot of color (although squirrels can bombard the unwary with acorns from above); in winter, these trails are admirably suited for cross-country skiing—gentle and wide—when the snow is deep enough. Because of the high elevation of the plateau, snow remains longer in Wawayanda State Park than in other areas. The terrain undulates and winds in a relaxed way, making for very pleasant and companionable walking. This hike uses the Double Pond (yellow), Cedar Swamp (blue), Banker (yellow), Old Coal (red), Lookout (white), Laurel Pond (yellow), and Wingdam (blue) Trails, as well as sections of Cherry Ridge Road. The hike makes a loop, meanders through areas of huge rhododendrons arching overhead, passes under tall hemlocks, and traverses the shores of several lakes.

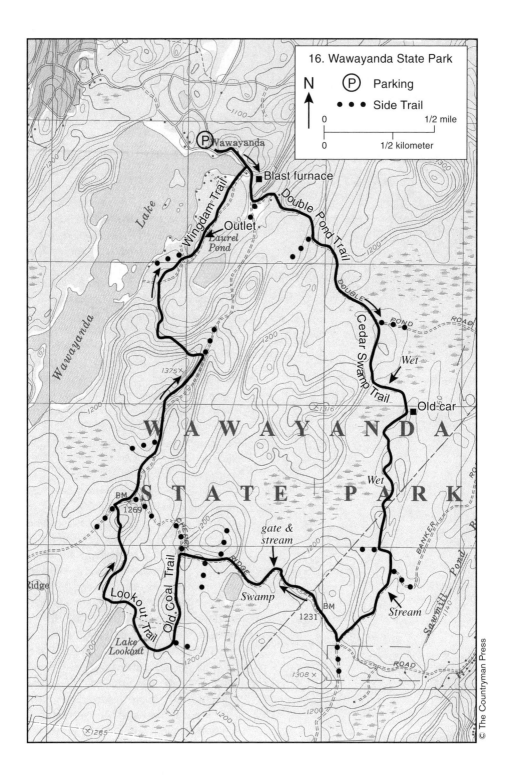

16. Wawayanda State Park

Ⓟ Parking

• • • Side Trail

0   1/2 mile

0   1/2 kilometer

N

Ⓟ Wawayanda

■ Blast furnace

Wingdam Trail

Double Pond Trail

Outlet

Laurel Pond

Lake

Wawayanda

DOUBLE POND

ROAD

Cedar Swamp Trail

Wet

1375 X

■ Old car

W A W A Y A N D A

Wet

S T A T E   P A R K

BM
1269

gate &
stream

BANKER

Sawmill Pond

Ridge

Old Coal Trail

Lookout Trail

Swamp

BM
1231

Stream

Lake
Lookout

1308 X

ROAD

1265 X

© The Countryman Press

HOW TO GET THERE

Access the park office in Wawayanda State Park from the northern section of Warwick Turnpike, approached from the north on NY 94 and from the south on Clinton Road. The park entrance is on the west side of Warwick Turnpike, approximately 1.25 miles north of Upper Greenwood Lake. A good road map is an asset. Just beyond the park entrance, stop at the office to obtain the park map and other literature. The hike actually begins at the boathouse area, the second parking lot after the lake. Out-of-season parking is free, but in season a fee is charged. During the summer months, it is advisable to arrive before 10 AM to be sure of a parking space.

THE TRAIL

Many old roads bisect trails in the park, and because this hike uses multiple trails, watch carefully for each turn. Also be sure to park at the boathouse-fishing lot, which is different from the beach parking location.

With Wawayanda Lake on your right, leave the parking lot, walk left to a wide gravel road, and follow it by the side of the lake, noting that the yellow blazes here indicate the Double Pond Trail. From time to time during the hike, you'll see signs indicating the degree of difficulty for mountain bikers.

Wawayanda Lake was once two separate bodies of water called Double Pond. The narrow strip of land that divided the two ponds is still visible on the west side of Barker Island, now in the center of the lake. In winter, when the lake is frozen solid, it is pleasant to walk across to Barker Island and watch the people fishing through the ice. The Thomas Iron Company built the stone dam at the northeastern end of the lake in the middle of the 19th century. On the lake,

admire the many yellow pond lilies and white fragrant water lilies and note, as you reach the dam, that there are picnic tables and a disconnected water pump. The blue-blazed Wingdam Trail, your return route, joins from the right within a few minutes, and very soon the remains of the old charcoal furnace come into view.

Walk across to the information boards and pause to imagine the busy scene of yesteryear when Wawayanda was the center of the New Jersey iron industry. The old structure is all that remains of a charcoal blast furnace built by Oliver Ames and his three sons, William, Oaks, and Oliver Junior. William was in charge. His initials W. L. A. and the date 1846 are still visible on a lintel in the main arch. Iron ore from local mines was smelted here continuously from 1847 to 1857, when cheap coal became available in Pennsylvania, making it more economical to transport the ore for smelting to those hotter and more efficient furnaces. In an average day, 7 tons of iron was produced from the Wawayanda furnace and poured off twice daily, at noon and at midnight. Wawayanda iron was of such superior quality that it was used to manufacture railroad wheels. During the Civil War, the Ames factories also filled government orders for shovels and swords. A small village grew up in the vicinity during the time of greatest activity, but nothing remains. The furnace building is currently supported by metal framing and protected from vandals by substantial fencing.

When you have absorbed enough history, walk toward the two portable toilets, and turn left in front of them, crossing a small wooden bridge across a stream and walking toward a sign indicating a left turn for the Double Pond Trail. The trail passes through group campsites, and for a short distance is rocky and climbs slightly. The

Stringers, Wawayanda State Park

Red Dot Trail enters the Double Pond Trail approximately a mile from Wawayanda Lake. Continue straight ahead, following yellow blazes for another 0.5 mile to a fork. Three blue blazes on a tree to the right alert you to the commencement of the Cedar Swamp Trail, which is now the route of the hike.

The 1.5-mile Cedar Swamp Trail is one of the highlights of Wawayanda State Park. The huge rhododendrons arch high overhead, and hemlocks soar above these shrubs. Look for the unique stand of inland Atlantic white cedar trees growing in this very wet environment, but be aware that parts of the trail are sometimes muddy. There is a 750-foot boardwalk on part of the trail. About 0.5 mile along the Cedar Swamp Trail, watch on the left for an old rusted car in a clearing, and follow the footway as it makes a sharp turn to the right.

The Cedar Swamp Trail emerges at a T-junction with the wider, yellow-blazed Banker Trail. Turn right and follow this old road for a short distance to its connection with the wide, gravel Cherry Ridge Road, where you again need to turn right.

Cherry Ridge Road is routed past an extensive swamp on the left side. The road has a broken gate along its route, passes over the gullied outlet from the swamp, and, approximately 1 mile from the parking circle, the Red Dot Trail joins from the right. Very soon after this junction you may notice a grassy road joining from the left. Ignore this attractive route and proceed ahead until you reach the junction with the red-blazed Old Coal Trail.

Leave Cherry Ridge Road here where it makes a right turn, and turn left on the Old Coal Trail, walking until the red blazes leave to the left at a wide grassy junction, and you see three white blazes on a tree to the right, which indicates the beginning of the

Lookout Trail. The footway is pleasant and grassier here, and soon reaches the outlet of Lake Lookout with its beaver house. The peaceful and seldom-visited lake is an attractive place to take a break. Cross the dam and follow the white markers back into the woods.

The footway is now narrow and a little indistinct, but marked clearly with white paint and white metal patches. The trail climbs steeply for a short distance among large boulders wearing hairpieces of fern, then turns right and proceeds north along a valley floor with the heights of Cherry Ridge above on the left. This section winds among large silent fallen trees and through a wet and rocky area dark with mountain laurel. Fifteen minutes brings you out onto Cherry Ridge Road, less than 100 yards west of the junction with the Laurel Pond Trail. Turn right, pass through a gate, leave Cherry Ridge Road to continue ahead, and turn left onto the yellow-blazed Laurel Pond Trail.

After about 0.75 mile watch for the blue-blazed Wingdam Trail and turn left onto the more traditional and agreeable footway. (The Laurel Pond Trail is a rocky road, but leads back to the Wawayanda Furnace.) The Wingdam Trail climbs at first, but soon descends and flattens out with some obscured views of Laurel Pond to the right. Ignore the woods roads that join the marked route, and continue until you reach the attractive outlet of Wawayanda Lake about 0.75 mile after leaving the Laurel Pond Trail. The benches here make a tempting place to dally before finishing your walk. When sufficiently rested, continue on the Wingdam Trail through mature hardwood trees and cross the dam you saw at the beginning of your hike.

The wing dam was constructed by the Thomas Iron Company and, together with the previous dam you crossed, raises the lake level by about 7.5 feet. The water comes over this dam in a wide, swift fall and rushes on its way to feed Laurel Pond, out of sight on the left. Wildflowers abound in this lush area at most times of the year.

Walk through the barrier of large boulders, turn left and retrace your earlier route back to the parking lot, perhaps taking the time to swim in the cool waters of Wawayanda Lake.

SJG

17

Appalachian Trail Stairway to Heaven

Total distance: 5 miles

Hiking time: 3 hours

Vertical rise: 1,000 feet

Rating: Moderately strenuous

Maps: USGS Wawayanda; NYNJTC North Jersey Trails #21; NJWB #19; NY/NJ Appalachian Trail Guide Map #4; DEP Appalachian Trail and Wawayanda State Park maps

The Appalachian Trail (AT) is our nation's first designated National Scenic Trail. It extends 2,152 miles from Springer Mountain in Georgia to Mount Katahdin in Maine. The AT is a unique partnership among 14 states, the National Park Service, the US Forest Service, and a network of hiking clubs coordinated by the newly renamed Appalachian Trail Conservancy (ATC, PO Box 807, Harpers Ferry, WV 25425). Volunteers with the New York–New Jersey Trail Conference manage and maintain the almost 74 miles of the AT in New Jersey.

Entering from Pennsylvania at the Delaware Water Gap, the trail follows the crest of the Kittatinnies to High Point State Park, where it turns east along the New York–New Jersey border. After crossing Wawayanda State Park and traveling through Hewitt State Forest, the trail turns north into New York State just west of Greenwood Lake.

The main part of this hike follows an AT segment built mostly by volunteers with help from ATC trail crews, local Boy Scouts, New Jersey correctional inmates, and Wawayanda park personnel who completed their huge three-year cooperative effort in May 1991. You are about to see, appreciate, and enjoy the results of everyone's labors.

This relocation is a fine example of the concern trail builders now show for the environment. The old trail (about 0.5 mile south) had changed little since it was first built in 1937. It shot straight up the mountain in just more than 0.5 mile. Without a

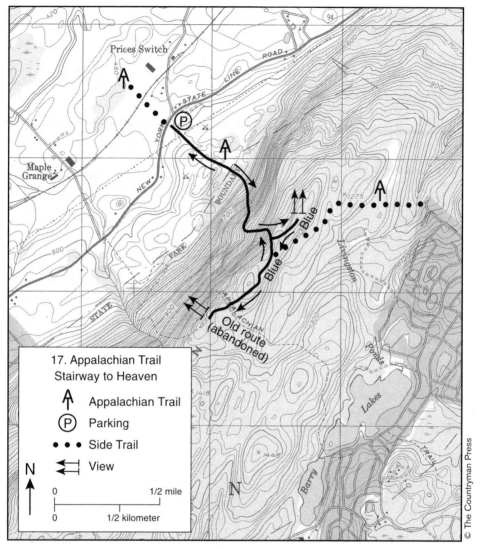

17. Appalachian Trail
Stairway to Heaven

Ⱥ Appalachian Trail

Ⓟ Parking

●●● Side Trail

⇇ View

N ↑

0 — 1/2 mile

0 — 1/2 kilometer

switchback, the climb was an exhausting boulder-hop and rock scramble up an ugly, erosion-scarred ditch. The new route, however, loops gracefully up the 900-foot elevation gain. Long switchbacks skirt patches of mountain laurel instead of cutting right through them. Water bars and some 300 stone steps protect the steepest sections. About two-thirds of the way up is the impressive 60-step "stairway to heaven" built in 1990. Some people walk here and actually think this all happened naturally! You know better.

HOW TO GET THERE

You can access the trail from a signed AT parking area on NJ 94, about 2.4 miles north of Vernon (0.7 mile north of the Maple Grange Road junction) and 2 miles south of the New York–New Jersey border. The parking area is on the east side of the road just south of the Amity/Pine Island directional sign and the Heaven Hill Farm Stand. There is room for about eight cars.

THE TRAIL

Your hike starts on the same side of the road as the parking area. Proceed up a small embankment on a grassy path (poison ivy abounds on the sides of the footway) past some stone drains and into a large field. The path is well marked with the traditional 2-inch-by-6-inch white paint blazes. In this first section, often lush with wildflowers, the blazes are on wooden posts embedded in the ground. Soon you'll cross an old stone wall, enter the woods, and reach the base of Wawayanda Mountain. After traversing an area strewn with rocks from eons of tumbledown from the heights above, the route begins the 900-foot ascent of the Wawayanda escarpment. In about 0.25 mile, it ascends two small switchbacks and Annie's Bluff on the right (named for a favorite trail builder, we assume). If you are here in the summer, especially July, those healthy people you see with the large packs are AT through-hikers, folks trying to do the entire trail in one long go. They are usually taking a steady pace trying to make miles, but more often than not will stop for a short chat and tell you about their lifetime adventure. Offering some chocolate or fruit is almost always deeply appreciated and gets the conversation going.

Some 1.3 miles from your car, after the trail takes a right bend, you may notice a blue-marked trail to the left. You'll be exploring this side route on the way back. If you miss it (don't be concerned—most people do), you'll arrive at the top of Wawayanda after about an hour's hike. There, at a junction with another blue side trail, is a hikers' registration box nailed to a tree.

Wawayanda is, according to one source, a Munsee word that translates to "winding, winding water," used by the Native Americans to refer to the creeks and meadows in the area. Another source indicates that Wawayanda is a phonetic translation of the Lenape term for "water on the mountain." In either case, the name was applied to the mountain before the Revolution, and given to the nearby lake in 1846. You are now at the western edge of 13,000-acre Wawayanda State Park.

At the top of the mountain, leave the AT, taking the blue-blazed Wawayanda Ridge Trail right (south) less than a mile to a fine view and lunch spot. The trail stays on or just below the ridge in open forest and along rock slabs. In 20 minutes or so, it descends somewhat off the ridgeline into a dark, wooded hollow filled with hemlock trees. After going through an old stone boundary wall, the trail swings right along the edge of a mountaintop swamp and steeply up a short distance, through a jumble of large rocks. Watch for the blazes as it twists and turns up to a modest view. Here it leans slightly left as it goes off the tip of the ridge and passes above some large trees in a gully above the swamp you just passed. After descending into the woods on a clearly defined footway, the trail again climbs into a more open summit area. You will notice a large grassy open area off to your left. This spot, with a spectacular view, is the end point of your hike. Scramble down, or go 50 yards farther on the blue trail and circle back to the viewpoint.

Here, on a clear day, is an unobstructed view of the Kittatinnies, High Point Tower, and the lush Vernon Valley with Pochuck Creek flowing through. Off to the right rise New York's Shawangunk Mountains, a geologic extension of the Kittatinnies. Behind the "Gunks" rise the peaks of the Catskills,

New growth

several more than 4,000 feet high. You can easily see three states: New Jersey, New York, and Pennsylvania.

The way back is the way you came, except for the short side trip to another fine view. After returning along the blue trail to the junction with the AT, proceed downhill on the AT the way you came. Soon the trail turns right at a large rock outcropping, makes a modest descent on some steps, and then swings left. It is in this area, only a few minutes from the Wawayanda summit, that you should notice two piles of stones to your right, and the three-blazed start of a blue side trail. Follow the blue blazes for a few minutes to a rock outcrop area. There are two view areas here: one at the end of a clear (but unmarked) trail on the left and the other a few yards farther along the blue blazes.

Return to the AT and resume your descent. Please remember to stay on the designated footway. Shortcutting the switchbacks leads to erosion problems and is considered very poor hiking etiquette.

HNZ

18

Pyramid Mountain

Total distance: 3 miles

Hiking time: 2.5 hours

Vertical rise: 390 feet

Rating: Easy to moderate

Maps: USGS Boonton; NYNJTC Pyramid Mountain Trails #31; Morris County Park Commission Pyramid Mountain Natural Historical Area map

At 920 feet Pyramid Mountain is not the highest summit ridge in northern Morris County, but it has much to offer the hiker. It is crossed by foot trails that can be steep and rugged in places, has several overlooks, and contains a mysterious glacial erratic that may be part of an ancient Native American calendar site. To the west and below the mountain ridge is Stony Brook and its wetland. Here is found the gigantic Bear Rock, a granite monolith that towers over the brook and swamp. Some of the land containing these wonders is still privately owned, but much has been saved in recent years because of the work of an active grassroots committee, the Friends of Pyramid Mountain, and also the New Jersey Conservation Foundation, the Morris County Park Commission, the Mennen Corporation, and state agencies. Thanks to these organizations and many dedicated individuals, particularly Lucy Meyer, the next generation of New Jersey hikers will find this area as it is today—not developed with condos.

The Pyramid Mountain Natural and Historical Area is a hiker's paradise. Although the area is heavily used at times, there are many trails to disperse hikers. There are actually two trail systems to choose from: the Pyramid Mountain section, a small portion of which is the focus of the hike described below, and the Turkey Mountain section on the east side of County Route 511. Mountain bikes are not permitted in either section. A number of very long loop hikes in the general area are possible, including one around the Butler Reservoir (see NYNJTC map #31, Pyramid Mountain Trails).

While not long, this hike takes in some of the outstanding features of the area. It begins at the visitor center (973-334-3130), currently open Friday, Saturday, and Sunday 10–4:30, which contains displays and information about the area and its natural history. An excellent map of the area is also available. Wildflower lovers will appreciate the first leg of the hike, which passes near a power line cut. The exposure to the sun allows many species not found in the darker woods to thrive. This section has some wet areas, so wear boots; you should also take the usual precautions against ticks. The two most famous rock formations of the area, Bear Rock and Tripod Rock, are on the walk, as well as two vistas, Lucy's Lookout and the summit of Pyramid Mountain.

HOW TO GET THERE

From exit 44 on I-287, drive west on Main Street to the center of Boonton and turn right onto CR 511 (Boonton Avenue).The Pyramid Mountain Natural and Historic Area is on CR 511, 3.3 miles north of West Main Street in Boonton (0.8 mile north of CR 511's intersection with Taylortown Road) or 4.4 miles south of NJ 23.

THE TRAIL

Follow the access trail from the parking area. It quickly meets a power line cut and connects with the blue-blazed Butler–Montville Trail. The trail turns left here and crosses a brook on a long bridge. Next, the trail follows a dirt road, passing a junction with a yellow trail. After a jog to the left, it veers sharply right, leaving the road, and begins a short but steep climb to the shoulder of Pyramid Mountain. The stone steps leading up the hill were apparently constructed

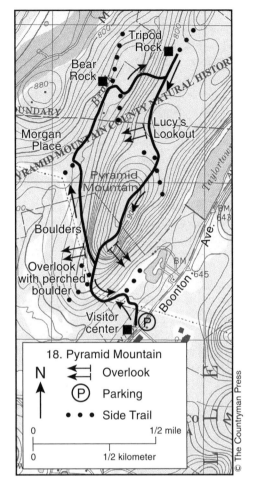

by the utility company many years ago. The climb ends under a high-voltage tower, which is also trail junction #3. Remember this junction—you'll come back to it later. Turn right here, following the blue markers into the woods to a rockpile that marks the junction with the red trail. Turn left here, now following only red markers.

The red trail is a relatively new trail in the system. After a short uphill you'll pass a viewpoint to your left over the power line cut. Some interesting boulders are nearby, erratics dropped during the previous glaciation.

For the next 0.5 mile the red markers lead through a rocky section of the mountain and then gradually downhill to a junction with the white trail. A left here will take you to an old house foundation located near the power line cut.

According to old newspaper articles, the notorious Morgans once lived here back in the late 18th century. They had a terrible reputation. People knew them as the Tar-Rope Gang, and they used to make raids into nearby Boonton, robbing people and terrorizing women. But to continue the hike, turn right at this junction and follow the white markers away from the power lines on an old lane. On both sides of the path are remnants of former occupation, and rock walls parallel the lane as it penetrates the woods. To the right is Bearhouse Brook.

Just 0.35 mile from the power lines, you come face to face with Bear Rock. Standing alone in the woods at the edge of a large swamp, Bear Rock has been used as a boundary marker for at least 200 years. Even today it marks the borders of the Kinnelon and Montville boroughs. Although it is difficult and even dangerous to scale, there are some very old surveying markers found near its highest points. Bear Rock is a glacial erratic, plucked from the side of Stony Brook Mountain and dragged several hundred feet by the glacial ice sheet that covered the area as recently as 12,000 years ago. To the northwest, about 150 yards away, is a waterfall that cascades over bare rock during the spring and after heavy rains.

From Bear Rock turn right, now following both white and blue markers, to the bridge over the brook and then along the edge of the Sachem Sajapogh of Minising Swamp, also known as Bear Swamp. Along the path are many dwarf ginseng plants, pepperbush, and spicebush. The trail will swing to the left and then to the right, where it begins to climb steeply the ridge of Pyramid Mountain over rocks. The climb, though only about 150 feet of vertical rise, is stiff. Lining the trail are clusters of mountain laurel, which create a tunnel effect in places. As you reach the ridge summit, the trail comes to a T-junction. A left turn here following white markers will lead you, in 150 yards, to Tripod Rock.

Perhaps the most massive perched boulder of its kind in the entire Northeast, Tripod Rock is the focal point of what may be an ancient calendar site. The sheer size and bizarre appearance of it–a 160-ton boulder standing on three medicine-ball-sized rocks–staggers the imagination. If it is simply a chance product of the last Ice Age, as most geologists believe, then it is unique. Others suggest that it was modified by humans. Nearby are two smaller stones partially perched on exposed bedrock. An observer seated on a lip protruding from a piece of bedrock 4 feet high will see, through the gap between these two stones, the summer solstice sunset. The alignment constitutes a simple solar observatory. Whether or not it was used by the early inhabitants of the area is an open question.

From Tripod Rock, retrace your steps to the junction and continue heading south along the ridge, now following only blue markers. This section of trail is overshadowed by tall rhododendrons and mountain laurel, a beautiful sight in winter. Just before the trail swings sharply to the left and meets a yellow trail, look for a small side trail on the right. Marked with blue and white, it leads west in 100 yards to Lucy's Lookout, named for Lucy Meyer, who led the long crusade to save this beautiful area from development. You will have a view to the south and west over Stony Brook Mountain from this rocky point. Return to the main trail and continue heading south following blue markers. (Yellow markers share the route for a short distance.) Little Cat Swamp, where peepers croak in spring, is off to your left.

After a gradual climb, the blue trail will bring you near the open southern end of the Pyramid Mountain ridge. Just beyond, over bare rock, are expansive views to the east and south, including a view of the New York City skyline when visibility is good. Many years ago a fire tower was located here, but evidence of it is scant today. It is said that on some old maps this summit was labeled High Mountain, though this does not seem to be the case. (The next ridge to the west, Rock Pear Mountain, was apparently the one with that name.) How the name Pyramid came to be associated with the mountain is a fairly recent story. In the 1920s the *New York Walk Book* directed hikers walking near where the visitor center is today toward the "pyramidal shaped mountain."

Indeed, the mountain has a triangular shape when viewed (without foliage) from that direction. Later editions of the book simply referred to it as Pyramid Mountain, and the name stuck. In the 1990s, a conflict erupted over the proper name for the peak, and the matter was handed over to the US Geological Survey for a decision. Pyramid Mountain is now the official name.

After taking in the view of woodland, hills, and encroaching suburbia (conflicts over development still rage), return to the blue trail and travel down the western slope of Pyramid Mountain, past the junction with the red trail, to the power line cut and junction #3. You should recognize it as a place you passed earlier in the hike. Bear left and downhill here, retracing your steps, and follow the blue markers east to the visitor center on CR 511 and your car.

BCS

19

Mount Hope Historical Park

Total distance: 2.5 miles

Hiking time: 2 hours

Vertical rise: 350 feet

Rating: Easy

Maps: USGS Dover; Morris County Park Commission Mount Hope Historical Park map

Most of the hikes in this book lead you through forests to natural areas such as ponds, lakes, mountaintops, rock formations, interesting botanical areas, and the ocean itself. On this hike you tour a natural area (assuming humans are a force of nature) of a different sort—a human-modified area. What this area looked like 100 years ago is hard to imagine, but whatever was going on there left a powerful imprint. There is nothing quite like the landscape you will traverse on this hike. Some may find it disturbing, others may find it utterly fascinating. There is a wildness to the park that stands in sharp contrast to its obvious human disturbance. You have to see it to understand what I'm getting at. Please note that mountain bikes are not allowed at Mount Hope Historical Park.

Iron mining in the Dover area of New Jersey has a long history and towns like Mine Hill and Mount Hope were built around this economic activity. The oldest mines in the region date back to 1710. The Dickerson Mine in Mine Hill is the oldest iron mine in the United States. The Mount Hope Mine, just to the north of our hike, has been the largest iron ore producer in New Jersey, 6 million tons have been produced since its beginning, and it is still being worked. Mount Hope Historical Park itself is a historic site that preserves the remains of one of the more active mining and processing sites in the region. It is composed of three separate historic mining operations: the Allen Mine, the Richard Mine, and the Teabo

Mine. Three veins of high-grade magnetite iron ore that ran the length of the park were mined here over the course of about 150 years. Approximately 5.7 million tons of ore were removed from these mines. During the early 20th century the mines were consolidated into one holding, but in 1958 operations ceased and the property was abandoned. This fact alone, the very recent ending of mining in the park, will give you much to think about—especially in regard to nature's power to heal itself.

Mount Hope Historical Park mines are located in the New Jersey Highlands province, a belt of mostly Precambrian (roughly 500 million to 1 billion years old) gneisses that have limited deposits of iron and zinc ore. Veins of iron ore vary from a few inches to over 50 feet in thickness, and can be a mile or more wide. These belts follow the fold patterns of the gneiss and trend, as do the Highlands, in a northeast-to-southwest direction. Mining operations would follow a vein as far as was possible as it dipped into the ground. The landscapes at Mount Hope Historical Park are the remnants of collapsed mine shafts that today look like huge craters.

The hike described below is not particularly strenuous, but some considerations should be taken. First, the mine pits present something of a hazard. Tailings from the mines are not always stable, and hiking with small children will require that you restrain them. Much of the pathway on the hike is quite rocky, and sturdy boots are recommended. There is no shortage of wildlife in Mount Hope Historical Park. Deer are common and once I came across a doe standing on the trail less than 20 feet away. She and I made eye contact and stared at each other for at least a minute—she made no movement nor did I. Slowly, she began to walk away into the forest.

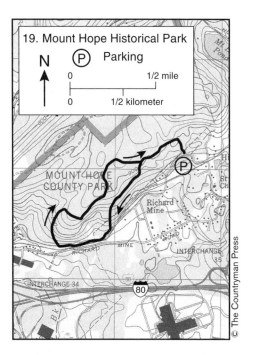

HOW TO GET THERE

From I-80 take exit 35 and turn north onto on Mount Hope Ave. You'll pass Fox Hills condos and after about 0.5 mile turn left onto Richard Mine Road. Signs will direct you through winding roads in a residential area—drive carefully. Follow Richard Mine Road for 0.7 mile and turn right onto Coburn Road. The park entrance is 0.7 mile ahead on the left. The parking area for Mount Hope Historical Park is located is just below the power lines that mark the southern boundary of the park.

THE TRAIL

The main trailhead is at the east end of the parking area near the directory. A historic plaque for Richard Mine and a picnic table are located here also. The trail begins as a footpath (this was not well maintained at the time of this writing), which then turns left

of Picatinny Arsenal (federal property) is prohibited. By now you will notice that the surroundings are not like most Highlands woods. All around you are piles of rocks, pits, and small rock walls—signs of human activity that has shaped the landscape. After making this left turn, the pathway becomes rockier and soon you will begin to notice that the pits on your left are getting progressively deeper.

The Red Trail forks where you reach a junction. The large collapsed mine pits to your left are those of Teabo Mine #2. Keep left at this junction and continue following the red markers around a huge pit, a veritable crater, on your left and then past a series of pits on your right. At another junction, leave the Red Trail and begin following orange markers that lead downhill. Just before the trail crosses the high-voltage lines again, look for unmarked paths that lead up to an overlook through the power lines. The vista includes the Rockaway Town Square Mall with I-80 in the foreground. Here are also two old, rusted water tanks and the remains of a small reservoir.

Returning to the main pathway, the Orange Trail crosses the power line cut, turns right, then immediately turns left into the woods again. Now following a cinder path, the trail parallels the power line cut, passes under it again, and swings very close to paved Richard Mine Road, which it follows for a short distance before it swings to the right. Next, watch for another junction—keep right here on a gravel lane that begins to climb. At the next junction, which faces a vernal pond and lies in a wet area, turn right. After another climb the trail enters a dry oak forest and begins to level off. Just past a mine pit on your left, you will arrive at a junction with the Red Trail again. Turn left here.

The trail now climbs to the highest point in the hike and then swings gradually

onto a gravel lane. Walk uphill to the high-voltage lines, where you will come to a fork. It is in this vicinity that the trail system of the park actually begins. To the right are two relatively short trails. These are the Blue Trail, which terminates at a vista from the high-voltage line cut, and the White Trail, which leads to the northernmost mines. For this hike, we turn left onto the Red Trail and enter the woods.

At the start of the trail you may notice three red markers—three markers designate the beginning or end of a trail—and a plaque indicating that this trail has been adopted by the preservationist group Friends of the Forest. The markers follow the lane through a young forest and indicate a left turn at the first junction. A sign here indicates that continuing straight ahead toward the property around to the east. The land is very dry here and there are no mines. Just after passing two small boulders on your left, you will reach the junction you came to earlier, where the Red Trail splits. At this junction, make a left. Walk past the pits, keep right at the junction, and reenter the high-voltage line cut. From here, you could follow the path back to the parking area, or you could follow the Blue Trail along the open power line cut to a view toward the working Mt. Hope Mines. The New York City skyline is also visible to the east and the town of Dover to the south. Return to the junction, turn left, and follow the path downhill to the parking area.

BCS

20

Mahlon Dickerson Reservation

Total distance: 4.3 miles

Hiking time: 3 hours

Vertical rise: 238 feet

Rating: Easy to moderate

Maps: USGS Franklin; Morris County Park Commission Mahlon Dickerson Reservation map

The Morris County Park Commission (PO Box 1295, Morristown, NJ 07062; 973-663-0200, www.morrisparks.org), steward of this reservation, believes that only 10 percent of its parkland should be developed for intensive recreation (picnic sites, ball fields, and playgrounds), while most of it should be left in its natural state. As a result, hikers in Morris County have a number of excellent nearby parks to enjoy. The largest county park is Mahlon Dickerson Reservation, known to park personnel as simply MDR. It is more like a state park and contains tent sites, several Adirondack-type shelters, and trailer camping areas. There is also a ball field, 20 miles of multi-use trails, a picnic area, and Saffin Pond. The park covers 3,200 acres at the time of this writing and seems to be expanding at a steady pace. It is used by hikers, mountain bikers, and equestrians.

The reservation was named for one of Morris County's great achievers, Mahlon Dickerson (1770–1853). Dickerson, who lived near Dover, lived a model life of political service. He never married but was successful in nearly everything he tried. He mastered several languages and attained distinction as a botanist. He owned and operated the Succasunna iron mines, some of the largest in the county. He was a general in the military, served in the state legislature, and was governor of New Jersey for a short period. He served as a member of Congress between 1817 and 1829 and, during the presidency of Andrew Jackson, served as Secretary of the Navy. He was said to

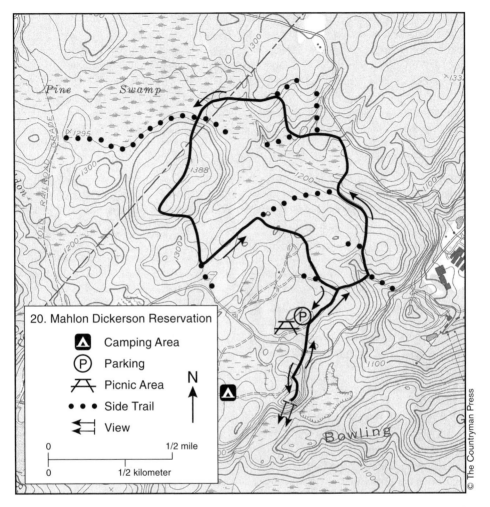

20. Mahlon Dickerson Reservation

🔺 Camping Area
Ⓟ Parking
🪑 Picnic Area
● ● ● Side Trail
⇇ View

N

0   1/2 mile

0   1/2 kilometer

have been popular with everyone and very consistent in his political faith.

In the reservation are a number of marked trails that are, for the most part, old logging roads and fire lanes. Some are covered in gravel. Unlike narrow footpaths, these wide lanes facilitate conversation with companions. They are also well suited for cross-country skiing, and because the average elevation in the park is 1,200 feet, snow remains on the ground longer than in many other areas in north Jersey. Many are open to horses and mountain bikes, and you may encounter them along the way. A section of the 150-mile Highlands Trail (see the Introduction) also passes through the park.

Although this hike does not offer sweeping views of the countryside, the change in woodland environments more than makes up for it. Along the route are deciduous forests, rocky scrub growth, damp hemlock groves, laurel thickets, and remote swampland. The reservation is located on a high plateau in the New Jersey Highlands Province. The bedrock, which is very close to the surface because of glaciation, is

Precambrian gneiss, a granitic rock that contains large amounts of iron. There are a few long-abandoned iron mines in the reservation. Because the park is large and located in the most remote part of Morris County, many species of wildlife, including red-tailed hawks, deer, and an occasional bear, make their homes here.

HOW TO GET THERE

From I-80 (Exit 33), take NJ 15 north for 5 miles. Turn right, following signs to Milton and Weldon Road. After 2 miles on Weldon Road, you'll see a sign indicating that you've entered the reservation. The road will swing around to the right and pass the large parking area for Saffin Pond. In roughly another mile, you will come to the reservation's three main entrances, the first two for campers. At 4.3 miles from NJ 15 take the second entrance on the left, which leads to a large parking area, a picnic area, and the trailhead.

THE TRAIL

Walk north on the wide asphalt path past a water pump, a workout station, a picnic area, and a ball field. The access trail you are following is part of the Highlands Trail, marked in turquoise, with some white markers as well. The pavement will soon become gravel, and in just 0.1 mile you will arrive at a junction with the Pine Swamp Trail, a 3.5-mile loop marked in white that passes through the northern part of the reservation. The blue markers of the Highlands Trail share this route for the first third of the hike. Make a right turn at this junction; walk downhill and cross over a small brook. At the next junction, bear left, staying with the white and blue markers. After a short climb, the trail veers to the right at a grassy intersection, heads downhill, then swings to the left through an open forest.

After a short level stretch, the Pine Swamp Trail comes to a triangular junction with the green-blazed Boulder Trail and turns to the right, down a long hill (there is a parallel path here) to a brook. This unnamed brook is one of the principal drainages of the swamp that dominates the interior of the northern portion of the reservation. Notice that the brook's water is a dark color. As in the Pine Barrens, the tannins in the roots of hemlocks and other swamp evergreens color the water. After crossing on a small bridge, be alert for a left turn off the main path onto a cut trail through a corner of the swamp.

In this section of trail, mountain laurel and rhododendron dominate, putting on a display of flowers in June and July. The footing is much rockier here, and there can be a few wet areas that may require some stretching. As you reach the end of this part of the swamp, the trail climbs up a few feet to higher ground, connects with a woods road, and turns left. Because this part of the trail passes near Sparta Mountain Road, you may hear an occasional motor vehicle.

In 0.1 mile the trail turns to the right, crossing over a bridge, and gains in elevation. When you come to Sparta Mountain Road on your right, turn left onto the Pine Swamp Trail, now following only white markers. After a short rise, the trail levels off and gradually descends, entering the area of the Pine Swamp itself. Just ahead on your left, at the edge of a small cliff, look for an area that overlooks the dense foliage of the swamp. This rocky spot is a pleasant place to stop for a rest or to have a snack or lunch. Below you is not a typical swamp of grasses and water, but a pine swamp with tall spruce, hemlock, rhododendron, and laurel.

Continue farther along on the trail, which now heads downhill to the level of the swamp, and get a closer view of this peculiar area. About 0.2 mile ahead, the trail—a woods road and very dry—comes closest to the main swamp itself. Off to your right you can see how wet the area is and how huge boulders protrude from the ground, providing drier areas in their cracks for plants incapable of growing in water or very wet soil. You are now in one of the most remote areas of the reservation. On your right, the swamp extends for perhaps a mile into Sussex County. It is virtually inaccessible, and no paths cross it. You get a feeling of wilderness here, broken only by the calls of birds or an occasional aircraft. In fact, some years ago a small private plane crashed in the swamp one May. It wasn't until that November that the wreckage and the bodies were found.

The trail, which travels a high area between two parts of the swamp, continues under tall hemlocks, crosses a small brook, and then begins a climb, leaving the swamp for good. You'll pass a junction with a bike trail on the right marked with yellow tags. For the next mile, you will share the route with this bike trail. Continue climbing gradually to the flat, rounded summit of an unnamed hill that, at 1,388 feet, is the highest point in Morris County. The trail passes just to the northeast of the height of land, but unfortunately there are no views except through the trees during winter.

The trail, which in this section is part gravel and used occasionally by maintenance vehicles, swings to the left, then to the right as it descends to lower ground. Follow it through a low area and up a gradual climb. You can find a few remnants of 19th-century iron mining—mostly pits and rockpiles—by exploring the woods to your left and uphill. At a three-way junction, the trail turns left (the bike trail turns right) and heads roughly east on a wide footpath. After about 0.25 mile, keep right at a junction with the Boulder Trail and continue walking on a wide lane, keeping to the left at the next junction. In about another 0.2 mile, you'll arrive at the trail junction where you began the loop hike, marked by signs. Make a right here and walk the path through the picnic area and back to your car.

If you still have energy and would like to take in a vista, the Headley Overlook is less than 0.25 mile away. Follow the blue markers as they leave the parking area in back of the directory across Weldon Road and then out to the overlook. The rocky overlook offers a view to the south and west that includes an arm of Lake Hopatcong.

BCS

21

Jenny Jump State Forest

Total distance: 4.5 miles

Hiking time: 3 hours

Vertical rise: 900–950 feet

Rating: Moderate

Maps: USGS Blairstown; DEP Jenny Jump State Forest map

Jenny Jump State Forest was named for a young colonial girl. As the tale goes, Jenny was out picking berries with her father. Some hostile Native Americans came across the pair and her father yelled out for her to jump from the cliff—if only to save her chastity. Although Jenny was successful in keeping herself pure, the result was her death . . . or so the tale goes.

HOW TO GET THERE

To reach Jenny Jump from exit 12 off I-80, drive 1.1 miles into the town of Hope. Bear left onto County Route 519. After little more than a mile, turn right onto Shiloh Road (near a small pond) at a marked junction. After going another 1.4 miles uphill, bear right at a fork, then right again after an additional 0.6 mile. The state forest entrance road is 0.4 mile farther on your left. After I-80, most of the route is marked with Jenny Jump State Forest directional signs, but some are rather small. Stop at the park office (PO Box 150, Hope, NJ 07844; 908-459-4366) for a free map, then drive uphill following the sign pointing to the trailheads. There is a new comfort station, several new rental cabins, two small parking areas, and the start of the hiking trails. There is also a trail sign here. Consider combining this short hike with a picnic lunch. There are lots of tables around.

THE TRAIL

You'll begin your hike on the red-marked Swamp Trail, which co-mingles with the yellow-marked Summit Trail for the first few

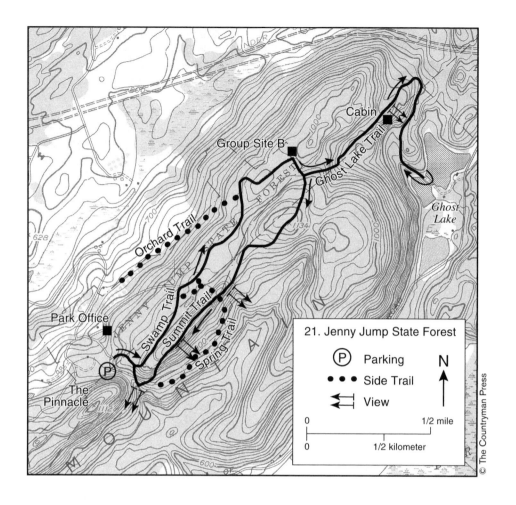

21. Jenny Jump State Forest

Ⓟ Parking
••• Side Trail
⇐ View

N

0   1/2 mile
0   1/2 kilometer

© The Countryman Press

minutes. In the mid-1990s the New York–New Jersey Trail Conference accepted trail maintenance responsibility within Jenny Jump State Forest, and the trails here are well maintained and are marked with standard one-color blazes.

Your trail (red) goes somewhat uphill along a woods road as it turns right and heads toward the crest of the ridge. Pass a few picnic tables as the path swings left. After less than five minutes, you will reach a well-marked junction. Stay to the left following the red markings. The yellow is the Summit Trail, upon which you will return.

The Swamp Trail is wide and proceeds gently through the woods. Continue straight ahead, avoiding a fork to the left. The small gorge off to the right contains some small wet areas that probably gave the trail its name; however, the going is generally dry and easy. As the trail descends into the lower tract, you reach Campsite #19 near a bathhouse and children's playground. This state forest has many such campsites available to the public for a small fee. Reservations are advisable. There are also eight cabins for rent, with four bunks each and a maximum capacity of six.

Jenny Jump State Forest

Proceed ahead, past the sign to the Summit-Spring Connection Trail and onto the paved road. Bear right, going along the road and passing several more campsites, some water faucets, and another bathhouse. Just afterward, near campsite #34 note the large glacial erratic on the left side of the road—as well as the small tree growing right out of the rock. Imagine the strength of the ice sheet that ripped out this monster, then left it here after melting and retreating north. I guess the tree is not all that impressed.

Continuing ahead on the road, pass a sign for the Orchard Trail. Continue straight ahead. Just before Group Site B, there is a trailhead sign. Turn right here, onto the Ghost Lake Trail, marked in light blue. This first section co-mingles with the yellow-marked Summit Trail.

Back again in the woods, the course sways gently to the left and back again through a small grove of hemlock trees.

After a gentle decent and traverse of a wet area, the Summit Trail makes a sharp right turn at a well-marked junction. Note this spot for your return trip. Unless you want to really shorten the hike (and forgo a 500-foot, up-and-down elevation change), stay on the blue Ghost Lake Trail, which goes straight ahead, soon skirting the side of a hill. For a while, the sounds of nearby I-80 intrude on the solitude, but then the trail begins a rocky descent over some loose rocks. I hope you're wearing your boots!

In a level area, the marked trail joins a woods road, which it will follow the rest of the way to the lake. Shortly after swinging left, the sharp-eyed will notice a wide woods road to the right. This is the now messy site of a former cabin that was removed in 2005. The view east is toward Allamuchy Mountain State Park and the Pequest River Valley. One local insists that this is the actual site where Jenny jumped.

Continuing down, the trail passes some house-sized rocks. The descent moderates as it swings left and parallels a stream. To your right are some dramatic moss-covered cliffs. Soon the lake is visible through the trees. The trail ends just before the grass-covered causeway across Ghost Lake, about 45 minutes from Group Site B.

There is some debate about how Ghost Lake acquired its name. One story involves a massacre between two warring Native American tribes, the other a mucky, pre-lake swamp where mosquitoes bred and spread sickness and death. The local road leading to the lake is named Shades of Death Road—the subject of a page or two of the Weird New Jersey Web site (www.weirdnj.com/_roads/shadesofdeath.html).

From here, retrace your steps to the junction of the Ghost Lake and Summit Trails. Make a left, going south, onto the yellow-blazed Summit Trail. This junction is clearly marked with a wooden post. If you start seeing both blue and yellow markers together, you've passed the junction; retrace your steps.

You'll follow the yellow blazes of the Summit Trail for the rest of the hike. The path becomes narrower and woodsy as it first moderately, then more steeply, gains the summit ridge of Jenny Jump Mountain. When the terrain begins to level off and you approach the top, note the mountain laurel off to the right. The path undulates along the ridge, not always on the very top, with some evidence of old yellow blazes. As it approaches the summit and several viewpoints, the woodland begins to thin and the trees are shorter.

Fifteen minutes of walking from the junction will bring you to a concrete post in the ground marked NJ 78, probably a former park boundary. The park map shows the Summit Trail crossing outside the forest boundary for a short distance. Here a short side trail to the left will take you to the first of three eastward views. Beyond the blue-marked Spring Trail crossing, another side trail to a view is 10 minutes away. This one is signed VIEW and has a nice rock outcrop-ping where you can pause for a final snack or water break. If the conditions are normal or wet, the moss and grass along the trail will be especially lush and green.

Continue ahead. Through trees to the right are some limited views toward Pennsylvania. There are usually more people encountered along here. Many take the short hike up from the parking area for the vistas. The hill protruding through the woods ahead is part of Jenny Jump and is called the Pinnacle. A microwave tower stands on its top.

As the trail turns right and starts downhill, there is an open area to the left marked vista. Walk out to a viewpoint some 30 yards off the trail. This lookout is the best view in the region. To the left is the vista you saw previously (the Hackettstown region), in front of you is the Pinnacle, and to the right are the Kittatinnies and Pennsylvania. Notice, too, the rock surface underfoot. The striations were made by the glaciers during the Ice Age.

Back on the Summit Trail, proceed downhill through a grove of hemlocks, passing the Swamp Trail junction. Bear left and return to the parking area. I hope the juice machine still works.

HNZ

22

Point Mountain

Total distance: 3.5 miles

Hiking time: 2–3 hours

Vertical rise: 535 feet

Rating: Moderate

Maps: USGS Washington; Musconetcong River Reservation Point Mountain Section Trail Map and Guide

As you drive along NJ 47 south of Hackettstown you will notice that you are in a very fertile valley nestled between two long mountain ranges. On your left will be the distinctive Musconetcong Mountain Range, a long ridge that is the remains of an ancient thrust fault in the Precambrian rock of the New Jersey Highlands. This thrust fault pushed older resistant rock on top of younger and softer rock, resulting in a ridge and an accompanying valley through which the Musconetcong River flows. The Musconetcong Mountain ridge and Musconetcong River are located in the northern portion of Hunterdon County. The highest point on the ridge is Musconetcong Mountain in Bloomsbury, where it reaches an elevation of 955 feet. The vertical relief from river valley to the nearby summit ridge is substantial—from 400 to 500 feet. Point Mountain is an outstanding feature of the Musconetcong Mountain Range and attains an elevation of 935 feet.

Point Mountain, named for its sharp profile when seen from the south, is contained within the larger Musconetcong River Reservation, a property acquired by the Hunterdon County Department of Parks and Recreation (PO Box 2900, Flemington, NJ 08822; 908-782-1158; www.co.hunterdon.nj.us/depts/parks/parks.htm). Located at the northernmost portion of the county, this section contains more than 700 acres of riverside and ridge forest that can be traversed via several trails. A portion of the hike described below also utilizes NJ Fish and Wildlife property. The mostly undeveloped area (no facilities other than parking) is open to fishing, hiking, horseback riding, cross-country skiing, and mountain biking. It is planned that in the future, the 150-mile Highlands Trail will traverse Point Mountain on its route from the New York border to the Delaware River. The region is also the focus of The Musconetcong Mountain Conservancy. This group was formed in 2002 and is dedicated to the preservation of New Jersey Highlands and surrounding environs and is concerned with the establishment of continuous greenways and trails along the ridges.

There are two access points to the trail system on Point Mountain. One is located on Penwell Road and passes through a series of working farm fields before entering the forested mountain ridge. This section is the site of Penwell Mill, named for a descendant of the Penn family in Pennsylvania. An 1830 farmhouse and barn (a private residence) are located here. The other access point, the one used for this hike, is located just below the summit of Point Mountain. The hike described below first leads alongside the Musconetcong River and through some open working farm fields. It then climbs the long mountain ridge to arrive at the spectacular vista near the summit of Point Mountain. A short but steep descent from this vista brings you back to your car. Those with less time and interest in the vista may wish to walk directly from the parking area to the viewpoint, a short but very steep hike.

HOW TO GET THERE

From Exit 26 on I-80 (Budd Lake/Hackettstown exit) drive 8 miles to the center of Hackettstown and turn left onto NJ 182/57. In under 1 mile make a right onto NJ 57, following signs to Washington and Phillipsburg. Drive just under 7 miles and turn left onto Point Mountain Road. The parking area is 0.5 mile ahead on the left, just past the

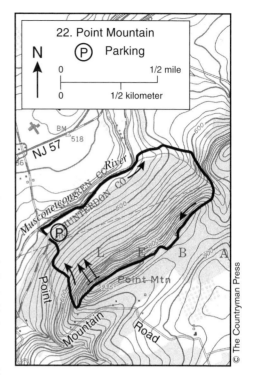

river bridge. From I-78, take NJ 31 north for 8 miles and turn right onto County Route 632 (Asbury–Anderson Road). Drive 4 miles to NJ 57, follow NJ 57 to Point Mountain Road, and turn right to the parking area on the left.

THE TRAIL

From the parking area (trail maps may be available here) walk back down Point Mountain Road toward the Musconetcong River. After passing some boulders, turn right onto a footpath located immediately before the bridge over the river. Follow this trail, marked with blue tags, alongside the river in a northeasterly direction. You may encounter some muddy sections, but also a few places where rocks rise over the water and invite exploration of the river itself. Keep walking with the river on your left, passing

Point Mountain

BRUCE SCOFIELD

rock outcrops and boulder fields composed of Precambrian Highlands gneiss on your right. At a small clearing, the trail jogs right and then turns to the left onto a more established path. At the next fork, keep left, hugging the river. Not far ahead, the trail leaves the river and, traversing NJ Division of Fish and Wildlife property, rises up to an open field. This field is planted with winter wheat—keep out of the field itself, but you may walk along its mowed edges.

As you enter the field, turn right and follow its south side along the edge of woods. There are blue posts with markers here to indicate that you are still on the marked trail. Where the path jogs to the left is the terminus of the Blue Trail and a junction with the Orange Trail. (A left here following orange markers leads uphill alongside the field to a wide view of the Point Mountain Ridge.) Turn right onto the Orange Trail, passing an owl box on a tree in a patch of woods. Turn right and follow the orange markers along-side the south edge of the field as it rises up the hill. At the end of the field is a bench overlooking a view of the hills (and microwave towers) in the distance. Here, after at least a half hour of hiking, the trail enters the forest and begins the steady climb up the ridge to Point Mountain.

The trail first utilizes an old road—it is flat, graded, and heads relentlessly uphill. When you cross a wet area, look for a small spring to your left alongside the trail. Just past the spring, pay attention as the Orange Trail veers to the right and off the lane. The trail now continues on a cut trail that immediately clambers over rocks through a wet area. A brook is crossed here under high canopy of maples—this is the halfway point of the hike. The trail then climbs out of the wet area and continues uphill on rockier footing. Before long you'll realize that the trail has reached the Point Mountain ridge—evidenced by both the narrowness of the ridge and the presence of a stronger breeze as well. To your right small openings through the trees reveal the other side of the Musconetcong Valley. To your left the land drops off steeply. Be careful on these rocks—the footing is very rough. Ahead, the trail turns sharply left and descends to an old rock wall, veers right, and follows it briefly before leaving it and climbing back up to the ridge. Skirting boulders and rocks, the trail now swings over to the other side of the ridge. After a steep rocky climb, the trail settles back to the center and continues its gradual climb. There were many blowdowns in this section at the time of writing, making a relatively difficult trail even more challenging.

As the trail climbs ever higher, tantalizing views over the Musconetcong Valley begin to appear to your right. The trail becomes increasingly rugged as it works its way past boulders and rock outcrops. Huge boulders jut out from the ridgetop, and you may need to use your hands in places. One last short descent and the trail finally arrives at the rocky Point Mountain overlook. Here the markers, which you will need to check carefully, lead through splits in the rocks. You'll have to pick your way through the boulders to reach the spectacular west-facing vista. Two huge rock outcrops extend out from the mountain's mass over the Musconetcong Valley. A trail coming from the southeast is also found here. Be sure not to take it on the way back.

To continue, leave the lookout and follow the orange markers downhill. This will be a very steep descent over rocks. Be aware that poison ivy may be found here, more near the first part of the descent. Watch your step on the way down! The trail swings to the right past a small building. Point Mountain Road is nearby and a few residences are located off of it. Trail builders have made a few stone steps in places that offer some relief from the steady downhill walking—and you will thank them for their efforts. After the steepest part of the descent, the trail levels out and comes to a four-way junction. Here the Blue Trail comes in from the left and turns just ahead of you, utilizing the lane on which you are walking. Walk straight through this intersection, now following blue markers, and down to the parking area where you left your car.

BCS

23

Schooley's Mountain County Park

Total Distance: 3 miles

Hiking time: 2.5 hours

Vertical rise: 500 feet

Rating: Easy

Maps: USGS Hackettstown; Morris County Park Commission Schooley's Mountain map. Available by calling 973-326-7600. Other information may be obtained from www.morrisparks.net.

Schooley's Mountain County Park is a comparatively small park of less than 800 acres, but has much to offer the outdoors enthusiast. The hiking trails are mostly easy, excepting the first part of this hike, where the footing on the Falling Waters Trail is quite rocky. However, the gorge and falls made by the Electric Brook are well worth the trip. Electric Brook takes its name from the old electric generating plant once installed here, which used the brook for power. There is only one vista, but the shade trees make for a very pleasant outing on a hot summer day. The high point of the park is at 1,104 feet. The Highland Cut bisects the park at this point, though there are no views because of the dense tree cover. The park is administered by the Morris County Park Commission, and in addition to the hiking trails—some of which are used by horses—paddle boats and rowboats may be rented for use on Lake George. Attractive benches are placed at intervals on the trails. Fishing is permitted, dogs must be leashed, and there is currently no swimming. Rest rooms, a picnic shelter, a playground, and a lodge are close by. The lodge may be rented for such functions as weddings and parties.

The park is named for the Schooley family, who owned much land in this locality in the 1700s. Originally a large part of the park was used for a Morristown YMCA camp called Camp Washington, but it was purchased by the Morris County Park Commission in October 1968, opening to the public in May 1974.

Highlands

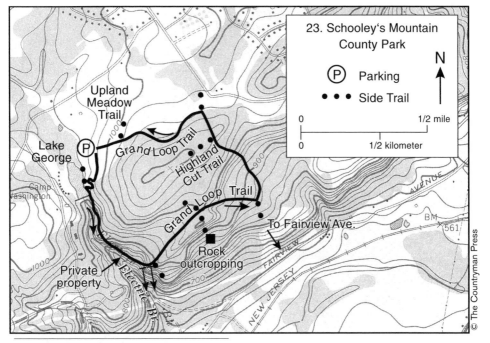

23. Schooley's Mountain County Park

N

Ⓟ Parking

• • • Side Trail

0   1/2 mile

0   1/2 kilometer

© The Countryman Press

HOW TO GET THERE

Take I-80 to Exit 27A, proceeding south on US 206 for 4.4 miles. Turn right onto Bartley Road (County Route 612, though it may not be signed), and continue for 3.5 miles. Turn right onto Naughright Road, and after 2.2 miles turn left onto East Springtown Road. The park entrance is on the left, 0.5 mile down East Springtown Road. Parking is available at the end of the park entry road.

THE TRAIL

Begin your trek by walking uphill on the grassy area toward the restrooms, and at the fork, take the wider shale path down to the right, passing an old foundation on the left. Do not take the Grand Loop Trail straight ahead, nor the narrow path to the left, which leads to an overlook of Lake George. Turn left at the base of the short descent and follow Lake George's west bank to access the blue paint-blazed Falling Waters Trail. Before continuing, take the short walk to the right leading to the bridge over Lake George's spillway, where you can see a different perspective of the lake.

The Falling Waters Trail descends steadily by the pools and cascades of Electric Brook. The path is rocky and care needs to be taken, particularly after rain, when the footway may be slippery. Be sure to stop and look around to admire the unspoiled scenery. The two attractive waterfalls are reached within 0.3 mile, and a break is suggested here.

Falling Waters Trail now swings away from Electric Brook and traverses the left-hand side of signed private property. The footway climbs steadily and more easily to the end of the Falling Waters Trail, marked by the traditional three triangular blazes on a tree. On your right at the top of the climb is a huge jumble of big boulders remaining from a rock quarry, and the junction with the

Falls on Electric Brook at Schooley's Mountain

white-blazed Patriots' Path. Turn right and follow these white blazes for a short distance to the only vista to be found on the hike. You have now covered 0.5 mile. The valley is serene and beautiful. Rest awhile and enjoy the view before retracing your footsteps to the Falling Waters–Patriots' Path junction you just left. Walk ahead following white blazes for about 20 yards to where the Patriots' Path leaves to the left. Here, bear right onto a wide gravel-based woods road called Quarry Stone Path. (Ignore a similar path coming in on the left a little way further on.) There are no reassuring paint blazes in this section, but the footway is wide and easy to follow.

Within 15 minutes a junction is reached with a welcoming bench. The path that turns to the left returns the walker to the parking lot, but the hike described turns right, taking the Grand Loop Trail pointing toward the Beehive Trail. Horses are permitted on this loop. Just before reaching this junction, look for a trail to the right, and take the time to follow this path, which quickly leads to a most unusual rock outcropping.

The Grand Loop Trail descends on a narrower footway with few rocks until a junction is reached. Ignore the right turn, which leads to Fairview Avenue and the Columbia Trail and turn left to walk consistently uphill for 15 minutes until the height of land is reached. Here there is a cairn, a signpost, and three red paint blazes indicating the start of the Highland Cut, which travels across the mountain toward the southwest. Do not take the Highland Cut, but continue ahead on the Grand Loop Trail, which now descends gently to a trail junction with a cairn and a pink ribbon flag. The signpost is temporarily missing here, but turn left on a narrower path through luxurious ferns. Stay with the yellow-blazed Grand Loop Trail, ignoring the first junction with the Upland Meadow Trail, which joins the Grand Loop Trail from the right within a few minutes.

Fifteen minutes through a lush forest brings you to a T-junction—the second junction with the Upland Meadow Trail. Turn left, passing another bench and signpost before you reach the parking lot and your car within a few more minutes.

SJG

24

Black River Trails

Total Distance: 6.6 miles

Hiking time: 4 hours

Vertical rise: 400 feet

Rating: Moderate to strenuous

Maps: USGS Chester. Black River County Park Trails map is usually available at the visitor center, at the bulletin board at Cooper Mill, or at the Bamboo Brook parking lot. Call the Morris County Park Commission at 973-326-7600 or consult their Web site at www.parks.morris.nj.us /parks/trails/edktr.htm

This hike requires a short car shuttle, and is a strip hike from north to south in Chester Township. An option is offered at the end of the Conifer Pass Trail if only one car is available. This trek has much to recommend it. In addition to the hike itself, there are interesting historical features at both ends to visit when time permits. The terrain used by the hike is varied. At first following an old railroad grade, the trails used parallel the Black River as the water rushes through its rocky gorge, then climb through cool and dense deciduous and pine forests to finish with a meander through several meadows. Dogs must be leashed.

Cooper Mill, at the northern end, is a gristmill dating from 1826, and is open to visitors at certain times, with tickets available at the nearby visitor center. Fees for the tour of the mill are graded among adults, seniors, and children. Both the visitor center and the mill are closed during the winter, and opening times vary from May through October. You should endeavor to obtain a pass from the visitor center before starting, because this hike passes briefly through a designated natural area. For information call 908-879-5463.

The Bamboo Brook Outdoor Education Center at the southern end of the hike offers a self-guiding trail brochure for $2, available at the parking lot bulletin board. The Willowood Arboretum is also close by. The hike uses the Black River, the Conifer Pass, and the Bamboo Brook Trails, and crosses two paved roads—Pottersville Road and Longview Road. These trails are used

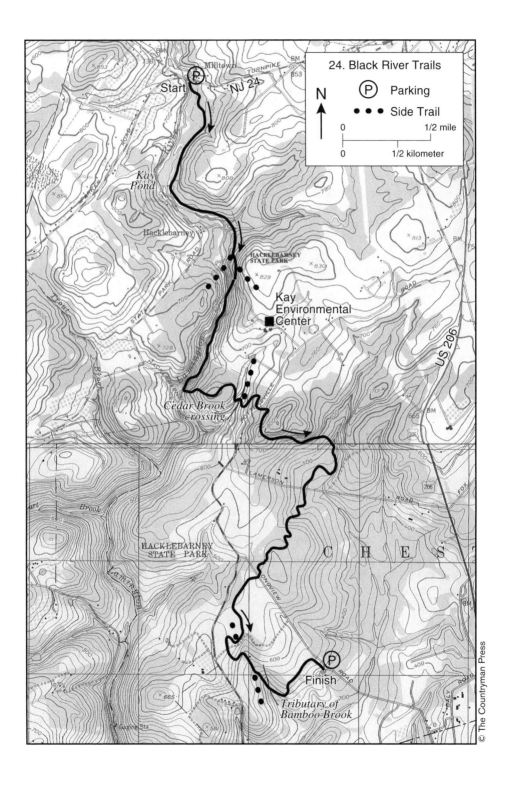

for the Patriots' Path National Recreational Trail (PP) and occasionally you will notice the green path-and-tree logo in addition to paint blazes.

HOW TO GET THERE

Drive both cars to the Bamboo Brook Outdoor Education Center parking lot. Travel south on I-287 to Exit 22 (Bedminster/Pluckemin) and drive County Route 206 north just over 4 miles to Pottersville Road (CR 512). Turn left for 0.5 mile, and then right onto Lisk Hill Road. Continue for 0.1 mile to a T-junction. Turn right onto Union Grove Road and continue for 0.3 mile to a Y-junction. Turn left onto Longview Road. Bamboo Brook Outdoor Education Center parking is on the left, about 1 mile from the Y.

Leave one car at the Bamboo Brook parking lot, and drive north to the Cooper Mill and visitor center. Turn left out of the parking lot onto Longview Road and drive 0.8 mile to a T-junction with Pottersville Road. Turn right and after 0.7 mile turn left onto the unsigned Hacklebarney Road. Infrequent brown signs for Cooper Mill will confirm your route. Travel on this narrow, partly gravel road for 0.7 mile to its end and turn right onto State Park Road. On the way you will pass the old Kay Pond ice house. Continue another 2 miles to CR 513, where a right turn leads almost immediately to the parking at the Cooper Mill and visitor center, also on the right.

At the end of your hike and return to the Cooper Mill, a right turn on CR 513 leads to US 206, where a left turn (north) accesses I-80, and a right turn (south) takes you to I-287.

THE TRAIL

Walk to the northwest corner of the parking lot toward the Cooper Mill County Park sign, and continue to the bulletin board in the direction of the mill. When the demand for local grains declined in 1913, this last operating mill in Chester was closed. The pump on your right-hand side has recently been capped. Descend the small flight of wooden stairs by the side of the mill and begin the hike on the Black River Trail, marked with blue paint blazes. The Black River (aka the Lamington River) is now on your right, but the trail soon leaves its banks. The area is lush, with some large trees, and the dirt footway, which crosses several small plank bridges, is crisscrossed by tree roots. Within 0.3 mile the trail turns left onto the abandoned route of the Hacklebarney Branch of the Central Railroad of New Jersey, built in 1873 to transport ore from the Hacklebarney Mine, and abandoned in 1900. The now wider trail passes through a cut with piles of rocks to the side and blasting grooves in the rock wall. In this section there are several informational signs.

After about 20 minutes, lily pad-covered Kay Pond can be seen on the right. Great blue herons and other wildlife can often be seen around the pond, which is man-made. The pond takes its name from Alfred and Elizabeth Kay, who moved from Pittsburgh in 1924 and built their summer home here, called Hidden River Farm. During the 1930s, Mrs. Kay grew herbs that she sold by mail, and she also opened a local tearoom called the Herb Farm. The Kays donated much of their property to the Morris County Park Commission, and in 1994 Hidden River Farm was dedicated as the Elizabeth D. Kay Environmental Center. The building is now an office for The Nature Conservancy. Kay Pond offered community swimming in the 1940s, and the facilities here at that time included parking and a bathhouse. A few steps to the right of the

Cooper gristmill

trail, the dam makes a pleasant place to take a quick break. One of the remaining ice houses still stands just on the other side of the dam.

Very soon the trail passes the old Hacklebarney Mine on the left. This mine was closed in 1896 and is now protected by a fenced-in area. Hacklebarney was Chester's oldest and most productive iron mine. At first limited to surface mining, Hacklebarney was developed into an underground mine after large iron deposits were found. This mine recorded more accidents than any other in Chester.

Almost immediately the trail crosses a tributary on a substantial bridge with a handrail and, on the right, approaches a barred paved road–State Park Road. The blue blazes indicate that the trail veers left, and on the right of the trail, which has now become rougher, a short herd path leads to some abandoned concrete abutments in the river. Within a minute of ascending the now rougher path, the blue blazes indicate a turn to the left, which should be ignored in favor of walking straight ahead. Look back to check this location by spotting a PP marker, and a maroon marker indicating no bicycles, both posted on a double-trunked tree at the junction.

There are no blazes on the grassy woods road, which now passes through the natural area for which you obtained a permit. A wide junction is reached after a couple of minutes on this flat trail. There is a green marker on a tree straight ahead, and you should take the gravel, uphill path on the left. The end of the green trail, marked with the traditional method of three blazes, and a Y-junction, is reached in about five or six minutes. Take the Conifer Pass Trail, marked in red, which uses the lower right-hand, slightly narrower trail from the Y.

Conifer Pass Trail is narrow, often marked with brown trail signs, and switchbacks on sidehills on its way down to the

Black River. The river with its waterfalls can be glimpsed through the trees on the right, until the trail begins to descend more steeply. The river then becomes more visible as it tumbles through its deep and narrow gorge. The trail, marked with cairns, parallels the Black River for a short distance before beginning to climb on switchbacks away from this wild and scenic spot. Take care to follow the red trail blazes, as the trail is sometimes a little indistinct here, and notice the indications of some test mining.

After 15 minutes, the Conifer Pass Trail crosses an old stone wall and a large cairn on the left and begins to descend. At times the trail is a little overgrown, and as it drops down through huge conifers is reminiscent of trails in the American West. The footway leads down to a crossing of Cedar Brook and then climbs, passing another stone wall and an old fence post on the right to lead, within 10 minutes, through another stand of evergreens, to a crossing of Pottersville Road. The sign here gives an emergency contact telephone number for the park police (973-326-7654), and indicates that hunting is permitted on some sections of these trails.

The trail now climbs away from Pottersville Road, passes another cairn, and after a turn to the right, levels out, and reaches a wooden signpost at the end of the Conifer Pass Trail. (One-car option: Turn left at the signpost to reach the Kay Environmental Center in 2.2 miles, and the Cooper Gristmill in 3.6 miles. This route will, however, entail a short walk on paved Pottersville Road.)

Our hike continues by turning right and using the Bamboo Brook Trail, marked in blue. After about 10 minutes of walking downhill, the trail reaches the brook itself, veers left, and parallels it. Also on the left is an old stone wall that the trail crosses a couple of times before reaching Lamerson Road, only about five minutes after arriving at Bamboo Brook.

Cross directly over Lamerson Road onto a woods road, bearing left after a few minutes. (In this section there are several intersecting woods roads, so be sure to watch for and follow the blue trail blazes.) After the Bamboo Brook Trail bends first to the right and then to the left, the trail becomes more open and receives more sunshine. In another 10 minutes a woods road joins the trail route from behind on the right. Watch here carefully for an almost immediate right turn. This junction is marked clearly with the routine turn signal, a PP logo, and a hiker sign. The trail now reaches an old rock wall and turns right. Pick your way along this wall for about 20 yards, then leave it by turning right away from it onto a smoother path, until Longview Road is reached. The trip from Lamerson Road to Longview Road takes about 25 minutes.

The remainder of the Bamboo Brook Trail uses some open meadows. If the sun is very hot and you wish to avoid baking in it, the next section can be avoided by turning left and walking paved Longview Road downhill for 0.6 mile to the Bamboo Brook parking lot and your car. This option is not our recommendation, because this next trail section is very pleasant and only takes approximately 45 minutes.

Cross Longview Road and follow the blue blazes through a wooded section until the Bamboo Brook Trail veers to the left and emerges onto an open meadow. Turn right and walk along the side of the field. Here there is no real footway, but there is a reassuring blaze on a post halfway along. At the end of this first side, a turn signal indicates that the route turns left and follows a second side of this first meadow. Leave the first field on a wide swath and walk the short distance into another field. Look for a marked post to the left, walk toward it, and around two sides of this meadow, noting a reassuring blaze on a tree to the left, halfway along the second side. At the end of the second side the trail goes back into a wooded section and quickly bears right indicated by a blazed turn signal and a PP logo.

Within a couple of minutes the trail crosses a rock wall, and a herd path, and continues to a blazed post indicating a right turn. Continue down this wide woods road to the second marker, and here make a sharp left into the woods. If the weather has been wet and the foliage has grown this turn may be a little indistinct, but the trail soon opens out into another wooded section, paralleling a tributary of Bamboo Brook on the left of the path. Now a little more rocky, the trail crosses the stream, leaving it on your right, as you begin a short climb away from it.

The Bamboo Brook Trail enters another field after this climb. There seems to be no turn signal here, but turn left, walking slightly uphill on a seasonally mown part of this meadow. At the next blazed post, leave this field and bear left onto a wide trail that leads to another meadow. Again turn left, and follow the side of this field as it makes an S-bend partway along, and at another marked post, turn left, back into the woods. The footway is distinct, and emerges onto another meadow with the Bamboo Brook parking lot visible down to the right. Walk around the sides of this last field down to your car.

SJG

25

Merrill Creek Reservoir

Total distance: 8.5 miles

Hiking time: 4 hours

Vertical rise: 800 feet

Rating: Easy

Maps: USGS Bloomsbury; Merrill Creek Reservoir trail map

The Merrill Creek Reservoir (34 Merrill Creek Road, Washington, NJ 07882; 908-454-1213) is located on Scotts Mountain in Harmony Township, Warren County. The area is designed and managed specifically for low-impact recreational use—possibly because of the opposition to the reservoir's planned enlargement in the late 1980s.

The present reservoir replaced a smaller one built by Ingersoll-Rand to supply water to its plant in nearby Phillipsburg in 1903. Ground was broken for the new reservoir in September 1985 and, because of the workers' long hours—sometimes as many as 20 a day—the reservoir was completed in April 1988. Seven electric utility companies combined their efforts on this project. The 650-acre lake thus formed is stocked with a variety of gamefish. It has a maximum depth of 225 feet and more than 5 miles of shoreline. The reservoir stores 16 billion gallons of water for release to the Delaware River during low-water periods to augment the river water used by its generating stations. A 3-mile pipeline, 57 inches in diameter and about 6 feet below ground, links the reservoir to the Delaware. Water is pumped up the mountain from the river by three 8,000-horsepower pumps and returned through the same pipeline when needed. The inlet/outlet tower controls water flow. Ports are provided along the tower to permit water to be released from whatever depth best matches the river's temperature.

A 290-acre wildlife preserve that surrounds the shore of the reservoir is only a small part of the 2,000 acres of open space

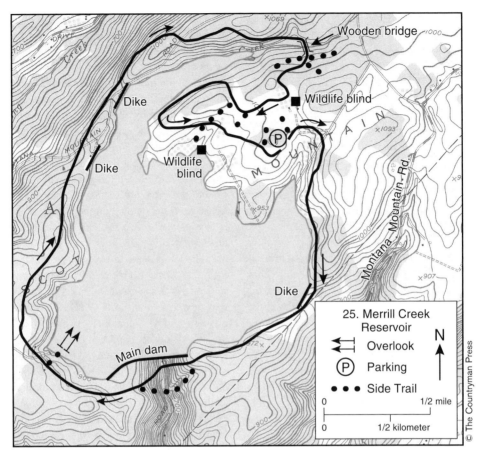

surrounding the lake. The visitor center contains an excellent display of the methods used to move the water. Another exhibit uses a unique method to illustrate in sand the tracks left by wild animals. A large collection of animal skulls is displayed in a glass case, and in the back room stuffed birds are suspended from the ceiling. The visitor center is open year round, although it's closed for certain holidays. Information may be obtained by calling 908-454-1213.

This hike is easy walking, largely on flat, wide trails, but with a few rocky sections. The trails used are the Perimeter (black) Trail, a circular trail; a bit of the Creek (orange) Trail; parts of the Orchard (green), Farmstead (yellow), and Timber (red) Trails, and all of the Shoreline (blue) Trail. The markers are metal and have MCR beneath the trail color. Benches are provided along many of the trails, and the first part of the Perimeter Trail is signed at 0.5-mile intervals. Neither bicycles nor horses are permitted on the trails, and only electric motor-driven boats are allowed on the water. No kayaks or canoes are available for rent. Deer and other wildlife are often seen. Nesting bald eagles have been noticed at Merrill Creek Reservoir since 1997, and during January and February of 2005 a pair was observed adding sticks to a nest. No one knows why the nest failed and the young didn't survive, but since then there have been only occasional sightings of adult birds.

HOW TO GET THERE

From I-78 take exit 4 (Warren Glen/Stewartsville). Turn right at the bottom of the exit ramp and drive 1.8 miles on County Route 637 to a blinking stoplight in Stewartsville. Turn right onto CR 638 (Washington Street, then New Village Road). Ignore the turn on the left signed for NJ 57 and drive 2.3 miles to NJ 57. Cross diagonally (your destination is signed from this point, sometimes with just a street sign), and proceed up Montana Mountain Road for 2 miles. Bear left at a fork and after 0.3 mile turn left onto Merrill Creek Road. The boat ramp is straight ahead, but take the road that veers right to the visitor center. Instructions for reaching Merrill Creek Reservoir from other directions are available by telephone or at www.merrillcreek .com/directions.html. A copy of the park map is available from www.merrillcreek.com or from the visitor center.

THE TRAIL

With your back to the front door of the visitor center (the lake is to your right), proceed toward the hiker-and-arrow sign immediately across the blacktop and to the right. On the first tree there are two markers, one green, the other black (both labeled MCR) and this first small section of the hike is dual-marked. Do not take the Orchard Trail to the left, but head downhill to the boat ramp and parking area. Cross the wooden bridge and follow the black markers of the Perimeter Trail.

Leave the dock and lake on the right, go straight across the paved area toward the DO NOT ENTER sign, find the black marker, pass through the metal gate, and walk slightly uphill on a wide gravel and dirt road across a field. Bluebirds, a common sight at Merrill Creek Reservoir, like to nest in the open, and nesting boxes are erected at every opportunity. The first is on a slope to the left of the trail. The two dams that carry the Perimeter Trail are visible. A gentle upgrade, followed by an equally gentle downgrade, brings the southeast dike into view. Ignore the trail leading down to the left (it eventually crosses a boardwalk), and walk straight ahead across the dike. At the end of the dike the trail heads slightly uphill again and becomes narrower. It is only lightly marked in this section, but continue straight, ignoring any other path coming in from the left or right, until you approach the main dam about 30 minutes from the start.

There is a choice at the main dam. The trail downhill to the left involves a steep descent and an equally steep climb back up, so in order to avoid this extra effort we recommend walking straight across the main dam, which is has wire gates at both ends. Halfway along on the left is a wooden instrument-access staircase, closed to the public. The pipe under the rocks is used to release water from the reservoir into Lower Merrill Creek; the flow is regulated at 3 cubic feet per second.

Ten more minutes brings you to the end of the main dam. Go through the gate and turn right at the base of the hill facing you. Black markers lead you through a stand of tall pine trees planted in rows. Poison ivy in vine form covers many of these trees; it is easy to spot because of the furry appearance of the vine. Stay very clear at all times of the year.

Continue walking through hardwoods for approximately another 10 minutes until you reach a T-junction. Turn right, toward the lake. Ignore the trail, passed shortly, that leads to the water's edge. Soon a flat expanse to the right of the trail with some brickwork, a large white pine, forsythia, daffodils, daylilies, and periwinkle denotes the site of an old homestead. The trail is a little rockier here and climbs slightly until it curves toward a parking lot to the left. The observation deck, a large wooden structure at the water's edge, is a pleasant place to take a break. It can be reached via a side trail to the right that leads downhill to the lakeshore. By now you have covered just over 2.5 miles.

Backtrack from the observation deck and continue to follow the black markers gently downhill. In about 10 minutes the trail makes a 90-degree turn to the left and, as it approaches a paved road, turns again, this time to the right. Continue until you have walked across northwest dike #1, passing the inlet/outlet tower on the lakeshore to the right. Go through the gate at the end of the dike and walk across the parking lot to admire the views across the reservoir. Here there is a bulletin board and a portable toilet screened by a wooden fence.

Follow the arrow on the sign and walk through the metal protective barrier to northwest dike #2. The view across the valley to the west includes two gaps. The more northerly is the Delaware Water Gap, and it is through the tunnel under this valley that the water makes its way back and forth between the reservoir and the Delaware River. From this vantage point you also look down on paved Fox Farm Road.

At the end of the dike, watch for a wooden post carrying black markers that indicate a right turn back into the woods on a rockier trail. Skirt a dry creek bed from the left and continue right, close to the lakeshore. In this section you will see many dead and submerged trees, indicating that the water level was once much lower. Look as well for tulip trees with their long straight trunks, a spruce fir stand, and at the top of

a short rise, a large tulip poplar to the right of the trail with a bulbous base and bark that grows in interesting patterns. Naturalists cannot account for the way this tree has grown.

In about 45 minutes the trail leads to a wooden bridge over Upper Merrill Creek. This bridge incorporates seating into its design and is a good place for a lunch break. You now have walked approximately 5 miles—over half the total mileage for the hike.

Almost immediately after crossing this bridge a T-junction with the orange-marked Creek Trail is encountered. Turn left on the Creek Trail, which climbs slightly and uses a wide woods road to a junction with the green-marked Orchard Trail. Ignore both the old trail straight ahead and the orange-marked trail, which now swings to the left. Turn right on the Orchard Trail (green markers). The path meanders a little and, at the beginning, is a more traditional hiking trail until after about 15 minutes it emerges onto a gravel road. The trail immediately opposite leads to a substantial wildlife blind overlooking a grassy area. Visit the blind, backtrack, and turn right, still following green markers that shortly lead to the ruins of Upper Beers Farm (#5 on the park map).

At the farm's signboard, turn right behind the ruined building onto the Farmstead (yellow) Trail, noting the lilac trees along the edge of the field. If you wish to cut the hike short at this point, follow the green-marked trail that crosses the main entrance road and leads back to the visitor center. Otherwise, follow the yellow markers, at first through a field and then into the woods again and after just over 0.5 mile on the yellow trail, watch carefully and turn right onto the red-marked Timber Trail, which actually crosses the Farmstead Trail.

The beginning of the Timber Trail was a little overgrown on our last visit, but soon

Dead trees at Merrill Creek Reservoir

the footway changes into a wider woods road, descends, bears right at a T-junction, and after just over another 0.5 mile reaches a junction with the blue Shoreline Trail. The orange Creek Trail, which here co-mingles with the black Perimeter Trail, leaves to the right. Now follow the Shoreline Trail, which is perhaps the hardest part of the hike because the trail is more rocky. The blue markers vary in color. Across the water is the trail used earlier to reach the bridge over Upper Merrill Creek. Trees in this area were deliberately submerged to create a better habitat when the reservoir was scoured and quarried. Northwest dike #2 is also visible from here. A side trail leads down to the water's edge, indicating that the trails in this area were relocated uphill when the water level rose. This probably accounts for the more difficult walking.

Continuing gradually uphill, emerge into an open field with views of the pumping tower and often geese and other waterfowl. The trail is located close to the trees that border the upper side of the field. Within 20 minutes from the junction of the Shoreline and Creek Trails, a wooden bench provides an enjoyable resting place. The tall post with the nesting platform is intended to attract ospreys.

Walk downhill until, almost at the water's edge, the blue markers direct you left onto a wide woods road. Soon a side trail to the right leads to another wildlife observation blind, this time on the water's edge. From this point the Visitor Center is approximately 1 mile away.

Several trails enter the Shoreline Trail from the left and a ruined lime kiln (#4 on the park map) stands at the next intersection, one of many in the area. Lime kilns were built on high ground where timber was plentiful and where the elevation caused an updraft, rather than close to the source of the raw materials needed for making lime. The kilns resembled huge stone fireplaces and sometimes served more than one farmstead. A wagon path was built to the top. The kiln was loaded with alternating layers of fuel—usually wood—and limestone chunks. When the fire was lit, temperatures frequently reached 2,000 degrees Fahrenheit, sometimes breaking up the stone with an explosive bang. The burnt lime filtered down and was used on the fields as a fertilizer. The word limelight is thought to have been derived from the light of the kiln when in action.

Continue on the blue trail until the yellow trail joins at the Cathers–Shafer Farm site. The ruins here include the Bank Barn Farm and Farmyard, the Shafer–Tenant Farmhouse, the Spring House, and, a little farther down the trail, the Cathers House (#3, #2, and #1 on the park map).

The pond is a man-made bog created in the 1980s to replace habitat lost in the reservoir construction. The bog turtle is an endangered species in New Jersey and was found in the inundation area. Nonnative grasses, which arrived here along with the soil used to build the dam that created the bog, still need to be eradicated, and studies of the bog turtle continue. Small transmitters are glued to the top of turtles' shells, but tracking their movements is difficult because the animals spend most of their time beneath the mud, emerging only to breed and bask in the May sunlight. The bog is fed by the spring and, because the spring still functions, the trail has been elevated on two sections of boardwalk.

Do not leave the blue trail. (If you wish to take a shortcut here, the next junction to the left leads to a right turn on the red trail, and thence to the visitor center.) Otherwise, go straight ahead on the Shoreline Trail, still following the blue markers, to another bench at the water's edge. From this point the blue markers take you inland where, at the top of a rise, the red trail joins in and the visitor center can be seen immediately ahead.

At the back of the visitor center is a small garden whose plants were chosen to attract butterflies, bees, hummingbirds, and beneficial insects—a pleasant place to unwind after the hike.

SJG

26

Jockey Hollow

Total distance: 5.6 miles

Hiking time: 2–4 hours

Vertical rise: 670 feet

Rating: Easy to moderate

Maps: USGS Mendham; NPS Jockey Hollow Area trail map

At just under 1,000 acres, Jockey Hollow is the largest section of the Morristown National Historical Park (Morristown, NJ 07960; 973-539-2085; www.nps.gov/morr), about 3 miles south of the city of Morristown. The site, operated by the National Park Service, is open year-round, but some of the buildings are closed on Thanksgiving, Christmas, and New Year's, and possibly on a few weekdays, depending on the year's budget. Call ahead to be sure the buildings are open, for they are well worth the visit. There is a modest admission fee for those over age 16. Holders of Golden Age, Golden Access, or Golden Eagle passes are admitted free.

Be sure to allow time for the visitor center. As well as the usual helpful ranger, there is a book nook, orientation film, and a "talking" display of a soldier's hut. Simple trail maps are available. For cartographic fans, a very detailed orienteering map is available for $3.

You should allow time, before or after the hike, to visit Wick House, just behind the visitor center. Henry Wick built his house around 1750 and made his living from farming and from his large woodlot. While better off than most, the family was by no means wealthy. During the winter encampment of 1779–80, the farm served as both the Wicks' home and as the headquarters of Major General Arthur St. Clair.

The main building has been restored, and there is usually a ranger in attendance in period dress to explain the fascinating history. Wick Farm is often less crowded in the morning. We have been there on a

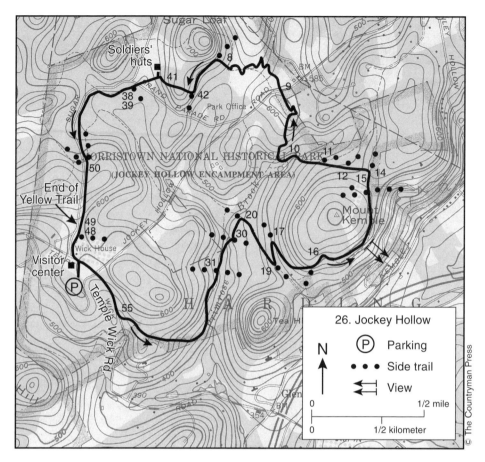

26. Jockey Hollow

N

ⓅParking

• • • Side trail

◁ View

0   1/2 mile

0   1/2 kilometer

magnificent fall Saturday yet had it all to ourselves for an hour; but it became crowded later that afternoon.

The whole hike, indeed this whole park, is fine for cross-country skiing as well as hiking. Signs are posted at almost every trail junction and include a trail map and corresponding location number. These location numbers are indicated in this text within parentheses.

HOW TO GET THERE

Take I-287 to exit 30B and follow US 202 north about 2 miles to Tempe Wick Road. Turn left on this road and drive 1.5 miles; this will bring you to the entrance and main visitor center. The route from the I-287 exit is well marked with the traditional brown National Park Service (NPS) signs.

THE TRAIL

Leave the rear door of the visitor center and proceed to the NPS sign describing the Wick Farm. This sign is about 80 yards behind the center at the end of a graveled path. The Wick House is off to your left. However, turn right and proceed along a wide grass path, flanked by a fence on the left that surrounds the orchard. Crossing a paved park road, continue through the opening in a wooden "snake" fence. A little farther on, take a few minutes to read the NPS sign on Hand's Brigade, and then continue straight ahead on the grass-covered woods road (named the Mendham Road Trail on the park map) that descends slightly.

After about five minutes, you will reach a junction (55). Turn left and proceed into the woods on the Patriots' Path, marked with white blazes and its own distinct logo blaze, a tree with a path underneath on a white background. This multi-use trail (no bikes are allowed in the national park, but horses can use the trails) is a partially completed linear park, running generally alongside the Whippany River from Mendham to East Hanover.

The trail is now a wide woods road, and the walking is easy. Take time to note the surrounding forest. The huge tulip trees are not typical of New Jersey. Since the National Park Service began managing the area in the 1930s (and probably for some time before that), there has been only inconsequential cutting of timber. The result is an unusually mature forest with a lush understory. Unfortunately the lushness is mostly the invasive Japanese barberry, a big problem in this area. For 10 to 15 minutes the route ambles through this forest with slight ups and even more downs on a generally straight course.

After skirting the side of a hill, the path becomes narrower and more trail-like and arrives at the junction (31) with the Primrose Brook Trail, which makes a red-blazed loop path that you will cross again as the Patriots' Path continues. Continue ahead, crossing two streams flowing under wide wooden bridges, the first one with a railing and the second without. Just across the second bridge is a sign (30) and the second crossing of the red trail. Continue ahead as the trail bears left.

You are now about 45 minutes (this time will vary widely) from the start. At the next sign (20), the Patriots' Path turns left. You turn right and continue slightly uphill for 10 minutes to yet another signpost (19). Ahead is a ranger residence, but your route turns sharply left toward the Mount Kemble Loop. A few minutes later you reach another sign (17). Going straight ahead would shorten the hike about a mile by avoiding the loop but, unless you're tired, make a right as the trail, still marked with blue blazes, now starts to circle the mountain. The house seen through the woods is the NPS ranger residence mentioned previously. Stay on the main trail (16). The sounds now heard are from I-287—the eastern boundary of the park is close by. Off the trail on the right is a fenced-in enclosure. This and four others in the park, were erected in the late 1980s to keep the deer out of these small areas and to study the effect their browsing has on the local vegetation. You'll pass two more of these later in the hike.

You will shortly reach an opening in the woods with a view to the east. If you are lucky enough to have a clear day, the tall building in the distance is the top of the Empire State Building. The rest of New York City is hidden from view by the Watchung Mountains. This area was the camping grounds of Stark's Brigade—New Hampshire frontiersmen who fought at Bunker Hill, Trenton, and Princeton. Take a few moments to read the signs and plaques. This is a good spot for a break or lunch. The Watchung Mountains are the reason George Washington chose this tract for his winter encampment. Some 30 miles from New York City, and Howe's British troops, they provided a fine natural defense. Lookouts posted on ridgetops could easily spot enemy troop movements toward Morristown or across the plains toward the "capital" of Philadelphia. How easy it is, if you close your eyes, to imagine this area as a Colonial wilderness.

Soldiers' huts at Jockey Hollow

After about five minutes of additional walking, you reach a metal gate and sign-post (15). Go past the metal gate onto the gravel road (there are private homes on the right) and continue straight on the road, following the blue markers, for about a minute, avoiding the woods road on the left, which heads into a grassy area. Look for a second woods road on the left, which is signed (14) and marked with blue. Make a left, through another metal gate and slightly downhill. You'll know you made the correct move when you reach a sign noting the Mount Kemble Loop (12), which is where you'd re-join the hike if you shortened it.

Take the right fork, again following blue markers, slightly downhill. Soon passing by a junction (11), bear left following the blue markers, and cross a small stream running through a culvert. Just beyond the culvert, the blue path now branches off to the left (10). Your route switches to the white-marked Grand Loop Trail going ahead and winding uphill. You go close to the north-eastern boundary of the park, where you can see more private residences to your right.

Cross paved Jockey Hollow Road (9) past the metal gates on both sides. The trail, after a gentle downhill, will soon become a moderate climb and then a fairly steep one—but the ascent is short. This section is the only one on which most novice skiers may have to walk.

Another of the many junctions is at the middle of the rise (8), where this hike makes a left turn off the white-marked route. At first the path is level, then it undulates for some four minutes until reaching a junction (42) with a yellow trail. Make a right turn over the hill, toward the soldiers' huts. You can see some NPS informational signs off the trail. Go over and read them, of course, but return to the trail. You are headed for the soldiers' huts, a major tourist attraction, and there are signs to direct you. The main path comes out behind the soldiers' huts (44).

The NPS has reconstructed five huts as typical examples of those built by Continental troops. The one you come to first was for officers; the ones with 12 beds were for the troops. Some 200 huts lined this hillside during the winter of 1779–80, while perhaps as many as a thousand stood in all of Jockey Hollow. Washington ordered all of them to be constructed alike, in neat lines, with officers' huts in the rear. The majority were finished by Christmas, and those for the officers in January and February.

Proceed down and across the open field to the visitors parking area, where there are some informative signs explaining the harsh winter spent here.

With your back to the huts, make a left through a grass field with some mature cedar trees. Passing by a boulder with a plaque commemorating the war dead buried here, you'll come to a trail post (number 39) at the edge of the woods with a yellow blaze. The Soldiers Hut Trail, marked in yellow, will take you back to Wick House generally paralleling Jockey Hollow Road. The trail passes through some brush, tall clinging grape vines, and blackberry bushes. The trail is level and easy to follow.

After about 10 minutes, observe a narrower path parallel to you on the left. Look down. The stone construction with the slate top is a springhouse. The trail described here circles above it and comes to a sign for Wick House (50). Continue ahead, bearing right and gently upward, still following yellow blazes and now on a gravel path. Here again are some especially tall trees and a lush forest floor—alas, now mostly barberry. Perhaps you'll be lucky enough, as were we, to have a deer pause calmly in front of you. The trail soon ends on the paved road just below the Wick House barn (49). Head toward the barn and the Wick House just beyond. It will be easy to guide yourself back to the visitor center and the parking area.

The amount of time spent on this hike depends, of course, on the time you spend at some of the many historic areas. You could even combine the hike with a visit to Washington's Headquarters and Fort Nonsense in Morristown, also part of the NPS Historical Park. Do you have time left for another visit to the ranger? You've covered a lot of turf and are sure to have some questions.

HNZ

27

Scherman–Hoffman Wildlife Sanctuary

Total distance: 3 miles

Hiking time: 1.75 hours

Vertical rise: 416 feet

Rating: Easy, but with some route-finding

Maps: USGS Mendham/Bernardsville; Scherman–Hoffman Wildlife Sanctuary park map

The sanctuary is named for Mr. and Mrs. Harry Scherman, who donated the first 125 acres of land to the New Jersey Audubon Society in 1965, and for Mr. Hoffman's estate and caretaker's houses, which were added to the sanctuary upon his death in 1981. The sanctuary covers almost 300 acres of open space, and supports more than 60 species of nesting birds.

This hike has much historical interest, and it travels through splendid woods and alongside the pristine Passaic River. The route is mostly on the Patriots' Path (PP), which at the beginning of the hike uses other named trails, such as the NJ Brigade Trail. Later, when the PP continues into Jockey Hollow on a bridge over the Passaic River, the hike transfers to a herd path by the water's edge, and continues on the yellow-blazed River Trail, and the green-blazed Field Loop, to finish on part of the red-blazed Dogwood Trail. No dogs are permitted in this sanctuary.

The PP logo is a tree with a path superimposed at the base, and the markers are white circular metal disks. The logo design in the Scherman–Hoffman Wildlife Sanctuary is mostly dark blue, with some other colors such as brown and red mixed in. The PP is gradually being developed by the Morris County Park Commission as a multi-use trail traversing open spaces in several Morris County townships, and at present is 20 contiguous miles on various surfaces.

The hike begins in the vicinity of the New Jersey Audubon Society facility in Bernardsville (11 Hardscrabble Road, PO Box 693,

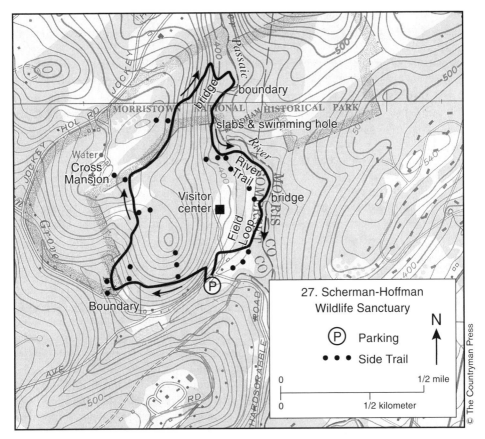

Bernardsville, NJ 07924; 908-766-5787). The Morristown National Historical Park at Jockey Hollow and the Cross Estate property are adjacent. The Hoffman Building, which houses the visitor center, should not be missed. It includes a well-stocked book and gift store, and an observation window overlooking a bird-feeding area. Stop here to obtain the park map, and the explanatory leaflet for the nature trail at the end of your journey. The Hoffman Building is usually closed on Monday, although the parking lot is open dawn to dusk.

HOW TO GET THERE

From the north, take exit 30B off I-287 and bear right at the end of the ramp onto North Maple Avenue. At the traffic light by the Old Mill Inn, go straight across CR 202 onto Childs Road; after a short distance, bear right at the fork onto Hardscrabble Road. The route is well posted with signs reading NJ AUDUBON. The Hoffman Building driveway is on the right, approximately another mile farther on.

From the south use Exit 30A from I-287. Bear right over the overpass and proceed to the light at the intersection of US 202. Turn left onto Childs Road and follow the above directions from there.

THE TRAIL

To begin the hike, leave the Hoffman Building and drive back down the sanctuary road. Turn right onto Hardscrabble Road at the end of the sanctuary driveway and almost immediately turn right again into the Scherman parking lot. Walk to the bulletin board. Just behind it the footway splits, and the Dogwood Trail is signed for both directions. The path ahead is the one on which you will return at the end of the hike, so for now turn left and walk uphill. A tree to the left carries PP markers and the red blazes of the Dogwood Trail.

The trail climbs steeply above the parking lot and in less than 0.25 mile a signboard indicates that the Dogwood Trail leaves uphill to the right. Continue straight ahead, confirming by the markers that you are still following the route of the PP. The trail's upward trend continues for about eight minutes before it starts downhill. Ten minutes from the start of the hike brings you to a national park boundary sign on a tree to the left. The PP markers are a little more sparse here, but old blue blazes that have been painted out can help in route finding. The invasive, nonnative species of barberry have a real hold on these woods. Seeds of these plants are spread by birds and animals, and the bushes are difficult to eradicate. A 13-acre enclosure has been constructed, inside which different ways of removing these unwanted plants are being evaluated, after which the best methods will be applied to the remaining 276 acres. Uprooting barberry only appears to create fresh, loose soil, which is attractive to other invasive nonnative species such as garlic mustard. There is some evidence that a controlled burn works well in fields.

A signpost is visible as the trail moves steeply downhill to a junction with the New Jersey Brigade Trail, and signpost #63, with a you-are-here map. Bear left downhill and walk straight on past the two interpretive signs and turn right at a junction where

signpost #64 offers another you-are-here map. (Turning left here accesses a gate to Hardscrabble Road.) The New Jersey Brigade section of Washington's army camped here during the winter of 1779–80, suffering greatly from cold, short rations, scant clothing, and late pay, because of roads blocked by winter conditions. It is believed this site was chosen for the iron ore and forge in the vicinity.

The trail, still marked with the PP logo, climbs again, paralleling the route of a small stream on the left. A short distance on there's an interesting six-trunked tree to the left of the trail, suggesting that this giant had once been logged. The white-blazed Connecting Trail, which leads back to the Dogwood Trail and the visitor center, enters from the right about a mile into the hike. In another 10 minutes, pass by a brown national park sign and bear right, ignoring the wide trail to the left, until signpost #62 is reached.

Turn left and walk the short distance to the Cross Estate Gardens. These peaceful formal gardens are recommended for your lunch break. The original house was built in 1905, but it wasn't until its purchase in 1929 by W. Redmond Cross that the gardens were developed by his wife. The property was added to the Morristown National Historical Park in 1975, but lack of funding prevented adequate maintenance of the gardens. Since 1977 a team of volunteers has been restoring the gardens to their original beauty.

Retrace your footsteps to the signpost after your exploration of the gardens, and continue to follow the PP markers down a wide and easy footway beneath tulip poplar trees. The trail to another parking lot enters the main route of the PP from the left, and the footway then begins to descend more steeply, following a rock wall on the right for

Tower at Scherman–Hoffman Wildlife Sanctuary

a short distance. Pass by signpost #60, bear left, and continue downhill, finally descending some wooden steps, until a small wooden bridge over the Passaic River comes into view. The bridge is another great place to take a break and to enjoy the tumbling water.

Here the Passaic River is an uncontaminated brook funneled between two hills, tumbling over rocks toward the Great Swamp and to Paterson and Newark beyond. Those familiar with the Passaic River farther downstream, where it is polluted and runs through industrial areas, will find this aspect difficult to believe. You will need to do some route-finding now for a short distance, but the navigational skills required are minimal. Do not cross the bridge, but turn right, following the faint herd path paralleling the river downstream, and passing inviting paddling pools, some tributaries, a cement boundary marker, and some slightly steeper riverbanks. Within about five minutes the river bends and invites you to stay and relax at some slabs and a good swimming hole.

At the slabs the herd path moves a short distance away from the river and climbs slightly. The path follows the water's direction for approximately another 10 minutes, and in this section there is a national park boundary sign, and a large downed tree that has been scooped out on top to aid the traveler over its bulk. Fifteen minutes on this unblazed footway brings you to another signpost.

Here is the junction with the Dogwood Trail going in both directions, and the three yellow blazes of the River Trail. Walk slightly downhill for a short distance on the River Trail until another wooden bridge is reached over a watercourse. Immediately after this bridge crossing is a T-junction with the Field Loop. Turn left, on a wide and grassy swath, which is obviously mown and has planking over the periodic wet patches. Occasionally there will be numbered posts relating to the nature trail.

Watch carefully for a fork in the Field Loop where the correct route turns sharply right, indicated by two green blazes on a slim tree. These blazes are not easy to spot, but the route ahead through a field is the wrong one, and if you see Hardscrabble Road and the New Jersey Audubon Society office on the right, turn back to seek the proper track.

Another signpost is reached very quickly, indicating that the Dogwood Trail goes right and also straight ahead. Walk forward and use the shale road until it crosses the entry road to the sanctuary and the trail reenters the woods. A sign confirms that this trail—the Dogwood—leads back to the parking lot, and within five minutes your car will come into sight.

SJG

Piedmont

28

Palisades

Total distance: 5.75 miles

Hiking time: 3 hours

Vertical rise: 1,100 feet

Rating: Easy

Maps: USGS Central Park (NY/NJ); NYNJTC Hudson Palisades Trails #108 & #109; Palisades Interstate Park Commission map; NYNJ WB #14

The Palisades Interstate Park Commission was created in 1900, mainly to curb the opening of quarries supplying traprock for the concrete used in building roads and skyscrapers. Most of the 2,472-acre Palisades State Park is in New Jersey. The average width of the parkland between the Hudson River and the clifftop is less than 0.2 mile. Apart from the talus at their bases, the cliffs are well wooded with a variety of trees and shrubs, some of them remaining from former estate gardens. The highest clear cliff is 520 vertical feet.

Numerous old woods trails complement the two main trails that run the length of the Palisades. This hike uses the Closter Dock Trail (orange) to descend to the Shore Path (white), ascends on the Forest View Trail (blue and white), and returns using a section of the Long Path, (parakeet aqua).

Enjoyment of the Shore Path is enhanced by the sound of lapping water, and on both the upper and lower levels there are many superb views of the river and its boaters. A visit to a historical house is also possible, but beware of the ubiquitous poison ivy.

HOW TO GET THERE

The hike begins at the administration building of the Palisades Interstate Park Commission (Alpine, NJ 07620; 201-768-1360). Access is east of Exit 2 off the Palisades Parkway, approximately 7 miles north of the George Washington Bridge. On weekends you may park in the large lot to the north of the building, but during the week parking may be limited, so check inside with the police department. Pick up the excellent park map, which has recently been updated, or find it online at www.njpalisades.org.

THE TRAIL

At the wooden sign near the road with NEW JERSEY HEADQUARTERS PALISADES PARK COMMISSION and the blue Long Path marker on it, walk south. After a very short road walk—Long Path markers are painted in the gutter—turn left, downhill and away from the road, on a wide path signed PATH TO THE RIVER and NO BIKES. The blue/green blazes of the Long Path and an orange blaze for the Closter Dock Trail are also visible on the signboard. There are frequent water bars; a seasonal stream runs on the left. Where the Long Path turns right to go through the stone tunnel, follow the orange blazes steadily downhill in a gentle zigzag. The descent is just under 500 feet in 0.6 mile. Passing a stream bridged with concrete on the right, the trail bends left and reaches a T-junction and the first view of the Hudson River. This junction is with the Shore Path, marked by a white blaze, and ends the Closter Dock Trail as indicated by three orange blazes.

If time permits, you might want to take the opportunity, before continuing on the hike, to visit The Kearney House, just 0.1 mile down the trail to the right from this junction. Part of the house probably dates to the 1760s, and is sometimes called the Cornwallis Headquarters. An informative brochure is available from the park headquarters, where you should find out before you go whether the house is open. Exploring the house is usually possible from May through October between noon and 5 pm.

Turn left (north) when you reach the Shore Path, and pass over a stream with one of many cascades you will notice on your walk. The main cascade is protected by

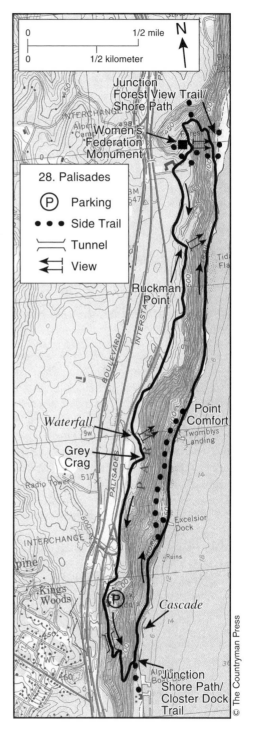

View from the Palisades

STELLA GREEN

a circular stone wall. There are several exploratory side trips in this area. The first takes you up two flights of steps to the left of the trail that lead through a gate in a wire fence to two small stone buildings. Side trips to the riverbank include one on the right that leads to a small rocky beach with views of the supporting pillars of George Washington Bridge and of Yonkers, immediately across the river. The Shore Path changes from time to time from being smooth and hiker-friendly to rocky and hiker-tricky, but there are many opportunities along the way to rest, such as at the Excelsior Dock, Twombly Landing, or Port Comfort.

After approximately 0.5 mile, look for a signpost on a rock and continue ahead on the Shore Path, now protected against erosion by large boulders on the left. The trail here is routed closer to the water's edge and is very attractive. Turning left uphill at this junction leads to a picnic area on the Upper Trail.

During the next stretch of the trail there are many signs of human activity. Several streams run under cemented rock covers, while paths and steps to the left indicate the way to sites where buildings once existed. Soon you'll see many attractive lunch sites, each with a natural rock table and chairs. This area features many cascades tumbling over man-made rock walls and is known as Twombly's Landing, after the man who donated this section to the park. Twombly's Landing is believed to have been a Native American campsite because of the layers of oyster shells found here. Because of the prevalence of *Giardia lamblia* and other pollutants, we do not recommend that you use water from the two places labeled DRINKING WATER. One cookout fireplace is provided at Twombly's.

Moving slightly uphill, the path is again edged on the left by rocks. Soon comes the first view of the cliffs. These outcrops are the two bastions of Ruckman Point, and it is interesting to know that in a little while you will be looking down from them to the Shore Path. Watch the cliffs to the north at this point to get a good view of Indian Head; at river level, observe the Tappan Zee Bridge in the distance.

After just over 2 miles on, the Shore Path turns left uphill on the blue/white-blazed Forest View Trail, indicated by three blazes on both a tree and a large rock to the left side of the trailhead. Originally maintained by Boy Scouts, the trail is now the responsibility of the New Jersey section of the Palisades Interstate Park Commission. Do not take the Shore Path, which continues ahead to the Giant Stairs, an intricate rock scramble. After climbing a few minutes, squeeze past a large rock on the left faintly marked STATELINE LOOKOUT.

The cemented rock steps that form the trail climb in a switchback, marked blue on white, to a trail junction. A stream crossing is ahead, and to the right beyond the stream is a Long Path turn signal on a tree. Ignore this turn and the signposted routes to the State Line and River Trails and bear left on the trail to US 9W, climbing uphill and south on three short flights of steps for another 100 feet of puffing. Long Path parakeet aqua blazes are to be followed for the rest of the hike, and the Scout Trail's blue-and-white blazes co-mingle here and lead to a wonderful vista and the Women's Federation Monument, a great place to take a break. This "castle" was built by the New Jersey Federation of Women's Clubs in 1929 to commemorate their efforts in the late 19th century to preserve the Palisades from quarrying.

A short distance from the monument, the Long Path crosses a wide gravel road and then turns left. (Ignore the right turn of the blue-on-white Scout Trail, which crosses a stone bridge over the Palisades Interstate Parkway to a small parking area on the side of US 9W.) Continue to follow the Long Path, disregarding the woods road to the left, until a broken wall at the cliff edge is reached at Ruckman Point. On the cliff edge there is a carving on the rock face dated June 1981; the Shore Path is visible below.

The trail goes slightly downhill to a boggy area with a stream. The damper, rockier section continues until you cross a larger stream on a substantial wooden bridge, then a boardwalk over a culvert. Just beyond, about 1.5 miles from the Women's Federation Monument, look for a short trail on the left leading toward the cliff edge with a super overlook of a seasonal waterfall pouring through a cleft, and a view of the Hudson. Take care, as there is no protective fencing. In the spring, drifts of snowdrops bloom here.

Only a short distance farther down the main trail, watch for a small footpath to the left, leading over a bridge to a secluded lookout called Grey Crag. A section of the main precipice has separated from the cliff and gives a tremendous feeling of isolation. The bridge has no handrail so take care, and again, watch for poison ivy.

Within 30 minutes, tall maples mark the next section of the trail, which runs very close to the Parkway until it finally emerges onto the administration building parking lot where you left your car.

SJG

29

South Mountain Reservation

Total distance: 8.25 miles (Short hike is approximately 5 miles.)

Hiking time: 6 hours (Short hike is approximately 4 hours.)

Vertical rise: 750 feet

Rating: Moderate

Maps: USGS Caldwell/Roselle; Essex County Park Commission South Mountain Reservation map

South Mountain Reservation has a lot to offer in the midst of such a built-up area. The 2,048-acre tract contains a substantial river, many streams and cascades, a 25-foot waterfall, and 19 miles of trails through gentle woodland. At certain junctions, the bustle of the world is encountered, but the trails are mostly free from traffic noise. The first and second of the three Watchung ridges of New Jersey form the eastern and western boundaries of the reservation. The name "Watchung" is a legacy from the Lenape Native Americans, to whom the ridges were the "high hills." These ridges were heavily lumbered, not only during the Revolution, but also in the late 19th century for firewood and paper making. Some very large trees remain in the reservation, some of them twisted into deformed shapes.

The Lenape Trail Committee, funded by the Sierra Club, proposed a multi-use trail system for Essex County, and this figure-of-eight hike in South Mountain Reservation uses the Lenape Trail, blazed in yellow, the Turtle Back Trail, marked in orange, and the white-blazed Rahway Trail. The name Lenape was chosen for the trail in honor of the state's original inhabitants and preeminent foot travelers; the Turtle Back Trail refers to the rocks in the area showing erosion markings similar to those on a turtle's back; and the Rahway Trail takes its name from the river that it parallels. Turtle back rocks were formed when the traprock fractured into small hexagonal blocks. The cracks filled with minerals, and, when erosion wore away the traprock faster than the minerals, the result

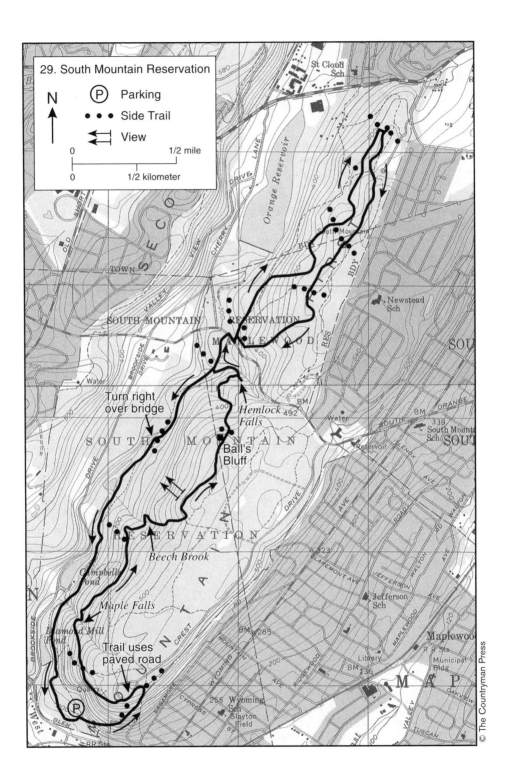

29. South Mountain Reservation

N

ⓟ Parking

••• Side Trail

⇇ View

0   1/2 mile
0   1/2 kilometer

Turn right
over bridge

Hemlock
Falls

Ball's
Bluff

Beech Brook

Maple Falls

Trail uses
paved road

ⓟ

was a patterned rock similar to the markings on the back of a turtle. There are several examples of this type of rock throughout South Mountain Reservation, and one on the northeastern side of the park is actually called Turtleback Rock. It is believed that the word "traprock" developed from a Dutch word, "trappen," meaning steps, indicating that the square hunks of rock were useful for step construction. The Essex Park Commission was established in 1895 and, drawing on Frederick Law Olmsted's ideas and in consultation with his firm, created 23 parks and three reservations within the county. Olmsted was also the creator of New York City's Central Park. Although the concept of South Mountain Reservation was Olmsted's, the smaller features such as bridges, trails, and steps were, in fact, built by the Civilian Conservation Corps in 1934.

There is no park office at which to obtain a map of the South Mountain Reservation. Maps will be mailed on request by calling the Essex County Environmental Center at 973-268-3500, Ext. 238 or may be picked up at the maintenance center off South Orange Avenue. This facility can be found by driving southeast on South Orange Avenue.

Dogs must be leashed in the reservation. Bicycles are not permitted, although there are signs of illegal use.

The distance covered in this hike is nearly 9 miles, but there are no difficult climbs, so the hike is useful for developing a good walking pace and to increase hiking stamina. The woods and rhododendron groves make the trail an excellent spring hike, although the area near the Rahway River is sometimes wet. The groves of rhododendron, wild azalea, and mountain laurel were deliberately planted, together with white pine and hemlock, when the land was acquired by the Essex County Park Commission at the beginning of the 20th century

in an effort to eradicate the previous damage done by logging and paper mills. The cost of the rhododendrons planted in 1910 was 43 cents each—a little different from the price of a rhododendron today. Watch for the tame herds of deer as you walk. In addition to this hike, Mayapple Hill at the northern end of the park is another area of South Mountain Reservation that warrants exploration, as well as Turtleback Rock, also in the northeastern part of the park.

HOW TO GET THERE

Driving from the east, take I-78 a short distance to Exit 50B (Maplewood, Millburn) and continue to drive north on Vaux Hall Road for 0.7 mile. Turn left onto Millburn Avenue, and in 0.5 mile, bear right to follow the one-way street system to Essex Street. Pass the Millburn railroad station, and turn right onto Lackawanna Place. Turn right at the next intersection (Glen Avenue) and make an immediate left turn into the Locust Grove parking area. Three yellow blazes indicating the beginning of the Lenape Trail are visible at the Glen Avenue T-junction.

Approaching from the west, you will need to make a U-turn at Exit 54.

Public transportation can be used easily to reach South Mountain Reservation, because Millburn Station is opposite the trailhead at Locust Grove parking lot. From the western end of the platform at the Millburn station, walk north along Lackawanna Place and cross Glen Avenue to enter the park at the Locust Grove parking area.

THE TRAIL

Walk away from Glen Road toward the back of the Locust Grove parking lot and then bear right uphill on a wide, rocky path following the yellow blazes of the Lenape Trail, which passes through a picnic area where there is a year-round spring on the left protected by a small, brick housing. Pass the rain shelter and picnic tables and begin climbing First Watchung Mountain on a narrow, rocky trail. Within a few minutes, ignore the wide road to the left and the light green-marked trail also on your left and continue on the yellow-marked trail as it turns right and moves across the side of the hill. During the climb, you will pass below and circle around a large concrete structure, which is part of the old waterworks system used to supply East Orange with water from the valley. At the top of the rise, the trail turns left and parallels the paved Crest Trail Road on the right, until it eventually emerges onto that road. At this point, the first large rhododendrons are to be seen. Turn left onto the paved road, which is now closed to motorized traffic, and walk by the side of the stone wall toward Washington Rock, located opposite a disused parking lot on the right-hand side.

The climb will have taken approximately 10 minutes from the parking lot, and a pause should be made to admire the view to the left. Looking down and over the old water-holding area, the panorama includes New York City, Newark Airport, 1-280, and, looking straight ahead, 1-78 in the valley of the Watchung Reservation, with the Bell Telephone tower on the ridge to the right.

The plaque on Washington Rock, dedicated in 1992, describes the events of 1780, which George Washington watched from this point. It describes British efforts to destroy the American supply base at Morristown, the burning of Connecticut Farms, now called Union, and other military events. The plaque records that, after the British efforts failed, they were forced to retire and "quit New Jersey soil for ever." History tells us that, at the time of the Revolution, all the suitable trees in New Jersey had been cut for shipbuilding and housing, giving good

visibility to observe the movements of the British in the valley. A sentry was posted at Washington's Rock, and as soon as he became aware of troop movements in the valley below, a bonfire was lit to alert the soldiers at Jockey Hollow. An additional stone marker commemorates Paul R. Jackson, a friend of the park.

Look for the yellow marker on the tree to the left, just at the end of the wall. Leave the commemorative rocks and walk downhill to an area of man-made steps and a decorative building-block viewpoint. There was once a roof over this shelter, but it was not replaced when the original building fell into disrepair.

Continuing downhill, the trail passes a rocky lookout on the left, a small stream and, also on the left, a large rock with a chain-link fence behind it. The rock is an example of traprock, and the fencing protects the walker from a traprock quarry. The first and second Watchung ridges are intrusions (or extrusions) of lava similar to those of the Palisades. As these layers rose from west to east and were glaciated, the top layer of the Watchungs cooled more quickly than the lower layers that formed the Palisades. Because the layers in South Mountain Reservation cooled more quickly, the hexagonal columns that formed are considerably smaller than those on the Palisades.

Proceed downhill on a wider path and cross a bridle path called Sunset Trail. Our route travels along the side of the hill in a slightly downhill direction until Maple Falls Cascade is seen on the left-hand side, about a mile into the hike. The stream here plunges downstream through a 25-foot sluiceway of exposed basalt, and is a good place for a short break. Cross the stream and climb away from the brook until the trail levels out and crosses several other smaller streams and Pringry Road. The yellow-

Rahway River, South Mountain Reservation

marked trail moves ahead on similar terrain, passing Lilliput Knob. This unusual rock is called a turtleback rock for obvious reasons.

Beech Brook Cascades, where two streams converge, is reached approximately 2 miles into the hike just before the trail crosses over Bear Lane, and reaches Mines Point. This site was named for the exploratory pits dug by copper prospectors around 1800. Ignore the two trails entering from the right, and proceed straight ahead to Ball's Bluff. The columns here were used to support a roof and are now all that remains of the shelter erected by the Civilian Conservation Corps in 1934.

Descend the short grade, leaving Ball's Bluff on the left, bear left, cross Ball's Bluff Trail, and walk downhill by the side of another small stream. Follow the yellow blazes to the right at the next wide woods road and, within two or three minutes at the next T-junction, turn left and walk steeply downhill through large rhododendrons and hemlocks to Hemlock Falls. You are now about 3 miles into the hike, and the falls are a wonderful place to take a more lengthy break. Picnic tables are provided, and for the energetic, stone steps lead to the top of the falls.

Cross the stone bridge, leaving the falls on the right, and at the end of the bridge turn left. At first, the trail is on a wide path, but soon after passing another pretty falls on the right and another substantial stone bridge on the left, which now leads nowhere, the foot-way becomes narrower and reaches a three-way intersection with a signpost. (If you wish to shorten your hike to approximately 5 miles, turn left on the bridle path and pick up the description in parentheses below).

The River Trail, a bridle trail to the left, will be the route for your return journey, and the white-marked Rahway Trail is straight ahead. Turn right, following the yellow blazes of the Lenape Trail uphill on a wide woods road to the top of the incline. Turn left at an enormous deformed oak tree just before a metal gate and a small parking lot on South Orange Avenue.

After a couple of minutes the trail crosses over South Orange Avenue on a bridge, and the hike leaves the Lenape Trail, which turns left into the woods. The hike now follows the red blazes of the Turtle Back Trail ahead on a wide path, soon to make first a left turn, and then a sharp right uphill into the woods on a narrower, more traditional trail, where a signpost clearly indicates the Turtle Back Trail. The Orange Reservoir can be glimpsed here, provided the leaves are gone from the trees. Continue to follow the red blazes as the trail turns left, crosses the Ravine Trail, and several small streams, the first one having a small plank bridge to ease your way. You encounter another crossing of the Ravine Trail before the Interpretive Trail marked with white/orange blazes is reached. Turn right, still following the orange blazes of the Turtle Back Trail. The new blazes co-mingle for a while with the solo orange blazes before they leave quite soon to the left. At this junction there is a large downed tree, with about a 6-foot-high root structure where you need to bear right. The hike is now about halfway through, and you are headed back toward your car.

The Turtle Back Trail crosses the Ravine Trail a couple of times, as well as the Hillspur Trail, but the route is clearly marked except at one point where it is easy to make a mistake and continue straight ahead on what may be an illegally marked white trail. The turn to the right is well blazed and descends slightly.

Road noise will be heard as you approach South Orange Avenue and turn right on a wide woods road. Follow the yellow-marked Lenape Trail as it turns left within a few minutes and again crosses the bridge over South Orange Avenue. Make a right turn at the familiar distorted old tree on your left and walk down to the signpost encountered recently. (If you have shortened the hike, then pick up the description at this point.)

Head south, straight ahead on the bridle path, the River Trail, and in about 0.5 mile, turn right toward a bridge over the Rahway River. Just before the bridge look for white blazes on a tree to the left, and follow the Rahway Trail to its end. The trail makes a few detours up to the River Trail to utilize the bridges over streams, crosses another woods road, and enters a prolific rhododendron grove just as Campbell's Pond comes into view.

Shortly thereafter, the trail passes Diamond Hill Pond, and throughout its remaining length is sandwiched between the bridle path on its left and the beautiful Rahway River on its right. Throughout this whole valley there is evidence of pumping stations now using electricity for fuel. The trail passes close to the buildings and chimney of the old, steam-driven pumping station. The large boilers housed in this building formerly provided steam for pumping water to a reservoir on the hills, using water from Campbell's Pond. Campbell's Pond is very shallow, probably not more than a foot in depth. Traffic noise from Brookside Drive is encountered along this section of the trail.

The white-marked trail continues in a southerly direction, using the bridges on the River Trail when necessary. It is interesting to look at the dams across the Rahway River. Some are derelict, with water seeping through the structures, and one in particular is sealed with a gate from the far side but unprotected from the trail side. The trail navigates the side of a small hill, just before the library and the parking lot for Millburn Station become visible to the right, where you arrive at the Locust Grove parking area and your car.

SJG

30

Watchung Reservation

Total distance: 6 miles

Hiking time: 4 hours

Vertical rise: 500 feet

Rating: Moderate

Maps: USGS Chatham/Roselle; Union County Department of Parks and Recreation park map

Watchung Reservation is a 2,000-acre patch of wooded land straddling the first and second Watchung Ridges in central New Jersey. The name Watchung stems from the Lenape word for high hills, *Wachunk.* Along with South Mountain Reservation and Eagle Rock Reservation to the north, Watchung Reservation has preserved what was for many years a long wall of mountain wilderness overlooking the flat plains that lead toward New York City and the Atlantic Ocean. General George Washington used the long Watchung Ridge as a natural fortification against the British during the Revolutionary War. He planted a number of lookouts along the ridge and kept his troops safely to the west in Loantaka and Jockey Hollow. At the end of the previous Ice Age, the Watchung Ridge formed the eastern rim of the basin that contained glacial Lake Passaic, a 30-by-10-mile lake of which the Great Swamp is but a remnant.

Although it sits in the middle of suburbia, Watchung Reservation is large enough for a good workout and also contains a number of interesting features, most of which you will see on this hike. Not that long ago, the construction of I-78 on the boundary of the reservation made access easier for many hikers not from the immediate area. More recently Watchung has been the scene of user conflicts. Mountain bike users loved it so much that they seriously damaged the trails. Today bikes are not permitted on trails in the reservation.

Watchung Reservation is laced with wide lanes and horse trails. Several shorter

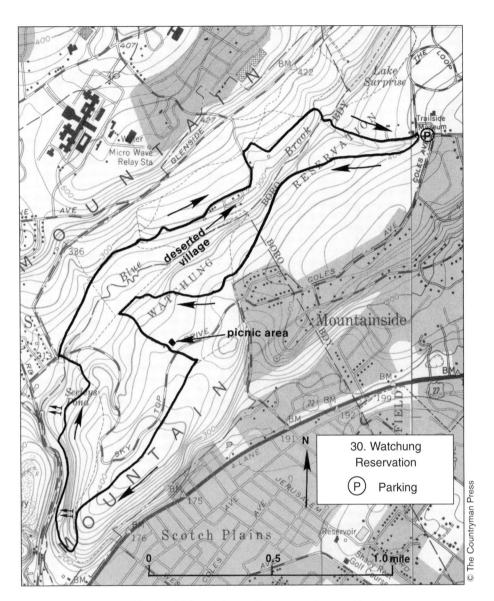

© The Countryman Press

30. Watchung
Reservation

Ⓟ Parking

N

0   0.5   1.0 mile

marked trails are found in the vicinity of the Trailside Museum. The longest trail is the white-blazed Sierra Trail, formerly marked with Xs, now with white squares. It is 10 miles long, has many ups and downs, and passes near just about every interesting feature the reservation has to offer. It is not a simple path, but one that links many trails in the reservation, making it necessary to watch for double blazes that signal turns. You will use a large portion of this trail for your hike.

HOW TO GET THERE

From I-78 eastbound (Exit 44), turn left at the traffic light onto Glenside Avenue, and look for signs for the Trailside Nature and Science Center. After 1.2 miles on Glenside Avenue, turn right into the reservation (County Road 645), on Tracy Drive, passing Lake Surprise and some picnic areas. At a circle, make a right turn onto Summit Road, then bear right onto New Providence Road. Directly ahead is parking and the Trailside Nature and Science Center. An excellent map of the reservation, which shows all trails and features, is available at the museum and also from a box near the parking area.

THE TRAIL

The trailhead, marked NATURE TRAILS, is located on the left side of the paved road that passes the museum. Begin your hike on the Sierra Trail, marked by white squares painted on trees. In addition, a green trail begins here and runs concurrently with the Sierra for a short distance. As you cross the brook on a bridge, note the exposure of bedrock in the streambed. These rocks are basalt, or traprock, which has been quarried extensively throughout the Watchung Mountains.

Once over the brook, bear right following the white markers. Pay close attention to the markers in this section. There are numerous paths, and it is easy to lose the correct one. The trail heads gradually downhill after this turn and then bears to the left through an area that is sometimes wet. Watch closely for white markers (ignore the orange markers) as the trail makes a subtle jog to the right.

The Sierra Trail takes you along the rim of a small glen, quite beautiful in any season. On the left, the brook is eroding the red shales that overlay the basalt. You will soon encounter exposed basaltic bedrock, and—as the glen widens—hemlocks. In this section, a blue-marked trail co-mingles with the white trail for a while.

After descending through the hemlocks in this beautiful section of the reservation, cross the brook, still following white markers, and begin to climb. Below, Blue Brook makes an oxbow bend as it snakes through the drainage between ridges. As you climb, watch the markers carefully. There is a steep climb at one point, which then levels off in a pleasant mixture of deciduous trees and hemlocks. Farther along, the Sierra Trail comes to another smaller glen with some fairly large boulders and even a grassy area. This spot is good for a break and perhaps some exploration. Deer are plentiful in this reservation—perhaps you've spotted one already.

Still following white markers, cross the brook and climb the opposite bank. After this small climb, the trail levels off and, as it swings to the right, passes a residential area. Next, cross a gravel road, head back into the woods, and begin another long, gradual loss of elevation. There are no hemlocks here, and the ground is higher and drier. Notice on the descent that where the trail has been deeply eroded there are some exposures of shale and sandstone, hardened mud, and silt deposited during the Triassic period. Later, volcanic magma intruded into these shales, forming the erosion-resistant, basaltic Watchung Mountains. At the bottom of the descent, the trail comes to an unimproved road and turns left. Tall cedars line the west side of this road, which was once a driveway. Within a few hundred feet, the trail turns left and cuts back into the woods in a pine plantation, heading uphill once more.

Look carefully for the markers here—the trail jogs slightly to the right and then heads straight through a row of tall pines. This is a peaceful environment with the exception of the ubiquitous motor traffic rumble. Little patches of sunlight decorate the uniform brown carpet of pine needles. These red pines were planted in the 1930s as part of a Civilian Conservation Corps project, and though some are shorter than others, all are the same age. If you are lucky, you might spot one of the owls that nest here. (*Note:* at the time of this writing some trail markers were missing in this section.) Too soon the trail emerges from the pines, crosses a trail junction, swings to the left, and, after crossing a small bridge, enters a picnic area with a shelter. The trail leads through this cleared area on a gravel service road, crosses Sky Top Drive, and reenters the woods on a lane.

At the first intersection, bear right and begin a long, nearly level walk on a lane that parallels Sky Top Drive. Along with the white markers of the Sierra Trail are some cross-country ski markers of green and white. You will cross several intersections before you arrive at a section that attains an elevation of over 400 feet above sea level, about as high as the first Watchung Mountain ridge gets. Bushwhack to the left to obtain a glimpse of the nearby urban world through the trees. From here the trail begins to head downhill, and, after another 10 minutes of walking, you will come to a small overlook to the south and west. Here you can see—and often hear—the effects of quarrying in the Watchung Hills during the week when the quarries are operating. Traprock, the popular term for basalt gravel, has been used for years to pave New Jersey's roads and highways.

At the overlook, the trail swings to the left and heads down the mountain. Now the sounds of civilization are more apparent. The trail makes a sharp right at the bottom, just before a row of condos, and may not be marked very well. This section of trail is washed out in places and tends to be clogged with leaves and branches washed down by the rains. (It is possible that this section of trail may be relocated in the future.) Soon you will see Green Brook on the left and, beyond that, New Providence Road. Green Brook is a stocked trout stream and attracts many anglers. As the trail heads north along the bank of the brook, it becomes rockier. The trail, the brook, and the road all pass together through a gap in the long wall of the Watchungs.

Above, you will see some outcroppings of basalt on your right. Look closely at the rock and observe the way it forms hexagonal columns much like the Palisades of the Hudson, only on a smaller scale. Next you will reach the remains of an old mill foundation. The mill that once stood at this site used the power of the brook to make paper; later it held a 10,000-gallon still operated by bootleggers, whose product is said to have been world renowned. The brook drops quite a few feet in a short distance here and once was diverted to turn a mill wheel. Look around to find where the water was channeled away from the brook and over to the mill. The trail swings to the right and climbs steeply uphill after leaving the ruins of the mill.

At the top of the climb, another rock outcrop offers more views to the south and west. I-78 is clearly visible. During the late 1970s and early 1980s, many conservation-minded people tried to prevent the construction of I-78, which planners had routed through the western and northern section of the reservation. It was a major regional issue that was finally settled by replacing the land used for the highway, which totaled about 70 acres, with land from a nearly adjacent rock quarry. With the deal came $3.6 million for the upkeep and development of the reservation. The highway was also built low in the ground and is flanked by walls that muffle the sound somewhat. In one place, a cut-and-cover structure—a 220-foot-wide bridge with soil and plants—allows animals to cross the highway safely. I am told that it didn't take the large local deer population long to find the way across.

From this overlook, the trail turns right and heads back toward the woods into a grove of old hemlocks. Now following a woods road, the trail bears to the left heading gradually downhill. Just before reaching Sky Top Drive again, the markers lead to a shortcut on the left, ending at the paved road near a bridge at Seeleys Pond. Cross the road, make a left, and walk toward the bridge.

Cross the bridge and immediately bear right to find the trail that heads back into the woods. This point is at the edge of the reservation, and suburbia is just across the street. At first on grass, the trail soon becomes a footpath in some fairly dense vegetation. In places it is crowded by wild roses; you will find violets and spring beauties where an occasional spring keeps the ground moist. Watch for poison ivy in this section, both as a vine on trees and as a bush.

After a few minutes you will come to a quiet spot where some large hemlocks dominate the land between two small brooks. The trail next crosses the second brook and makes a left on a badly eroded path. Almost immediately, at a small clearing, the trail swings sharply right and heads back into the woods, crossing several small streams that run only in the spring or after a rain. As the trail gradually gains elevation, it also becomes wider and more badly eroded.

Continue on this eroded path, heading gradually uphill. At the right turn just before the trail passes a hemlock grove on the right, you will find a partially exposed conglomerate boulder. This stone, which tech-nically is Shawangunk conglomerate, is not native to the area—it was dragged south by the glacier for a distance of more than 20 miles.

Suddenly you will see a large building facing you—you've entered Deserted Village, also known as Feltsville and Glenside Park. From 1845 to 1860, David Felt owned and operated a paper mill on Blue Brook. Feltsville was a factory town then, but when the mill closed, it became Glenside Park, a Victorian retreat with lawn tennis and pure water. Some say there is a salt brook and a magnesium spring in the vicinity, which may have been why the area was made a miniresort between 1882 and 1916. In 1991 a New Jersey Historic Trust grant was awarded for the preservation of Feltsville as a unique resource.

After passing the last two houses (one with a wooden tower attached to it), the trail bears right, turning off the road and onto a dirt road. It immediately turns again to the right and onto a footpath. In a few hundred yards is a small Revolutionary War cemetery where members of the Willcocks family, the descendants of the original settler Peter Willcox, are buried. William Willcox was a judge and advocate of the Revolutionary War, and he died in 1800. Joseph Badgley was a private in the First New Jersey Regiment and died in 1785. John Willcocks, Sr. died on November 22, 1776. He was in the Light Horse Company of the New Jersey militia.

At the gravesites the trail turns left. Continue along the footpath, following the white markers as the trail snakes through the woods at a nearly constant elevation. Soon the trail begins to descend, then meets a wide horse trail. Your trip on the Sierra Trail is over. Turn right here, head downhill, and cross the bridge over Blue Brook. At the junction, go right then left and follow a footpath marked with blue markers upstream, keeping the brook on your right. After a short distance, the blue markers change to orange. Continue uphill and keep the brook to your right. After a few more minutes you will reach a gate and a paved road. Bear right here and walk uphill. The museum and then the parking area will be on your left.

BCS

31

Washington Valley Park

Total distance: 4 miles

Hiking time: 2–3 hours

Vertical rise: 200 feet

Rating: Moderate, with rugged footing and many trail junctions.

Maps: USGS Bound Brook; Somerset County Park Commission Washington Valley Park Trail Map & Information

Long ago, George Washington defended the fledgling United States by positioning his troops between the first and second Watchung Mountains. The mountains served as a natural fortification and from the height he kept an eye on British movements. Prominent rock faces such as "Washington Rock" and "Chimney Rock" were important lookouts for the general, places from which intelligence on the British was gathered. A few of these strategic vistas remain. Washington Rock is located within a small county park near the town of Watchung.

Chimney Rock, another strategic vista, was for many years on private land that was used by the public. I can remember Chimney Rock as a youth in the 1950s, before New Jersey's latest massive population explosion. I went for picnics and walks there with my family, and years later I would scramble around the cliffs exploring the forest and brooks myself. But the area was never an official park. By the 1960s Chimney Rock had become the site of uncontrolled picnicking or partying on land owned by the nearby quarry, and it was placed off limits. But today, access is possible. Along with nearly 700 acres of surrounding forest and slope, Chimney Rock and its surrounding woods and ravines now comprise Somerset County's Washington Valley Park. This park, which is located in the midst of the densely populated suburbs of central New Jersey, offers a wide variety of trails for both hikers and mountain bikers. While this is no wilderness—residences can be seen from the trail and the motor traffic rumble is never

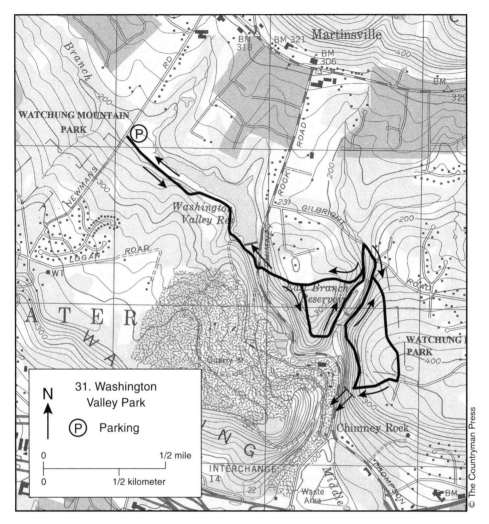

escaped–wildlife abounds and hikers will find the trails interesting and challenging.

The trail system in Washington Valley Park (www.somersetcountyparks.org) is, at the time of this writing, unmarked. The footing is rocky and sturdy hiking boots are recommended. For the most part, however, the trails are clearly visible and easy to follow, partly due to heavy mountain bike use, especially on weekends. Still, hikers are advised to pay close attention to the directions so as not to veer off onto any of the many other unmarked trails in the park. The hike described below leads past some of the more interesting features of the park, though it covers only a small portion of the total trail mileage. Those who wish to take much longer walks can follow the Middlebrook Trail for several miles northwest of the parking area on Newmans Lane, or explore many of the side trails that climb up the eastern slope of the ridge.

The geology of the park is simple. You will be walking on the first Watchung Mountain, a long basalt ridge that is part of an ancient rift valley (see Introduction). At a weak point in the ridge, a drainage developed and millions of years of erosion have carved out two gorges, each quite interesting. The larger one is that of the West Branch of Middle Brook, the route that Chimney Rock Road follows as it climbs from the Piedmont Plain to the valley between the first and second Watchung ranges. The route along the gorge is unfortunately not accessible to pedestrians, though you can see it from your car. The second gorge is hidden from the road and located just below Chimney Rock. This is the small gorge created by the East Branch of Middle Brook, and it has been dammed between some spectacular basalt formations.

HOW TO GET THERE

From US-22 north of Bound Brook, take the Thompson Avenue exit (County Route 525) and follow it north toward Martinsville. Thompson Avenue becomes Chimney Rock Road just past the Stavola quarry and in 2 miles ends at a set of traffic lights facing Washington Valley Road. Make a left here, pass through another set of traffic lights, and after 0.5 mile turn left onto Newmans Lane. In 0.5 mile the large parking area for the park will be found on your left. Maps of the park are available here.

THE TRAIL

Begin hiking on the unmarked trail that leads out of the far (north) end of the parking area. As you begin walking north, notice that you are in the valley between the first and second Watchung Mountains, a valley into which the hills drain, creating the West Branch of Middle Brook. This brook is to your left and is the water supply for the reservoir, which you will pass by shortly. The trail is not marked here, but is fairly easy to follow as it winds through the woods on a rocky surface. After a few turns you will

begin to see the south end of the reservoir and soon the trail passes through a stand of tall white pines. You'll pass near the shoreline of the reservoir, though not right up to its edge. Keep your eyes open for the few rocky points along the way that offer a better look at this peaceful body of water. Soon the trail leads right down to the water level, skirts a wet area, and then, passing through an opening in a wire fence, meets a gravel road. Turn left here and follow this lane past the dam and down to Chimney Rock Road.

Use caution as you cross Chimney Rock Road. Turn left after crossing, and walk along the side of the road (which is your bridge over Middle Brook) for 150 feet to the end of the guardrail. Here the trail continues and begins a steep climb up the hill using switchbacks on a solid footpath. Toward the height of land the trail widens and comes to a fork. Turn right here and follow the trail along the ridgetop through a mixed forest of oak, pines, and an occasional cedar. Soon you'll come to another junction—go straight ahead and downhill. At the next junction, keep to the left and follow the trail as it makes a hairpin turn and heads west and downhill. Stay on this main path; don't take the small path you'll pass on your right that heads steeply downhill. The trail soon arrives at a rock causeway made of huge slabs of basalt attached to each other with steel rods that extends across the small reservoir. It is sometimes possible to cross here, but this is not always the case and it is not recommended. Stay on the northwest side of the reservoir and continue hiking in a northerly direction following the edge of the reservoir, or at least parts of the reservoir that have become a wetland. You'll pass under a traprock talus slope and a short distance ahead the trail leaves the little valley and skirts up the slope on your left. After a short but brisk climb, the trail begins

BRUCE SCOFIELD

Washington Valley Park

to descend and approaches Gilbride Road. You'll come to a trail junction. Keep right and follow the heavily eroded path to the paved road. Turn right on Gilbride Road and follow it for about 100 yards over the brook and up to a trail on the right that leads back into the woods, now on the north side of the East Branch of Middle Brook.

Follow this path for only a very short distance and make a left at the first trail junction. You'll now be on a trail that follows a tributary of the East Branch of Middle Brook uphill, and you will be gaining elevation steadily. Ignore any side paths to your right. The trail soon makes a wide switchback and continues climbing through an open oak and maple forest with many large trees. As you crest the height of land (elevation about 400 feet), the trail descends and meets a gravel road. Turn right here, and walk past the parking area and through the gate. This is how most people visit Chimney Rock. A short walk down the wide lane leads to the historic rock and its bizarre vista. You should be 1 to 1 ½ hours into the hike at this point.

Vistas from mountaintops are inspiring because they expand your vision. You see more than you usually can see and, as your mind soaks in the view, you may find yourself waxing philosophical. The same thing should happen to you as you contemplate the vista at Chimney Rock. Directly in front of you is a gaping scar, the unfilled cavity of the traprock quarry. Is it ugly? Sure—but this is where our roads come from. You drove on these roads to hike here. Ask yourself how much of nature should humanity destroy in order to provide our bloated populations with the conveniences of the modern world? Look at Chimney Rock, painted white with red drippings. Why does a person want to paint a natural feature like this? Strangely, it's been white for as long as I can remember. Does humanity seek to cover nature, to deny it its own natural qualities and impose our species' visions over it? Are not golf courses, ski areas, and landscaped yards human-caused impositions on nature—although these examples are more aesthetically pleasing than the painted basalt chimney? If nothing else, the vista

from Chimney Rock should get you thinking about things larger than our own small lives. If it doesn't, I'd be concerned.

To the north of Chimney Rock, however, is a more natural view, a glimpse into the gentle folds of the Watchung range. To the south are the flat plains of suburbia. All around you other people may not be thinking about humanity's assault on nature—they may be holding binoculars to their eyes as they search the skies for raptors. It turns out that Chimney Rock is a major hawk watching site, and during the spring and fall migrations, many birders come here to add to their counts. They see the birds while the birds see the ridge and use it for navigation purposes on their long migration. Maybe the white paint on the chimney and the mountain with a bite in it serve as clear reminders to them that they are on course.

Leave the Chimney Rock viewing area and make an immediate left turn onto a wide path that heads downhill. As the lane descends, you'll notice two steep side trails that lead down to the gorge and dam over the East Branch of Middle Brook. Be careful following these side trails; the footing is rocky and potentially dangerous, but if you make the effort you'll get a good look at the former gorge and the unusual column-like qualities of the basalt. The falls here, partially destroyed by the dam, are called Buttermilk Falls. What a beautiful place this could have been if it hadn't been appropriated by engineering projects.

After visiting the gorge, return to the main path and follow it down to the reservoir, near the stone causeway you passed earlier. Under exceptional conditions you might be able to cross here, but most of the time you will need to continue ahead, following the footpath along the east side of the reservoir. Pay attention to the path as it becomes increasingly narrow, rocky, and very difficult in places. It is certainly passable, but with ice or slippery conditions, it can be dangerous. (If this is the case, return to Chimney Rock and use the trail you came up on.) Soon Gilbride Road becomes visible and the trail becomes far more walkable. Pass the trail junction you met earlier and walk straight ahead up to Gilbride Road. Turn left here and follow the road over the brook, and then turn left again onto the trail you followed earlier. Take the path up the hill and at the first fork, turn right. This trail, heavily used by mountain bikers, switchbacks up to the height of land. At the next fork, turn right and follow the trail past a stand of cedars, a favorite hiding place for deer. Soon you'll arrive at another junction, which you also passed earlier. Turn right and follow the path as it switchbacks down the hill to Chimney Rock Road. Cross the road (be careful), pick up the trail on the other side, and follow the lane you walked on earlier back to the reservoir. From here, retrace your steps back to your car.

BCS

32

Sourland Mountain Preserve

Total distance: 3.3 miles

Hiking time: 2 hours

Vertical rise: 360 feet

Rating: Easy to moderate

Maps: USGS Rocky Hill; Somerset County Park Commission Sourland Mountain Preserve trail map

Sourland Mountain is really a 10- by 4-mile sheet of Triassic traprock, similar to the Palisades, Watchungs, and Cushetunk Mountain (see Introduction). Here a portion of a buried igneous intrusion was tilted, with its eastern edge leaning up, then uplifted. Erosion left the harder igneous rock exposed, and it now overlooks the surrounding plain. The highest elevation on the mountain, attained in two places, is 586 feet. Contrast this with the 120-foot elevation of the eastern plain and you have one of the steepest gradients in central New Jersey. It is on this eastern edge that the hiking trails are located. The western portion of the mountain slopes off into the plain more gradually.

Two factors have allowed Sourland Mountain to remain mostly undeveloped. The first is the fact that the land has never been of much agricultural or commercial worth—something that seems to be reflected in the name. Sourland may have stemmed from the German term *sauerland,* meaning land that is not sweet. It is true that the soil is rocky and acidic and that there is little groundwater. The name may also refer to the reddish brown ("sorrel-land") color of the soil found on the plains beneath the mountain. In some old records is the name Sowerland.

The second factor is that Sourland Mountain is far from any major thoroughfares. It has served as a retreat for many, including Charles Lindbergh, whose child was kidnapped there. The broad, flat top of the mountain is quite rocky, mostly wooded, and includes about 400 acres of old growth. Many historical buildings still stand along the

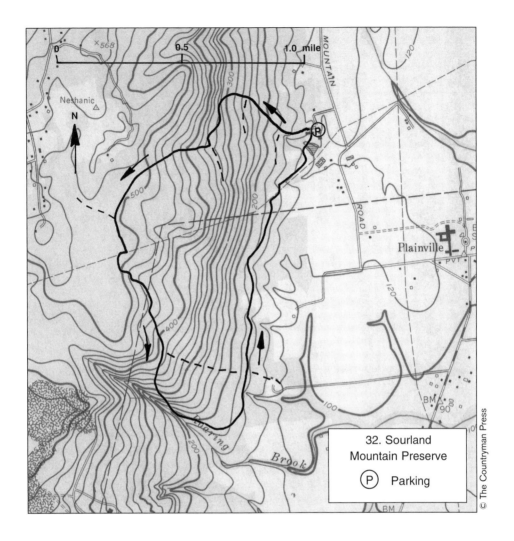

32. Sourland
Mountain Preserve

(P) Parking

several quiet country roads that cross over it. But developmental pressure in New Jersey is relentless, and many have become concerned. One such voice is the Sourland Regional Citizens Planning Council, which has pushed for preservation of the area since 1989. The matter is complicated by the fact that portions of the mountain fall in Mercer, Hunterdon, and Somerset Counties. To date, only Somerset and Hunterdon Counties have established a public reservation.

The Sourland Mountain Preserve is one of the newest components (opened in June 1995) of the Somerset County Park Commission (PO Box 5327, North Branch, NJ 08876; 908-722-1200, www.park.co .somerset.nj.us) and now totals more than 2,600 acres. One interesting feature near the preserve not currently accessible from the marked trails is the Roaring Rocks boulder fields, an area of large traprock boulders. Ask a naturalist or ranger about this

---

Sourland Mountain Preserve

In Sourland Mountain Preserve

area. Naturalists are present on Saturdays and lead walks at 10 AM and 2 PM.

HOW TO GET THERE

From the junction of US 206 and US 202 at the Somerville Circle, drive 8.6 miles south on US 206 and take County Road 601 South. This junction occurs as the highway veers sharply left–CR 601 goes straight ahead. (This turnoff is 2.7 miles south of where Amwell Road/NJ 514 crosses US 206.) Drive 1.2 miles on CR 601, then turn right on East Mountain Road. The Carrier Foundation buildings are located at this corner. Follow curving East Mountain Road for 1.2 miles to the entrance to the Sourland Mountain Preserve. Turn left here and drive to the large parking area.

THE TRAIL

There are three major marked trails in the Sourland Mountain Preserve marked with symbols and numbered junctions. They

were designed to meet all needs: an easy trail of 0.5 mile, a moderate trail of 1.4 miles, and the trail that you will take, the 4-mile Ridge Trail. The trails in the preserve were built by groups of volunteers that included the Boy Scouts (Troop 46), the Sourland Regional Citizens Planning Council, and the federal Youth Conservation Corps. Unlike other large tracts of land that open to the public and only later develop trails, the preserve sprang into being with a trail system in place, including bridges, boardwalk, and water-control features. At the time of this writing, mountain bikes are permitted to ride the trails.

From the parking area, walk past the directory/booth to the single trailhead for all trails in the preserve. Follow the footpath as it enters the woods and crosses a bridge. The trail follows a small brook for a distance, crossing it again before entering a section of boardwalk in a boulder field. After this boardwalk, a sign will direct you to turn right. At this point the concurrent trails begin to divide. Here the Pondside Trail, marked with a circle, turns off, leaving you now following only the Maple Flats Trail (triangle) and the Ridge Trail (rectangle). The path begins to climb. At the next intersection the triangular trail diverges; keep right, staying with the Ridge Trail and still heading uphill.

When you arrive at post #4, which is at the height of land and marks a junction, turn left. Just after this turn, look for an unmarked footpath on your right off the main trail. This leads to a large boulder field that is worth exploring. After a few more minutes on the Ridge Trail you should arrive at a pipeline clearing. The cleared pipeline is the Texas Eastern Gas Transmission Corporation right-of-way. If you turn left onto the pipeline clearing and walk a short distance up the slope, you'll come to an expansive vista that looks out to the east. This is also the high point on the hike.

To continue with the hike, return to post #5 and continue downhill on the pipeline path, cross a small brook, then immediately turn left into a small field of tall reeds called phragmites. These, the reeds of the Bible, are not native to the Americas but they seem to be found everywhere in New Jersey. Follow the trail here, which brings you to the other side of the pipeline cut and back into the woods.

Back in the woods the trail crosses a bridge, then follows a rocky path that snakes its way between a convergence of small streams. After passing this wet section, the path swings to the right onto a series of boardwalks. When you reach post #6, located near a fence, turn left and head steeply downhill (be careful—this area can be quite slippery when wet). The pathway widens as it reaches post #7. Bear right here. Next you'll pass through a wet area and arrive at post #8, which marks the point where the Ridge Trail comes closest to Roaring Brook, the largest brook on the hike.

The boulders in Roaring Brook are typical of the main rock type on the mountain. This igneous rock, called diabase, is mined by the 3-M Company, located nearby. The rock is ground down to make the abrasive coating on asphalt shingles. Farther upstream and in other parts of Sourland Mountain are large boulder fields where these rocks deny vegetation a foothold. One such place is named the Devil's Half Acre. If you are interested in exploring one of these boulder fields, which at present are not on public land, speak with a ranger.

At the next junction, keep left. You've now entered a different kind of forest than the one you've been hiking through, a tall cedar forest characteristic of the lowlands. You'll pass some old stoneworks here that may have served as a dam. Walk straight through the crossroads at post #9. Ahead is a section of trail that may be quite muddy during wet periods. As you approach the starting point of the hike you will again join with the other trails. Pay close attention now to markers and junctions. At post #10, turn right. Then walk to post #11, which is located at the lower end of the Texas Eastern Pipeline clearing you crossed earlier. Follow the pipeline down for about 0.1 mile and turn left on a path that leads to the pond. Keeping the pond to your right, walk back to your car, which is across the field in front of you. (*Note:* there are several paths that lead to the parking area off the pipeline and the routes can be confusing. If you come to post #12, which is in the woods off the pipeline, make a right and walk out to the pond.)

BCS

33

Washington Crossing to Scudder's Falls

Total distance: 6 miles

Hiking time: 3 hours

Vertical rise: 100 feet

Rating: Easy to moderate

Maps: USGS Pennington; DEP Washington Crossing State Park map; DEP Delaware & Raritan Canal State Park

Washington Crossing State Park (RR 1, Box 337, Titusville, NJ 08560; 609-737-0623) is #13 on the state's historical site listing, and this hike is a combination history lesson and long walk on a towpath. On the towpath you will be exposed to much sun—a blessing or curse depending on the season or the weather. There is plenty to do at this state park. In all, this 1,400-acre park boasts 13 miles of walkway and trails. Other hiking possibilities besides the one described here include several footpaths through a 140-acre natural area with an interpretive center.

The park's Visitor Center Museum (open year-round Wednesdays through Sundays, 9 to 4:30 pm with some holiday adjustments—call 609-737-9304 for details) contains a large collection of Revolutionary War artifacts, maps, and descriptive brochures. A short slide presentation on the history and offerings of the park will give you a feel for the momentous event that justified its creation, and full-length historical films are also shown at specific times. The importance of what happened here in 1776 cannot be overestimated. This was the site of probably the single most important offensive in George Washington's military career. At the very least, it kept him and the country alive during the early days of the American Revolution.

Since independence had been declared, the Continental Army, led by Washington, had not scored a point against the British. Washington and his men had tried to stop the British invasion of Long Island (Brooklyn) but were driven back to Manhattan and then across the Hudson to New Jersey. Denied adequate troops and supplies to meet the threat, Washington had no recourse but to retreat across the middle of New Jersey, cross the Delaware, and hunker down in Pennsylvania. Although the situation appeared to be cause for extreme depression, Washington took a risk and won, and in the process stirred hope for the revolutionary cause.

On the night of December 25, 1776, he ordered three divisions of troops to attack the Hessian garrison at Trenton. The plan called for each division to cross the Delaware at different points and then converge on the enemy. Washington himself and 2,400 men crossed the river in ferryboats at the site of the present-day state park. After a difficult crossing in the ice-choked river, he and his men marched south to Trenton, caught the Hessians by surprise, and took possession of Trenton. The other two divisions never made the crossing that night because of river ice. Washington immediately followed up the victory with a successful attack on the British at Princeton. Having pushed back the enemy halfway to New York, he took shelter for the remainder of the winter behind the long, curving natural wall of the Watchungs in central New Jersey. These two battles marked a major turning point in the war, and they kept Washington in place as commander in chief.

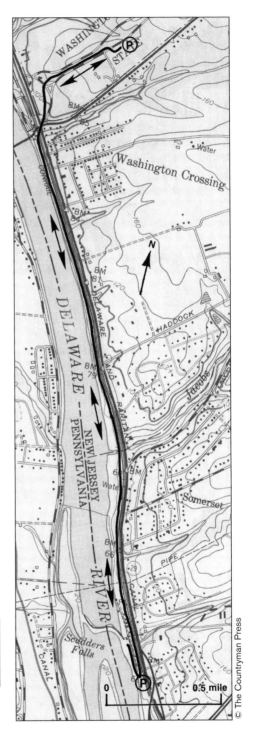

33. Washington's Crossing to Scudder's Falls

(P) Parking

HOW TO GET THERE

You will see signs for Washington Crossing State Park (State Park #13), as you approach it from any direction. From I-95, take Exit 1 north (the last exit in New Jersey) to NJ 29 north. About 3 miles from the exit, make a right turn onto County Road 546; you will find the main entrance to the park on your right in about 0.5 mile. Alternatively, take Exit 3 and follow signs to the park entrance. Between Memorial Day and Labor Day there is a $5-per-car entrance fee on weekends only. Pass the toll gate, follow signs to the Visitor Center Museum, and park in the large lot just to the north of the center. Parking is free just north of the Nelson House near the river—if there is room. You may wish to park here and walk back to the visitor center to see the museum's collection of artifacts or simply walk south along the towpath as described below. Limited parking is also free at an area located at the intersection of CR 579 and CR 546, just off CR 579. If you park here you will be able to walk along the historic Continental Lane to the Visitor Center Museum a mile away. Parking here will add an extra 2 miles to your hike. Another option is to spot cars at each end of the hike. A parking area for boaters is found 3 miles south of the park on NJ 29 near Scudder's Falls.

THE TRAIL

After a visit to the center, walk over to Continental Lane, the grassy walking path about 100 yards due west (in front) of the center. This path is marked with a red dot. You'll find it between a long line of trees and other plantings just across the paved road. Turn left onto the lane and head toward the Delaware River. Continental Lane is a pleasant, tree-lined walkway between two paved park service roads. Ashes, oaks, white

pines, and cedars line the path on either side. After a few minutes, you'll come to a few colonial buildings. To your right is an old barn that now houses rest rooms and a flag museum. In front of you is the Johnson Ferry House, fronted with an herb garden. You may wish to explore these buildings now, or perhaps on your return. At the terminus of Continental Lane, bear left for just a few feet on the paved road and turn right onto a path marked with a green dot heading south. This path will lead you past a walled-in overlook (overlooking NJ 29 and the Delaware) and out to a pedestrian walking bridge over the highway. This area is part of the memorial arboretum, and the varied plant life here may be of interest. Take the pedestrian walking bridge over NJ 29 and make a left, crossing the road leading to the bridge. A restaurant is located near here. Now head south (through the gate) on the canal feeder towpath. En route you'll pass two stone markers commemorating the crossing.

The towpath, which was used for a time as a bed for the Belvidere and Delaware Railroad, is very flat and is surfaced with a very fine, though loose, gravel. It gets much use from joggers and bikers as well as walkers. To the right and quite a drop below is the Delaware River. To the left is the feeder canal and, beyond that, NJ 29. It is unfortunate that the highway is so close, but that is an unavoidable reality in such a densely populated area. This section of towpath is very exposed to sunlight and, during hot summer days, it may be advisable to hike in the late afternoon when the shade of the taller trees on the west bank covers the entire path.

As you walk along the towpath, you'll see vegetation very different from that of the highland mountains or the Pine Barrens. The plants—weeds actually—are more typical of

Flag house

highways, urban vacant lots, and other places that receive much sunlight. Don't be put off by this; some of the most valuable medicinal herbs are found in such environments. For example, you'll see thistle, with its prickly leaves and round flower heads, which is used for fevers (it produces sweating). The common mullein, the tall, spikelike plant commonly seen along the roadside, is also found here; a tea made from its leaves and flowers is used for lung complaints and asthma. As for flowers, you'll find purple gentians, black-eyed Susans, goldenrod, and wild carrot (better known as Queen Anne's lace). Poison ivy is in abundance here as well, though it doesn't encroach upon the path. Pokeweed, edible as a young shoot but poisonous fully matured, is found here also. You'll find the staghorn sumac with its red berry clusters that, when soaked in cold water, make a lemonade-like drink. At the edge of the dense woods that separates the towpath from the river are flowering dog-woods and even a few catalpa trees with their large heart-shaped leaves and long, beanlike pods.

Where the canal curves slightly to the east, notice the outcroppings of red Brunswick shale, also known as brownstone, on the opposite bank. This rock is the primary bedrock throughout all of central New Jersey, except for the igneous intrusions that make up the Watchungs, Cushetunk Mountain, Sourland Mountain, and Rocky Hill. A little farther ahead, Jacob's Creek passes under the canal and empties into the Delaware. There's a nice view of this wild and rocky confluence from the towpath, which stands 50 feet above it. Blue herons may be wading in the shallows, where they are safe from intruders. Don't be surprised if you see deer hoof prints on the towpath; they've got a dense woods to hide in during the day.

After passing a flood-control structure, which allows the canal to drain into the river if necessary, you'll see a bridge across the canal ahead of you. Bear right here and head downhill on the paved road. Take one of the pathways to your left down to the river, and you'll come out near Scudder's Falls, a Class II set of rapids on the Delaware. At the time of this writing, the best path to the falls was directly opposite a parking lot off NJ 29.

Scudder's Falls was named for the Scudder family, whose 18th-century farmstead and mill were once located in the area. One well-known member of the family was Amos Scudder, one of Washington's scouts at the Battle of Trenton. John Hart, one of the signers of the Declaration of Independence from New Jersey, was married to a Scudder. Unfortunately, nothing is left of the original house.

Notice the huge sections of concrete on the island just across from the falls. A structure located here once utilized the immense power of the water, which drops several feet in a short distance. These falls, more like a channel or chute between shoreline and island, are popular with kayakers. If you are here during high water and on a weekend, you will no doubt be treated to a display of paddling skills. The area, also heavily used by anglers and partygoers, is quite pleasant and very interesting, making it a good spot for lunch. You can sit on some of the big rocks near the river's edge, listen to the roar of the rapids, and gaze out toward Pennsylvania, far off on the other side.

After watching the rapids, return to the towpath (or follow the road along the river to a gas line and then scramble back up to the towpath) and begin the long walk back to Washington Crossing State Park. The benches placed about every 0.25 mile can provide a welcome rest should you need one. Before taking the pedestrian walkway over NJ 29, you may wish to take a look at the Nelson House just below it toward the river. There is a portion of the original tavern here at the ferry dock. The building contains a large collection of period pieces, a flag collection, and, adjacent to the building, a reconstruction of one of the original ferryboats that took Washington and his men across the frozen river on that cold December night.

From the Nelson House, take the pedestrian bridge across the highway and bear left through the walled overlook. Continue retracing your steps toward the Johnson Ferry House and flag museum to find Continental Lane that, in 0.3 mile, will bring you to the visitors center and parking area—unless, of course, you parked elsewhere.

BCS

34

D & R Canal, Bull's Island to Prallsville

Total distance: 3 miles (or 6 miles using one car)

Hiking time: 2 hours (or 3.5 hours)

Vertical rise: Minimal

Rating: Easy to moderate

Map: USGS Lumberville/Stockton; DEP Delaware & Raritan Canal State Park map

The 22-mile-long feeder to the main Delaware & Raritan Canal is part of Delaware & Raritan Canal State Park. The towpath in this section was used by the Belvidere and Delaware Railroad and is surfaced today with fine stone chips. From Bull's Island to Stockton at the Prallsville Mill, the railroad bed is located on the east bank of the Delaware River. At Stockton, it swings over the canal to the towpath, which separates the canal from the river. Containing a large campground, Bull's Island is the main developed section of the state park and invites exploration. The Prallsville Mill, 3 miles to the south, is a restored historical area scenically located on the canal and overlooking the Delaware River.

Bull's Island is an artificial island created by the construction of the canal. Richard Bull, one of the original owners, gave his name to the island and also to Bull's Creek, displaced by the canal, which separated it from the mainland. In 1832 work on the Delaware & Raritan Canal was started, and by 1834 the Delaware River dam, which is used to divert water from the river to the canal, was completed. Here, the Delaware River water enters the canal and begins its long journey south to Trenton. This section, known as the canal feeder, was not only a source of water for the main canal but also a navigation channel that competed with the Delaware Canal on the Pennsylvania side of the river. The feeder meets the main canal at Trenton, where the canal turns north and, following first the Millstone then the Raritan River, terminates at New Brunswick. Along

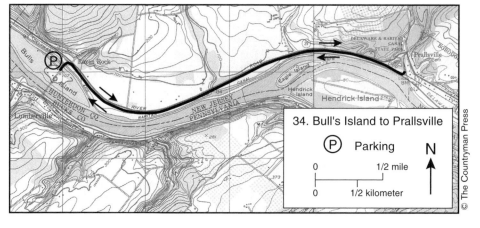

the way, the water level is maintained by a series of locks. A 24-acre state-designated natural area is located on the southern portion of the island. A trail through the area begins near the park office and provides views of both the canal and the Delaware River.

The D & R Canal parks in both New Jersey and Pennsylvania suffered sometimes severe damage during the spring floods of 2005. While the section used on this hike is in good shape, call ahead should you be planning more extensive use of the trails along the shores of the Delaware River.

HOW TO GET THERE

From its junction with US 202, take NJ 29 north for 6 miles to the Bull's Island section of Delaware and Raritan Canal State Park (2185 Daniel Bray Highway, Stockton, NJ 08559; 609-397-2949). The park, which offers car and tent camping, is located on a densely wooded floodplain of the Delaware. Park in the large day-use parking area, which will be on your left.

THE TRAIL

You might want to begin by hiking past the ranger's house toward a long suspension bridge for pedestrians that crosses the Delaware and allows access to Pennsylva-

nia. The views of the river from this bridge are outstanding.

Go back toward your car and the entrance road. Just before reaching NJ 29 (which the hike will parallel), find the abandoned Belvidere and Delaware Railroad bed, now a 17-mile multipurpose trail suitable for walkers, joggers, and bicycle riders. Pass around the gate and begin the 3-mile walk to the Prallsville Mill.

As you walk east along the railroad bed, the woods will be on the right and NJ 29 on the left. After only 0.5 mile, you will see the canal far below. Throughout most of Delaware & Raritan Canal State Park, the actual towpath—which lies between the canal and the river—is used as the recreational path. In this section, the towpath is cut by unbridged overflow points that present major obstacles for the walker. The railroad bed, covered with fine gravel, therefore serves as the main path until you reach the first lock at the mill. Occasional piles of old railroad ties lie along the route, which is quite straight and, of course, very flat.

On the way to the mill, the walkway takes you through a mixture of sun and shade, field and woods. At about the halfway point, cross over an inlet leading to the canal on a high bridge. Here, 50 feet or more above the canal, you will see a break in the towpath out to the Delaware.

Farther along, the path becomes more shaded and crowded in with honeysuckle and other vines. A rock embankment, which separates the path from the road, appears. The stone, the Stockton Formation, is better known as brownstone and is quarried locally. This stone has been used in the construction of many historic buildings in New Jersey, including some at Princeton and Rutgers Universities.

Ahead on the path, a bridge over a brook flowing into the canal is particularly picturesque. On a clear summer day you can look over an expanse of water to wooded islands, banks of purple loosestrife, and the mighty Delaware River. Ahead are the first locks on the feeder canal, and to the left are the buildings of the Prallsville Mill.

Located just north of Stockton, the mill is named after John Prall who, though not the original owner, bought the property in 1794. He enlarged the original gristmill and sawmill operation by adding a stone building used to mill linseed oil and plaster. In 1874 the original gristmill burned, ignited by a spark from a passing steam engine on the B & D Railroad, but the mill was rebuilt on the old foundations three years later. After milling came to an end in the late 1940s, the entire complex of seven buildings was acquired by the state and gradually restored by the Delaware River Mill Society, which leases the site. What makes the Prallsville Mill unique is that it is the only historic multiple milling operation remaining in the state.

Today, the displays at the restored mill include an industrial herb garden, an exact-scale model of the mill built by the last mill owner, and a crafts shop, along with the restored buildings themselves. Near the old sawmill is a picnic table, a good place to have lunch or a snack after the walk from Bull's Island.

After visiting the mill, head back to Bull's Island the way you came—or leave from here if you have arranged a car shuttle.

HNZ/BCS

35

D & R Canal, Kingston to Griggstown

Total distance: 5 miles (or 10 miles using one car)

Hiking time: 2.5 hours (or 5 hours)

Vertical rise: Minimal

Rating: Easy to moderate

Maps: USGS Monmouth Junction/Rocky Hill/Hightstown; DEP Delaware and Raritan Canal State Park map

From its opening in 1834 to its closing 100 years later, the Delaware & Raritan Canal served as a major transportation link between Philadelphia and New York. From the northernmost point of navigation on the Delaware River at Bordentown to the head of navigation on the Raritan River at New Brunswick, the canal totaled 44 miles. A water supply for the canal was created by digging a 22-mile-long feeder canal to divert water from the Delaware River at Raven Rock to the main canal at Trenton. Both main and feeder canals had towpaths (walkways for the mules that pulled the barges along). Today, about 34 miles of the main canal and towpath are used by hikers, joggers, canoeists, and nature lovers. The D & R Canal State Park (625 Canal Road, Somerset, NJ 08873; 732-873-3050, www.njparksand forest.org) is a green corridor through the center of the nation's most densely populated state, and though it is never far from suburbia, it offers many miles of walking.

HOW TO GET THERE

The linear D & R Canal State Park has many access points. For this hike, you will use a large parking area that is located near a canal lock on the south side of NJ 27 in Kingston, where the highway passes over the canal and river. (There is additional parking at the Flemer Preserve across the street.) If you wish to hike the full 10 miles, park your car here and begin hiking. A car shuttle is necessary for a one-way hike of 5 miles. To leave a second car at the northern end of the hike, drive east on NJ 27 uphill to the second traffic light in the center of Kingston. Turn left here onto Laurel Avenue. Drive north past the quarry and through the traffic light onto Canal Road. Continue for another 3.4 miles to Griggstown Causeway Road. Make a left here, and leave your car at the large parking area about 0.2 mile ahead on the left. Return via the same route to the Kingston parking area in the other car.

THE TRAIL

Take the paved path on the west side of the parking area through the tunnel underneath the highway. As you emerge, the Millstone River will be to the left and the canal to the right. This is the Millstone River floodplain, the densely vegetated—though muddy—strip of land lying between the river and the canal. The path, which swings to the right and toward the canal towpath, is marked with occasional metal markers.

Once you reach the towpath, walk north on a well-used multipurpose recreational trail. The path is wide enough for a vehicle (though they are not allowed) and is used mostly by hikers, runners, bikers, horseback riders, and anglers. Throughout the hike, the canal will be on the right and the river below you on the left. For much of its length, the Delaware & Raritan Canal is paralleled by roads, though most of these are secondary country roads. In the section covered on this hike, a road follows the river for a while but then veers away, and with it the sounds of cars. You will get a feeling of isolation through this stretch. All kinds of wildflowers

35. D & R Canal, Kingston to Griggstown
P Parking

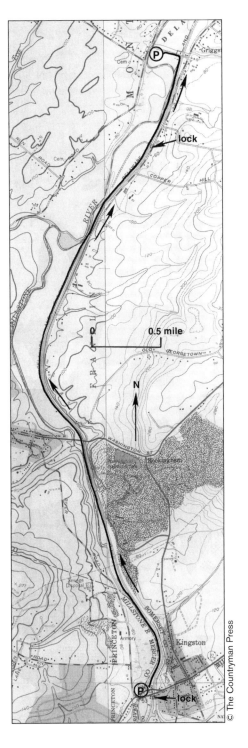

© The Countryman Press

grow along the towpath here, including yarrow, wild carrot, pokeweed, and lobelia, as well as clusters of arrowroot in the water, a favorite food of Native Americans. The trees that line the towpath are mostly oak and maple with some horse chestnut, ash, and sumac. The great blue heron is also frequently seen along the canal. A word of caution: poison ivy abounds along the towpath. This toxic plant is frequently found along the towpath as a tree-climbing vine. Although the walkway is wide enough to avoid any contact with the plant, when leaving the towpath and approaching either the canal or the river more closely, be sure you know how to identify it.

After 1.5 miles you will reach the edge of a traprock quarry that borders the east bank of the canal. One of the largest and oldest quarries in the area, it supplies crushed basalt, called traprock, to road builders. The rock is quarried from what was once a large igneous intrusion, similar to and contemporary with Sourland Mountain, the Watchungs, and the Palisades. If you are hiking during the week, your solitude may be spoiled by the activities of this large operation. In recent years an exchange of land between the quarry and the state has taken place, and the section of the quarry nearest to the canal is now open to the public. It is quickly reverting to its natural state.

Look for a square concrete pillar with a tapered top, not unlike a fat 3-foot-high obelisk. This is a canal milepost, actually a replacement for the original stone markers. Notice that the number 23 is facing south and that on the other side, facing north, is the number 21. These figures indicate the number of miles from New Brunswick and Trenton, respectively. Adding the two gives the total mileage between these points. The markers, at least the ones that have survived, are found at every mile along the tow-

path. Just before you reach Rocky Hill Road, an inviting rock outcrop extends into the Millstone River on your left.

After about 40 minutes (just less than 2 miles) of walking, you reach paved Rocky Hill Road. There is a new parking area here on the other side of the canal where the trail on the opposite bank of the canal begins. If you wish to shorten your hike and don't want to retrace your steps, cross over the canal and find the footpath on the opposite bank. It will follow the canal back to Kingston and your car.

To continue the hike, cross the road and continue past the small dock and back onto the towpath. From here to Griggstown, Canal Road, a small country road, parallels the canal on the opposite bank. A number of old homes are located in this area, some of them well over 200 years old. In fact, George Washington himself gave his farewell address to the Continental Army in 1783 from a house originally located not far from the canal. Washington was said to have enjoyed his three-month stay in this house on his way from Newburgh to Mount Vernon. It was here that he came to know of his great popularity, and history reports that he did much official entertaining—for a few months, this area was the social capital of the new nation. The house where Washington stayed, now called Rockingham, was relocated twice as the quarrying operation expanded. It is now about 0.75 mile from its original location. Within the next five years, it is due to be relocated again as per the state's agreement with Trap Rock, Inc. It will be moved closer to the east bank of the canal, somewhere between Rocky Hill and Kingston.

Ahead on the towpath, pass mile marker 22/22, the halfway point between New Brunswick and Trenton. Beyond this marker is a small wooden bridge over the canal, a

D & R Canal

BRUCE SCOFIELD

good spot for a rest or snack. Farther ahead on the left at milepost 23 is one end of a bridle trail, the Silver Maple Trail, which explores the Millstone River floodplain. Just beyond the trailhead, notice that the towpath is lower than usual. This area is a spillway, which allows a swollen canal to shed water into the floodplain of the river. At the end of this section are stones placed to prevent erosion of the towpath. Just ahead is the Griggstown lock.

Canal locks on the Delaware & Raritan, which measure 220 by 24 feet, allowed boats to change water levels between sections of the canal. Though seven locks were necessary in the 6-mile stretch of canal from Bordentown to Trenton, only seven more were needed for the remaining 38 miles, a low route that follows the river valleys of the Millstone and Raritan. The house behind the lock is one of the old lock tenders' houses found near every lock. Alongside the lock are some round concrete

posts known as snubbing posts, which were used to secure boats making the passage. The turbulence of water rising or lowering in the lock required a tight line, but also one that could adjust as the water level changed. Such lines were also needed for braking purposes–the boat had to be stopped once it entered the lock. Aside from the technical problems of stabilizing a boat in the lock, the passage through was also a social event. Exchanges of news would take place between the lock tender and the boatmen. Telegraph connections were in place, and information, such as the arrival of boats, could be sent on to other locations. The lock tender and his family would often trade with the canal boatmen who, like many of today's truckers, owned their own vehicles.

Returning to the towpath, find the other end of the Silver Maple Trail nearby. You may wish to walk a short distance on this trail down to the banks of the Millstone

River. The shagbark hickory tree may be found in this well-watered environment.

Milepost 20/24 is found at a point where the canal and the river are very close to each other, though the river runs well below the level of the canal. Ahead are the paved Griggstown Causeway and several historic buildings. Notice a steel bridge on your left, located just before a house. Turn onto this to reach the parking areas without walking along the road. The bridge spans a millrace that once existed at this site, the nearby house being set on the foundations of the old mill. Ahead of you, at the paved road, notice the long structure—built about 1800—of the Griggstown Barracks. This building was used to shelter the men who built and worked the canal. Today it serves in part as a small museum for the Griggstown Historical Society, which is open daily, weekdays 9–3 and weekends (if volunteers are available) 1–4. The bridge tender's house and station are on the other side of the canal; both were built around 1831. Griggstown Canoe Rental is also here; along with canoes, it also rents single-person kayaks.

If you haven't left a car in the parking area (to reach it, use the previously mentioned bridge), turn around and walk the 5 miles back to Kingston. At the Rocky Hill Road crossing, near the traffic lights, you may wish to walk the last section on the footpath on the other side of the canal.

BCS

36

D & R Canal, Weston to East Millstone

Total distance: 4.2 miles

Hiking time: 2 hours

Vertical rise: Minimal

Rating: Easy

Map: USGS Bound Brook; DEP Delaware & Raritan Canal State Park

A century ago the Delaware & Raritan Canal—now the site of a state park (625 Canal Road, Somerset, NJ 08873; 908-873-3050)—was the scene of intense commercial activity. Hard coal was the most important item shipped on the canal, accounting for 80 percent of its total tonnage. Many of the canal boats used on the canal were of the "hinge-boat" variety; they measured about 90 by 10 feet and drew about 5 feet of water. Long strings of these canal boats loaded with coal were pulled by steam tugs, while other canal boats were towed by mules. Towing charges varied according to the service used. At one point steam tugs were charged a flat rate of $22.22, plus an extra $11.11 per barge for the trip to New York City. Mules and horses were available from barns at Bordentown, Griggstown, and New Brunswick. The open season on the canal was about 250 days a year, from early April to mid-December. Canal hours were from 6–6 daily, and the speed limit for canal boats was 4 miles per hour. When steam tugs began to be used on the canal, the wash began to undermine the banks in places. A stone lining called riprap was installed and can still be seen today in many places.

HOW TO GET THERE

To locate this section of the Delaware & Raritan Canal State Park from I-287, take Exit 12, Weston Canal Road. When you reach the end of the exit ramp, turn left (south) on Weston Canal Road, following signs to Manville. In 1.7 miles, pass Ten Mile

36. D & R Canal,
Weston to East Millstone

Ⓟ Parking

Lock and the lock tender's house on the right and, after that, the religious community of Zarepath. In 3 miles, the road will swing around and cross the canal. The parking area, created from a remnant of older pavement, is located on the right just before the road crosses the canal.

THE TRAIL

Cross over the bridge and turn left onto the towpath, heading south. On the other side of the canal (the east bank) is the old bridge tender's house, built circa 1831. Originally, a swing bridge spanned the canal here. If you are hiking in summer or early fall, notice the duckweed, the miniature lily pad-like plant that floats in clusters on the water. This plant tends to accumulate, sometimes covering the entire canal surface for 10 or 15 miles before New Brunswick (the terminus of the waterway). The towpath, which receives an equal amount of sun and shade, is quite grassy here, though the actual walkway is worn to the dirt. The trees, mostly oak and maple, form an intermittent canopy over the towpath. Poison ivy is, unfortunately, abundant. On the other side of the canal is Weston Causeway Road, a country road with light traffic. On your right is the large Millstone River floodplain.

After a few minutes of walking, notice that the Millstone floodplain, undoubtedly very fertile, is being used as a cornfield. At about the point where the cornfield ends, Weston Canal Road turns away from the canal, and the towpath enters one of its very few sections not paralleled by a road. For the next 1.5 miles, the walking through this quiet and somewhat wild area—rare in densely populated central New Jersey—becomes very pleasant.

As the sounds of civilization fade out, the towpath takes on a wilder look. The Millstone River itself swings close to the canal,

D & R Canal towpath

but 20 feet below it. The sounds of insects, fish jumping, and the hurried scrambling of turtles startled by your intrusion fill the void left by the sounds of traffic. If you are lucky, a great blue heron may wing its way down the canal. The only evidence of civilization is the boat dock for a day camp on the opposite bank of the canal.

Just before a spillway, you will come to milepost 31/13. This original canal artifact tells you that you are 13 miles from New Brunswick and 31 miles from Trenton. Ahead on the opposite bank is a cleared section of Colonial Park, which has a small dock. Next, pass over a culvert through which Spooky Brook runs, going under the canal on its way to the Millstone. This an example of one of the many streams that were channeled underneath the canal in order to keep its water level stable.

In another 0.5 mile, and all too soon, the quiet and privacy of this section of towpath come to an end. Ahead are the bridge and parking area off Amwell Road in East Millstone. If you are interested, cross over the canal on Amwell Road and take a short walk into East Millstone, a small town that has changed very little over the years. The first road on the right leads to a small convenience store. On the way you'll pass a first-aid station and, in back of it, Turning Basin Park, a filled-in area where boats used to turn around. Today you'll find swings and other recreation for children. On the opposite side of the canal, but on the same side of the road as the parking area, is a bridge tender's house. Next to it is the historic Franklin Inn, its exterior refurbished and its interior now a nonprofit used bookstore run by volunteers of the Blackwells Mills Canal House Association.

After your visit to East Millstone, return to the towpath and retrace your steps to your car.

BCS

37

Six Mile Run Preserve

Total distance: 3.5 miles

Hiking time: 2 hours

Vertical rise: Minimal

Rating: Easy, but with a possibly challenging brook crossing.

Maps: USGS Monmouth Junction; NJ DEP Six Mile Run Reservoir Site Trail Guide

In the 1960s and 1970s, regional planners were anticipating high population growth and demand for water. Reservoirs were thought to be the solution, and acquisition of lands suitable for future water storage were acquired—a process that was not popular with some property owners. In 1970 a considerable acreage surrounding the large central New Jersey brook Six Mile Run (so named because it is about 6 miles south of New Brunswick on the way to Princeton) was acquired—but no reservoir ever appeared. Much of the land is being leased to local farmers for agricultural purposes. While it may someday be flooded to serve as a reservoir, the Six Mile Run Reservoir site is today being managed by the NJ Division of Parks and Forestry as an extension of the Delaware & Raritan Canal State Park. In fact, the headquarters of the park is located right on Six Mile Run.

The future reservoir status of the area has been a factor in the retention of its rural atmosphere. Many 18th century farmhouses and farms are located here as well as buildings that served canal traffic. The reservoir site is quite large, more than 3,000 acres, and offers miles of paths for hikers, mountain bikers, and horseback riders. For the most part, the trails follow edges, boundaries between forest and field, brook and wetland, habitats preferred by many animals and birds. Walking is generally not difficult here, although there are wet and muddy areas in the floodplain. The greatest challenge in creating a trail system in this

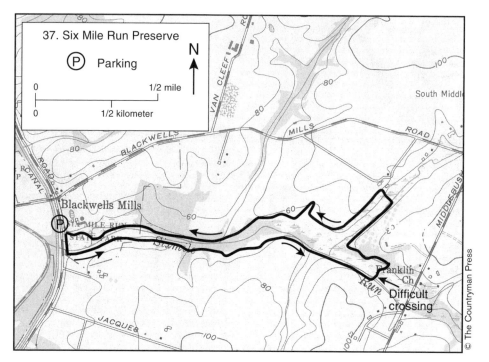

area is in crossing the many tributaries that feed the brook. The first section of the hike described below (the Red Trail) stays on higher ground, and even during very wet periods it makes an excellent hike.

The Six Mile Run Reservoir area is rich in wildlife, and hunting is allowed during the season. In the autumn, be sure to check ahead of time about the year's hunting schedules. Information on hunting and other recreational activities relating to Delaware & Raritan Canal State Park can be found at the park office adjacent to the parking area. The office is located in an old house typical of the area. Nearby is the Canal House, which is open to visitors.

HOW TO GET THERE

From I-287 South, take Exit 10 to Easton Avenue (CR 527) heading east towards New Brunswick. In less than 0.25 mile, turn right at the second set of lights onto Cedar Grove Lane. Follow this road for 3 miles until it ends at Amwell Road (CR 514). Turn right here. After 2.3 miles on Amwell Road you will enter the village of East Millstone. Turn left onto Market Street, which is located just before Amwell Road crosses over the Delaware & Raritan Canal and Millstone River. Follow Market Street 0.2 mile to its end on Elm Street. Turn right here and follow the curve to the left onto Canal Road. Drive south on Canal Road for another 2 miles with the canal on your right to a four-way stop at Blackwell's Mills. Drive straight ahead, still on Canal Road, to the park headquarters just 0.1 mile ahead on your left. Park in the large parking area.

Alternatively, Blackwell's Mills can be reached from I-287 north Exit 11. Follow CR 623 south alongside the canal and then Weston Road east to Mettler's Road. Turn right here and drive past Colonial Park to Amwell Road. Turn right here, then left onto

Market Street in East Millstone just ahead. Follow the above directions to the trailhead from here.

From Route 206 in Hillsborough, south of Somerville, follow Amwell Road (CR 5214) to Millstone. Turn right (south) onto CR 533, drive 2.1 miles and turn left onto Blackwells Mills Road. Cross the river and canal, and turn right onto Canal Road. The parking area and office are 0.1 mile ahead on the left.

THE TRAIL

Leave the parking area and walk south on Canal Road. The road is narrow—a ditch is to your left and the canal to your right—so pay attention to traffic. In under 0.1 mile the road carries you over Six Mile Run, a substantial brook, which runs under the canal and then out to the Millstone River. Just past the brook you will find the trailhead for the Red Trail, a trail for hikers only, on your left. Here is also a holly tree, its stiff leaves green all year long. The Red Trail follows the south bank of Six Mile Run and is marked with red circular plastic State of NJ trail tags nailed to trees, and flexible trail-use posts. Along the way are several informative signs that describe some of the natural features of the area. The south bank rises perhaps as much as 25 feet above the brook and consequently the trail is normally dry. In contrast, the north side of the brook, which is the route of the return leg of the hike, lies in the floodplain and can be muddy in places, depending on recent weather and the season. The woods along the trail are typical of those of central New Jersey: oaks, beech, and cedar, along with a rich understory of thorned plants, including greenbrier.

After a few minutes of walking, the pathway becomes brighter as the trail passes near the edge of a field. Not much farther ahead the trail dips down into a mostly dry drainage that allows access to the brook itself. Here you can see close up how the brook is cutting into the easily crumbled red-brown Brunswick shale. This rock was derived from ancient highlands and deposited during late Triassic times (roughly 200 million years ago) in floodplains as muddy hematite-stained shales and mudstones. It is thought that the Brunswick Formation, as it is known, is more than a mile thick. Other drainages just ahead allow for more close-up views of the brook and the erosion processes taking place, leaving behind low cliffs of crumbly rock.

After about a half hour of walking, the trail swings away from the brook and begins to follow a grassy lane bordered by a large grove of eastern red cedars. These hardy trees are common in the area and are known for their aromatic oil, berries that are used in making gin, and for the small wooden chests with that distinctive cedar smell, often sold at souvenir shops. The trail leaves the mowed grassy lane temporarily to cross a drainage, but then rejoins it near some black walnut trees. If you look carefully, you may notice a number of animal paths on your left that lead to the brook. Where the mowed trail swings to the right, look for the Red Trail to swing back into the woods and lead down to brook level again. Here is a fairly significant tributary crossing, one that may not be possible in times of high water. Be careful and use your best judgment. From here the trail passes alongside an older stand of cedars that darken the trail considerably. There are some pleasant views in this section overlooking the floodplain below. Just ahead you will arrive at a trail junction marked by a large sign.

At this trail junction, turn sharply left onto the Blue Trail. The Blue Trail leads down to the floodplain, which may be wet. At this location, as Six Mile Run makes an oxbow

Six Mile Run

turn, you will come to a possible crossing of the brook on several large stones. I say "possible" because it may not be possible to cross here at times of very high water! If the water is high, return to the junction and follow the Red Trail back to your car—this section, in itself, is a great hike. However, much of the time you will be able to cross the brook here (wading is a possibility also) and make a loop back to your car by using the Blue Trail and then the Yellow Trail.

Having crossed the brook, follow the path, now designated for both hiking and mountain biking, along the low floodplain, which may be wet or muddy in places. The trail comes up right alongside the brook in one place, but then turns away from it and climbs to a stand of cedars. For the next 0.5 mile or so, the Blue Trail heads north away from Six Mile Run in order to cross one of its tributaries on a small wooden bridge. Following this crossing, the next is at a wet meadow, which actually has some board-walks hidden among the reeds. It seems that bicycle traffic alongside the boards has established a dominant trail, and the lush growth of the floodplain has overwhelmed the boardwalk, at least at the time of this writing.

Once you are out of the floodplain, walk straight ahead up the rise to the edge of a farmed field and turn left. Continue along the edge of this field until it swings to the right, where you will find markings for the Blue Trail. Turn left here. The trail here is open to hikers, bikers, and horseback riders. After crossing another tributary on a wooden bridge, and following the edge of another open field, you'll come to a junction with the Yellow Trail. Turn left onto this trail, which is open to only hikers and bikers. The Yellow Trail immediately reaches Six Mile Run, then turns west following its north bank. As this trail is low, it can be wet and muddy in places. A major tributary is crossed on a high, wide bridge and just

Piedmont

beyond this is a trail junction where a board-walk comes in on the right. Continue straight ahead on the footpath, with views of the low shale cliffs on the other side of the brook. Soon the trail reaches the open floodplain following a grassy path through the reeds and milkweed. Follow the trail as it turns toward the barns, then swings left and right, leading you to the park headquarters and the parking area.

BCS

Coastal Plain

38

Sandy Hook

*Total distance: 4 miles with car shuttle
(8 miles without)*

*Hiking time: 3 hours with car shuttle
(6 hours without)*

Vertical rise: Minimal

Rating: Easy

Maps: USGS Sandy Hook; NPS map

Sandy Hook (Highlands, NJ 07732; 908-872-0115) is the only New Jersey unit in the Gateway National Recreation Area. The area is heavily used, so this hike is not recommended during the summer months, when the parking lots are closed as soon as they are full—sometimes as early as 10 AM. In addition, beach areas may be closed at any time from March 15 through Labor Day to protect nesting shorebirds, such as black skimmers, least terns, and piping plovers. It is impossible to know where these endangered birds will nest but, in accordance with state and federal law, it is forbidden to enter those areas that are posted as closed. Areas are clearly marked in the effort to keep the young from being disturbed. Avoiding the closed area means you must use part of the newly completed paved bicycle path to complete the hike into Fort Hancock—another good reason to hike here out of season. Be aware also that the Gunnison Beach area is a clothing-optional beach.

The Hook is a narrow, sandy spit 7 miles long, extending into the Atlantic Ocean and lower New York Bay. It is a barrier beach—the ocean on one side, a bay on the other. The beaches migrate because of littoral drift: the sand is slowly moved in the same direction as the nearshore current. Every time a wave hits the beach, some sand is picked up; it is redeposited as the wave ebbs. At Sandy Hook, the littoral drift is from south to north, so the beaches at the Hook's northern tip are increasing in size and those to the south are decreasing.

Coastal Plain

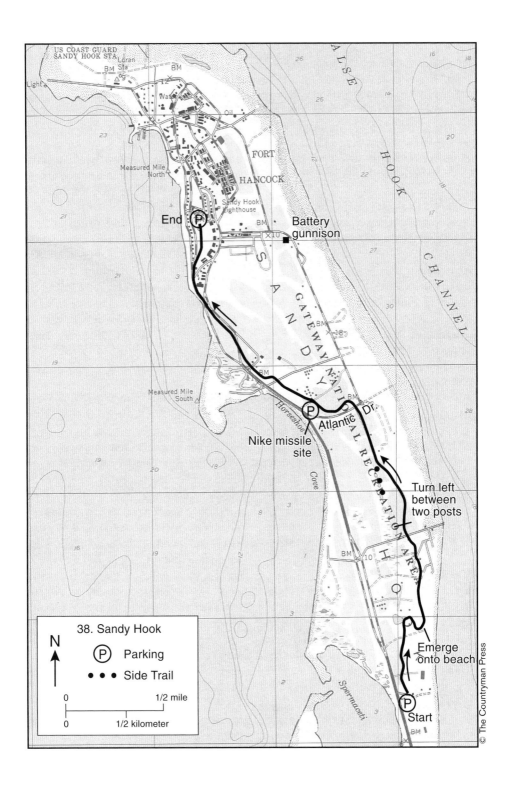

US COAST GUARD
SANDY HOOK STA.

Loran Sta.

BM

Light

Water

Oil

FORT

HANCOCK

Measured Mile
North

Sandy Hook
Lighthouse

End   P

BM

Battery
gunnison

×10

S   A   N   D   Y

G   A   T   E   W   A   Y   N   A   T   I   O   N   A   L   R   E   C   R   E   A   T   I   O   N   A   R   E   A

H   O   O   K

F   A   L   S   E

C   H   A   N   N   E   L

BM

BM

Measured Mile
South

Horseshoe

P

Atlantic Dr.

Nike missile
site

Cove

Turn left
between
two posts

BM   10

H   O

Emerge
onto beach

Spermaceti

P

Start

BM

38. Sandy Hook

N

P   Parking

• • •   Side Trail

0   1/2 mile

0   1/2 kilometer

© The Countryman Press

When the Sandy Hook lighthouse was built in 1764, it stood near the northern end of the spit, but now, as you will see during your walk, it is 1.5 miles south of the tip. There is some concern that Sandy Hook will again become an island, as it has been several times in the past. In addition to the Hook's island history, this sandy spit has twice before been attached to the mainland at Atlantic Highlands.

Sandy Hook is a major bird migration route, and 300 species of birds have been seen in the area, attracted by the wide variety of environments ranging from fresh to salt water and from beach to grassland and forest. Ospreys and great blue herons nest here during the warmer months, and the area has a wintering population of robins. Just north of Spermaceti Cove on the bay side is the oldest known stand of hollies, covering 280 acres. Some of the holly trunks measure 5 inches, indicating 300 years of growth. The area is closed to the public, except for occasional guided tours.

There is a great deal of history associated with Sandy Hook. In 1524, Giovanni da Verrazano (1485–1528) supposedly landed on the spit; Henry Hudson also stopped here early in the 17th century. Some of Captain Kidd's treasure is reputedly buried beneath a great pine tree on the Hook, though his booty remains undiscovered.

HOW TO GET THERE

At Exit 117 off the Garden State Parkway, take NJ 36 east, following signs to the villages of Atlantic Highlands and Highlands, and thence to Sandy Hook, and the visitor center, approximately 2 miles into the spit. There is a beach parking fee from Memorial Day to Labor Day, but again, the low-use months—late fall through early spring—are the preferred months for your visit. The parking fee is for beach use, and for walkers there is no charge, though there may be a parking time limit. Parking fees are halved for holders of the federal Golden Age, Golden Access, or Golden Eagle passes. Alternatively, you can leave a car at one of the northern parking lots for use at the end of the hike. A multi-use pathway was recently constructed, beginning at the park entrance, passing the visitor center, and ending after 5 miles at the Fort Hancock ferry landing adjacent to the Post Chapel. Extensions are planned for the future. The paved path is 12 feet wide with a central double yellow line, and it is recommended that you consider using bicycles for the return trip. Drive to Fort Hancock in the car, leave the locked bicycles, and return in the car to the beginning of the described hike. The ride back after your exploration is delightful and easy, passing ocean views at the beginning, and weaving through shady sections.

THE TRAIL

The visitor center building dates from 1894. Make a stop to look around the museum with its fish tank and slide program, shown on request. The center is housed at Spermaceti Cove, site of one of the first eight lifesaving stations built on the New Jersey coastline to provide rescue services following shipwrecks. One of the worst sea disasters occurred in January 1837. One hundred seventeen people died and whole families were found frozen in the rigging when, within sight of Sandy Hook, the American ship *Mexico,* full of English and Irish immigrants, was unable to sustain its anchorage in a tremendous gale and snowstorm and was swept aground off Long Island. Crews of these stations used the Lyle gun, which fired a rope to a ship in distress; when the rope was established, crew and passengers were pulled ashore. Regular practice sessions were held.

Be sure to stop at the visitor center to obtain brochures for Fort Hancock, the Sandy Hook Multi-Use Pathway, and the glossy National Park Service pamphlet about Sandy Hook, because these all contain useful maps. The Old Dune Trail handout is also useful in explaining the numbered stops as you walk, but this pamphlet must be returned at the end of your exploration for the use of future visitors. Signs at the visitor center indicate a two-hour parking limit, but permission can be obtained from an attendant inside to stay longer, provided you explain that you are planning to hike. Enquire about the location of the no-charge parking areas should they require you to move the car from the visitor center. Bear in mind that this hike is an out-and-back, giving you the option to turn around at any time to retrace your footsteps to the visitor center.

Find the trailhead, toward the bay side of Sandy Hook in the parking lot near the handicapped parking places. Study the guide, and stop at the numbered signs to read and learn about the area. The Old Dune Trail is only 1 mile in length and ends within sight of the visitor center.

As you walk, bear in mind that this area is under constant bombardment by salt and wind; plants have adapted to the harsh environment, but the area can still be easily destroyed by careless walking across the dunes. Please remain on the marked trail.

In season you will find many wildflowers here—apple blossom, honeysuckle, wild strawberry, and rhodora. In the open area, beach heather and prickly pear eke out a precarious existence. To discourage competition for scarce resources, the roots of these two plants secrete a poison that inhibits the growth of neighboring plants. That this strategy is successful is apparent by the concentrations of beach heather. Another botanical oddity to be found on Sandy Hook is an import called dusty miller, with furry leaves that catch dew on their velvety surfaces. A program is in place to eradicate the nonnative invasive plants, which change the local ecosystem. The Old Dune Trail passes a parking lot on the right and then crosses an entry road to that parking lot, then the paved bike trail, and bends right toward a service station.

Some magnificent specimens of holly grow in this section. Shortly, the trail becomes wider, and the increased breeze may tell you that you are walking toward the ocean. The trail snakes through the dunes to an area where trees left as upright skeletons testify to the damage caused by salty winds. After about five minutes the trail comes to a stop at a wide sandy crossroads with a signboard explaining soil conditions and the types of trees seen around you, and then continues to reach a wooden viewing stand on the left. Climb the small flight of wooden stairs for an unusual sight of a freshwater pond surrounded by a salty area. It is possible to get closer to the pond, supported on the left by a man-made stone wall, by walking for a few yards through tall phragmites down to the water's edge. Look closely along the shore, for a blue heron may be there. Some depressions occur in the midst of this salty area that access the freshwater table and create freshwater oases. Swamp rose mallow is a native plant that thrives here due to the fresh water.

Shortly after you leave the tranquil freshwater pond with its teeming wildlife, you will reach the remains of a Nike missile site, placed here to guard New York City against air attack—the missiles could intercept and destroy aircraft long before they could pose much of a threat. Concepts of defense changed, however, and the missiles were removed in 1974. At the end of that year, the military installation at Sandy Hook, Fort

Sandy Hook Light

Hancock, was officially decommissioned. The site is now protected by a chain-link fence, and garbage is the only thing to be seen behind the fence. The trail turns right, then immediately left to skirt the Nike site, becomes more open, and leads onto the beach. Walking the Old Dune Trail will probably take about 30 minutes longer if you linger at the numbered sites.

Once out on the beach, stay close to the dunes and look for the entry to the South Beach Dune Trail, marked with a white dot on a wooden post. This entrance can be found just beyond a broken-down wooden paling fence, approximately 0.3 mile from where you emerged onto the beach from the Old Dune Trail. (Ignore the break in the dunes leading to a gate and a wooden post that can be seen soon after you begin the beach walk.) Wend your way over the ridge

of the dunes on the left and begin walking inland on the distinct sandy trail. The path bears right, and then turns left within a couple of minutes between two hiker signs. The arrows on the signs are a little confusing, but the path straight ahead is the wrong one—so be sure to turn left. Within another few minutes herd paths join from both sides, but hiker signs indicate the correct route.

Should you fail to find this section of the South Beach Dune Trail, continue along the beach from the Old Dune Trail until you reach fishermen's parking area F. There is a portable toilet here, and the parking lot is very small and full most weekends. Turn left down paved Atlantic Drive until you arrive at the trail sign on the right just before a 35 mph road sign, indicating that the South Beach Dune Trail is 1.1 miles long.

Coastal Plain

After crossing the paved road to the fishermen's parking area, the trail continues northward at quite some distance from the shore. The trees are taller and include oak and cedar as well as holly. Herd paths enter from both sides, but the main trail is wide and frequently marked. Toward its end the trail passes a marsh—where you can see signs of the range-finding units that were once established here—and emerges onto paved Atlantic Drive between two metal posts connected by wire.

Turn right and reenter the signed South Beach Dune Trail on the right just before a 35 mph road sign and continue, to emerge onto the bike trail adjacent to parking area L, and the Nike missile radar site. Continue north on the bike path until the Sandy Hook lighthouse is visible on the right. Turn toward it to begin your exploration of the Fort Hancock area.

Exploring Fort Hancock can take considerable time, but the fort holds great interest for history lovers. Established in the 1890s, its buildings now mostly stand empty and deteriorating, but there are plans for its rehabilitation. Close to the lighthouse is a mortar battery open to visitors. Several mortars occupied a single pit here and were designed to fire simultaneously, lobbing 12-inch, 800-pound shells in high arcs to penetrate ships' lightly armored decks. However, these masonry forts proved to be no match for the new-style battleships, and the forts were abandoned in favor of individual gun batteries that were more easily concealed.

Visits to the lighthouse, the museum, and other buildings are offered at times posted in the glossy Sandy Hook brochure, and on a one-page handout listing visitor programs.

Concession stands are available at Battery Gunnison. Further north, Battery Peck's viewing stand offers great views of the Verrazano Narrows Bridge and Brooklyn.

Sandy Hook is the oldest operating lighthouse in the United States. The white octagonal tower was often the first beacon seen by travelers arriving in New York, because until 1907 the Sandy Hook channel was the only sea passageway for large ships to enter New York Harbor. Built in 1764, the lighthouse was one of 12 established by the original American colonies. It was occupied for a short time by British troops during the American Revolution and was fought over by British and rebel soldiers. The tower, visible 19 miles at sea, is 103 feet tall and still in use, though now unmanned and automatic.

Battery Gunnison was erected in 1904. Its 6-inch guns were intended to track and destroy small warships too speedy for Fort Hancock's huge coastal artillery. There are two separate gun emplacements, accessible by two small flights of cement stairs, and you also get an improved view of the ocean from this small elevation.

Search out the Rodman Gun close to the bay. After a large gun burst near Lieutenant Thomas Jefferson Rodman in 1844, he committed himself to improving the technology of cannon manufacture and invented the casting process that made possible this one-piece, smooth-bore barrel. At the end of your exploration, your route will depend on the choice you made at the beginning of the day: return on foot to the visitor center, use the second car previously placed at Fort Hancock, or pick up the bicycles and enjoy the trip back.

SJG

39

Cheesequake State Park

Total distance: 4 miles

Hiking time: 2 hours

Vertical rise: Approximately 200 feet

Rating: Easy to moderate

Maps: USGS South Amboy; DEP Cheesequake State Park map

Located in the transition zone between New Jersey's distinctive northern and southern plant communities, 1,361-acre Cheesequake State Park (Matawan, NJ 07747; 732-566-2161) may be of particular appeal to those interested in botany. There are a variety of habitats throughout the park, including salt- and freshwater marshes, northeastern hardwood forests, Pine Barrens, and a cedar swamp. Cheesequake is one of the oldest state parks in New Jersey, dating back to 1937 when acquisition of some farms, orchards, and salt marsh began. It was formally opened in 1940. Family camping is available April 1 through October 31.

The area was occupied as early as 5,000 years ago by Native Americans who hunted and fished here. The name Cheesequake was taken from a word in the language of the Lenni-Lenape tribe, which lived in New Jersey when the Dutch and English colonists first arrived. Some say the word means "upland people." During the 18th and 19th centuries, a fine-quality clay used to make stoneware pottery was mined in the area and shipped to pottery-making sites up and down the Atlantic Coast. Red clay was also mined to make bricks that some say were used extensively in the building of New York City. As late as the early 20th century, a steamboat dock existed on Cheesequake Creek, at the end of Old Dock Road; there, products and produce were sent to markets.

There are several marked trails in the park (mostly footpaths) that are color coded. The recently improved markers in

the shape of arrows will keep you on the trail and off the numerous unmarked side trails (also mostly footpaths) that could be misleading. This hike will use three of the parks four trails marked, especially the green trail, which begins after you walk a section of the red and yellow trails. The footpaths, and in some cases the sand roads, that the trail follows are soft and bouncy in places, covered by pine needles. There are many wet sections that have been covered by boardwalks or bridges; in a few places are rough stairs made of railroad ties.

Rugged footwear is not required. Mountain bikes are not allowed (there is a special multiuse trail marked for them in another section of the park), but evidence of their trespass is widespread. Because of the proximity to swamps and marshes, it may be best to visit the park during the fall when both insect and human populations are at their lowest.

HOW TO GET THERE

From the Garden State Parkway, take exit 120 and turn right (east) at the end of the ramp following the brown STATE PARK signs. Turn right at the first traffic light onto Cheesequake–Morristown Road. Turn right again at next light onto Gordon Road, which in 1 mile will take you to the park entrance. Pass the Visitor Contact Station (park office) and drive to the parking area on the left, about 0.2 mile ahead. A directory and map of the trails, as well as a fountain, are found here at the trailhead. A parking fee of $5 daily, $10 weekends is in effect from Memorial Day through Labor Day. There is no charge during the rest of the year.

THE TRAIL

Begin your hike at the trailhead, just to the left of the directory. At the first fork, just a few hundred feet from the trailhead, turn right onto the yellow trail and follow it to the Hooks Creek Lake. This section of the trail is noted for the many lady's slipper orchids that grow alongside the path. Follow the trail along the south shore of the lake and then descend the wooden stairs from the high area that overlooks the lake. At the base of the stairs, turn left and follow the trail back through an area that borders a freshwater floodplain. The trail then heads back to a junction with the red, green, and blue trails. From this junction, follow the red/green/blue trails across a small brook on a wooden bridge, the first of many. Pass (or visit) the Cheesequake State Park Interpretive Center. One of the last major developments in the park was the building of this center. In it are exhibits illustrating the natural and cultural history of the park. You'll find a turtle display with live turtles in a tank, a model of a Lenni-Lenape village, both fresh- and saltwater aquariums, and rest rooms.

Continue on the red/green/blue trails through some sweet pepperbush, perhaps the most common plant along the trail. Pepperbush is related to mountain laurel and blueberry, also common in the park. During the spring, wild honeysuckle is in bloom here and in other sections of the trail. After leveling off, the trail passes a protected wet area on the right filled with tall ferns. Ahead is a view through the trees to the salt marsh below. The trail, still primarily marked with red, bears to the left here and heads downhill, crossing a muddy area. After crossing a few bridges, arrive at the base of an incline on which wooden steps have been attached. At the top of the rise, the blue trail turns to the right, and the red and green trails continue to the left.

Bear left at the junction, and continue on the red/green trail as it passes through a large stand of lowbush and highbush blueberries among some large pines (more typical of the Pine Barrens of southern New Jersey) mixed with the usual hardwoods. In this dry section are some large clusters of mountain laurel that bloom in June. After crossing a large bridge over a small brook, the trail comes out to a sand road (Perrine's Road) near a bench. It is here that the green trail splits from the red trail. Turn right, not onto the sand road but onto the green trail to the right of the bench.

Along this level section are many small sassafras trees, as well as some chokecherry, beech, maple, chestnut oak, and white oak. Through the trees on the right, you can see the now-closed Sayreville landfill about 2 miles away. Head downhill. At the bottom of the drop, the trail passes close to the tall sedges, rushes, and grasses of the saltwater marsh, which forms the western boundary of the park. After a short climb, proceed down a slope to a long boardwalk running over a freshwater swamp, heavily overgrown with arrowwood, elderberry, and buttonbush. In the middle of the walkway are two benches surrounding a red maple. This quiet area, rich in plant and animal life, is a change from the woods and brush environments traversed so far.

At the end of the boardwalk, bear right at an unmarked junction, passing a bench, and out to another boardwalk, this one in a cedar swamp. Here is an even cooler and darker environment than the freshwater swamp of a few minutes ago. The eastern white cedars—which grow out of black clay—dominate, shutting out light for other plants. The extreme moisture and the decomposing leaves make the soil very acidic, preserving any cedar logs that become buried. In some similar areas of New Jersey, old cedar logs in good condition have been mined from the dense acidic soil. Great horned owls are known to frequent this swamp.

After leaving the swamp, keep to the right and follow the trail carefully through a muddy area. Come out to another sand road (Museum Road), which the trail crosses, and enter a woods dominated by huge white pines. Because of their height and straightness, these trees were used by shipbuilders during colonial times—particularly during the Revolution—for masts. Overharvesting of the original white pines eventually forced the lumbering industry out of the state. These trees are estimated to be between 100 and 150 years old and are used as nesting sites by owls and hawks. The trail through this section is narrow and crowded in by pepperbush, mountain laurel, and rhododendron.

After climbing an interesting ladder/stairway on the trail, you will reach the highest elevation on the hike. The woods are dry here and composed mostly of oak, which provides food for the gypsy moth that has left evidence of its appetite in the form of standing dead trees. On the floor of the forest are large quantities of false Solomon's seal. At the junction, the trail bears to the left, leading to a stand of pitch pines typical of the Pine Barrens of south Jersey. Pitch pine grows in dry, sandy soil as well as on rocky outcrops as it does in northern Jersey, and can survive with few nutrients.

From this high area, the trail gradually descends. The trail, which skirts the southern boundary of the park (houses visible), is sandy here as it passes through a forest of hardwoods. After coming close to, but not touching, Museum Road, the trail continues along a path through a forest floor with numerous wildflowers such as the wild lily of the valley and the pink lady's slipper, both of which bloom in the spring. You can find violets, starflowers, and jack-in-the-pulpits here as well. Only plants that can tolerate frequent inundations survive here. Farther along the trail swings around a small, stagnant pond that attracts wildlife. More boardwalk, built by Boy Scouts, keeps you dry and clean in this section of black mud, clear brooks, and wet swamps. After a rise, the trail comes again to Perrine's Road.

Turn left onto the road, following green markers past Gordon Field, a camping area used by the scouts. Just ahead the trail, now joined by the red trail, turns to the right and reenters the woods. There are many unmarked side trails in this section that head off to the left. Stay on the main trail, which follows the edge of the cleared area, until markers indicate a left turn leading downhill and onto Museum Road. Bear right here and follow the road, which in 0.2 mile leads to the trailhead and your car.

BCS

40

Hartshorne Woods Park

Total distance: 2.5 miles

Hiking time: 1.5 hours

Vertical rise: 160 feet

Rating: Easy to moderate

Maps: USGS Sandy Hook; Monmouth County Park System Hartshorne Woods Park trail guide

Hartshorne Woods Park (Monmouth County Park System, Navesink Avenue, Middletown, NJ, 732-872-0336 or 2670, www.monmouthcountyparks.com/parks/hartshorne.asp) contains 15 miles of marked and unmarked trails. The area, portions of which rise 245 feet above the Navesink River Bay, is surprisingly hilly for central New Jersey. The forest totally covers the 741 acres of the park and is primarily dry, upland, deciduous, and composed of oak, hickory, beech, and maple; however, the many ups and downs of the park's trails lead you through a variety of very healthy plant communities.

Hartshorne Woods was named for its original owner, Richard Hartshorne, who purchased the tract from Native Americans in the 1670s. Some of his descendants still live on part of the original family tract. The local pronunciation of Hartshorne is "harts horn," or horn of the hart, an old English word for deer.

As you will notice from the directory or map, there are several color-coded marked trails in the park. This hike uses the Laurel Ridge Trail, a loop trail that explores the Buttermilk Valley section of Hartshorne Woods. Be warned that most trails here are multi-use—expect mountain bikes.

In the late 1980s, Hartshorne Woods, formerly a relatively quiet woods for walkers, became extremely popular with mountain bikers (due in part to the closing of parks in nearby counties to bicycles). Trails in Hartshorne Woods quickly became de-

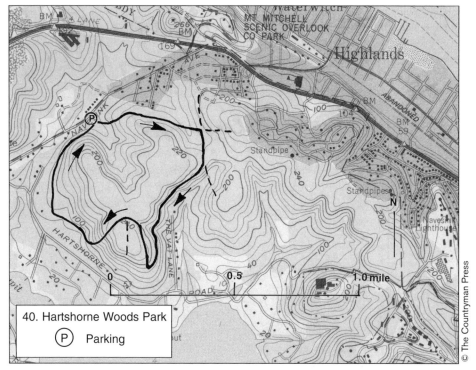

40. Hartshorne Woods Park

Ⓟ Parking

graded, forcing the Monmouth County Park Commission to find a solution to this problem. They launched a major trail rebuilding project and decided to go mostly multiuse—unlike other county and state agencies, which have chosen to keep bikers and hikers on separate trails where possible.

In 1991 the multiuse trail plan was devised and implemented with the help of some 40 volunteers. Worn and abused trails were covered and blocked with snow fence. New trails were cut and stabilized. Junctions were posted with signs and trails were color coded and labeled for differing degrees of difficulty. As with ski trails, a circle indicates an easy trail; a square one of moderate difficulty; and a diamond a challenging trail. A golden rule of this new trail system is posted and printed on the maps. It's shown in the form of a triangular logo

with symbols of a bike, a hiker, and a horse. Arrows between each symbol show who yields to whom—bikers to hikers, and both bikers and hikers to horses. When I was last here it worked most of the time.

Hartshorne Woods Park is divided into three sections: Buttermilk Valley, Monmouth Hills, and Rocky Point. Trails connect all three sections and hikers desiring a longer walk should consult a trail map. However, mountain bikes will be encountered on the trails. The hike described below is easy to follow and avoids areas more frequented by mountain bikes. You may wish to explore the Monmouth Hills section of the park on your own, perhaps during the week when usage is low. If you wish to avoid bikes entirely, two very short trails for foot traffic only begin at the main trailhead: 1.5-mile Candlestick Trail and 1.1-mile Kings Hollow Trail.

HOW TO GET THERE

From eastbound NJ 36 in Atlantic Highlands, follow signs to SCENIC ROAD, a right turn off the highway. Take Navesink Avenue 0.5 mile to the large Buttermilk Valley Trailhead and Parking Lot on the left side of the road. A directory (which includes a large topographical map showing contours at 10-foot intervals) and a box of free hiking maps are located in the woods about 20 yards from the parking area. State Highway 35 to Navesink River Road and continue 4.7 miles. Turn right onto Locust Road. Cross Clay Pit Creek bridge to five-way intersection. Bear right onto Navesink Ave and continue to park.

THE TRAIL

From the directory turn left onto the Laurel Ridge Trail, which is marked with blue blazes. This section of the trail is a wide and sandy service road that begins a gradual climb. Keep to the right at the first junction, then turn right onto Grand Tour Trail at the junction. A trail sign is posted here.

The Laurel Ridge Trail and the Grand Tour Trail are concurrent. Still following blue markers, follow the path along the side of a slope through thickets of mountain laurel, an evergreen shrub. It is for this plant, abundant throughout the hike, that the trail is named. The trail meanders up and down as it swings around the slope passing a few holly trees, also green throughout the year. In a thickly vegetated section look for greenbrier, a vinelike plant with a green, smooth, and thorny stem. In this vicinity are also a few monster-size hickory and tulip trees. Smaller sassafras trees are scattered about, and in the understory are jack-in-the-pulpits.

Stay on the Laurel Ridge Trail as it climbs gradually, moving deeper into the flat summit of an elevated peninsula of land. You'll notice chunks of conglomerate rock (sand fused with pebbles) along the trail here and for the next 0.5 mile. This resistant rock has acted as a protective cap over softer sediments, creating highlands among sea-level plains. Another change you may note is in the vegetation itself. Oaks are now the predominant tree. As you climb higher up the slope, a view of water appears to your left, particularly when the leaves are off the trees. This is the Navesink River. Ahead, the trail winds back on itself and continues climbing, eventually reaching a junction with the path to the Claypit Creek overlook, the highest point on the hike (elevation 248 feet). Turn left onto this path and walk about 200 yards to the fenced overlook. From here is a view (somewhat obstructed in summer) of the Navesink River and bridge. This area makes a good rest stop. Return to the junction when you are ready to continue the hike.

Turn left at the junction and follow the blue markers down the other side of the hill. The descent is over soft dirt that in places may be torn up from mountain bike usage. The frequent passing of hikers or bikers seems to have no effect on the squirrel population in this section, though, and the abundance of oaks makes this a perfect place for these animals to harvest the year's acorn crop. If you are lucky, you may spot a deer or two.

As the Laurel Ridge Trail progresses around the hill, the trail bed widens. It passes through more patches of mountain laurel on the slope, then gradually descends to the directory. Just a few feet away is the parking area.

BCS

41

Allaire State Park

Total distance: 4.5 miles

Hiking time: 2.5 hours

Vertical rise: 120 feet

Rating: Easy to moderate

Maps: USGS Farmingdale, Asbury Park; DEP Allaire State Park map

Allaire State Park (PO Box 220, Farmingdale, NJ 07727; (732-938-2371) was a gift in 1941 to the people of New Jersey from Arthur Brisbane, a prominent newspaper man. The original 1,000-plus acres has now expanded to more than 3,000 and includes a stream, narrow-gauge railroad, golf course, car camping area, and an entire historical village dating from the boom days of the bog iron industry in the last two centuries. The park, located in one of the northernmost sections of the Pine Barrens, straddles the Manasquan River, which is popular with canoeists. The recent completion of I-195, which bisects the park, pollutes the park with sound, denying it the isolation it once had. On the other hand, the interstate also makes the park more accessible to the public.

Within Allaire's boundaries are a large number of sand and gravel roads and an abandoned railroad bed that are used for hiking, biking, and horseback riding. These trails are marked with colored tags and directional arrows. Because the park is essentially quartered by the river and the freeway, a complete tour is not possible, and we have chosen a route that takes you through some wooded areas as well as the park's main attraction, historic Allaire Village.

HOW TO GET THERE

Take Exit 31B off I-95 and head east on County Route 524. The park is well marked with signs, and you should have no problem finding the main entrance. A map can be obtained in the same office where campers

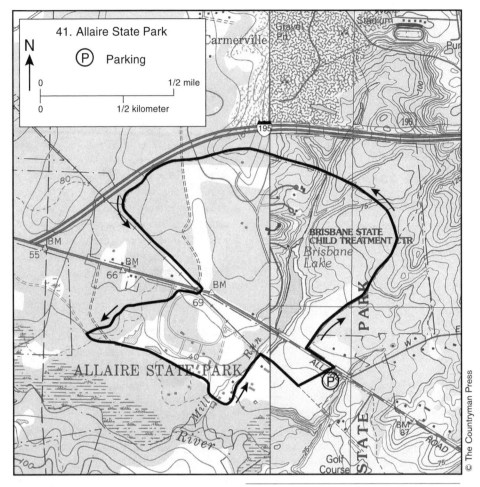

register. The park is also accessible from the Garden State Parkway, Exit 98; just follow the brown state park signs. This hike begins at an unmarked parking area on state land, 0.6 miles beyond (east of) the main entrance. If you are coming from the Garden State Parkway, this area is just after the entrance for the Spring Meadow Golf Course. (The main park entry is 0.6 miles farther down the road.) By parking here you avoid both the fees and the crowds of people who visit the park only to see the historic village. Most of the hike is on sandy trails. Sneakers as well as boots are fine here.

THE TRAIL

Cross the road and head west, back toward the main entrance. You'll be walking past a small horse ranch with a split-rail fence. At the end of the fence, look for a gate leading into a field. Just to the right of the gate is a post that marks the entrance to a lane running between the ranch and a field. Your route, occasionally marked with orange plastic disks, may be overgrown for the first 100 yards or so, but it soon widens and becomes more comfortable for walking. The lane—which is very straight because it is the border of a farmed field—is shadowed by tall sumac trees and vines. There are also a few patches of holly along the trail. As you leave the highway and the sound of traffic, the sounds of birds, plentiful in this area of field and woods, are heard.

After about 10 minutes, enter a typical south Jersey forest. The pathway widens into a sand and gravel road common to the Pine Barrens, and the walking becomes very pleasant. Ferns and blueberry bushes form the ground cover, and huge clusters of mountain laurel rise up from the forest floor. At first some oaks and maples appear; farther along come sassafras and the inevitable pitch pines. When the road comes to a fork, keep left.

This trail (or, more accurately, sand road) forms a large horseshoe, eventually returning to the county road you started on, though a little farther west. As it swings left and west, it parallels I-195 (always busy with cars heading to and from the Jersey Shore) for about 0.5 mile. In this section is a short uphill climb to a gravel quarry and water tower, and then a long downhill when the trail comes within sight of the interstate. Stay on the main road/trail, now quite wide, which eventually swings away from the noisy highway and heads south toward the main park entrance and a quieter environment. The sounds of birds once again become more prominent. A wood thrush or two may resent your intrusion into its territory. In this section the trail parallels the bed of the former Freehold–Jamesburg Railroad, used in other sections of the park as a hiking and horse trail.

The trail will bring you to the main road at a gate similar to the one at the beginning of the hike. Cross the road here, bearing a little to the left, and follow the narrow-gauge railroad tracks to the right toward where they enter the woods. Look for the occasional orange trail markings and follow the

parallel path—not the tracks—into the woods. After only a few yards, cross the park entrance road and reenter the woods, still on the trail. The route next crosses a dirt maintenance road, zigs left and then quickly right (at a NO HORSES BEYOND THIS POINT sign), across another bridle path, and eventually comes to a T-intersection with a gravel road. Bear left here, cross a creek, and make a sharp left on a gravel road known in the park as a Raceway.

Follow the Raceway (at first marked both green and red) straight ahead, keeping the water to your left. After a short distance you should see a wooden bridge on your left. This bridge leads to the park nature center, which has some interesting displays and an accurate wall map of all the sand roads and trails in the park.

From the bridge, continue along the Raceway past the pond and through a large picnic area. This is the developed section of the park, and you should expect to see many people here, especially on summer weekends. After passing the large parking lot on the left, enter historic Allaire Village. Back in the 18th century, this village site was known as Monmouth Furnace and later as the Howell Works, after the first iron maker here. He leased the property to James P. Allaire of New York in 1822, who was already very much established as a brass worker. At the Howell Works, Allaire put together a community of more than 400 people to turn bog iron into pots, kettles, cauldrons, stovepipe, and other common items. The self-contained community included a wide variety of craftspeople to both run the industry and serve the population.

Bog iron, found in the Pine Barrens, is smelted from iron oxides leached from the sand and deposited in accumulations of decaying swamp vegetation. Interestingly, bog iron is a renewable resource as long as the vegetation decay cycle is not interfered with. The operation at Allaire's village prospered until around 1850, when competition from products made of higher-grade iron ore lowered profits. After its abandonment, the Allaire community was used for a time by the Boy Scouts as a headquarters; in 1941, it was deeded to the state. Today, the village of Allaire is remarkably well preserved and nearly intact from its heyday in the middle of the 19th century.

The visitor center, a long brick building, is on your left and offers a number of interesting displays about the park and the village. A map and guide to the village can be obtained here. A seasonal food concession is located in this area also. From here, continue straight ahead to the end of the visitor center, make a right, and follow the main road that heads downhill to the left and out to the main buildings of the village. Follow this main road as it swings to the left and heads north, eventually leaving the village area through a gate.

Follow the gravel road (which ultimately leads to CR 524) away from the village. To avoid walking back to your car on CR 524, turn right on a wide, grassy pathway that crosses the lane. This is actually an abandoned Freehold–Jamesburg Railroad bed. Be alert, because after only a few minutes, you'll find a narrow unmarked trail coming in on the left that will lead you through a field to the parking area and your car. This trail, which skirts a swampy area, may occasionally be too muddy to walk. If so, retrace your steps along the old railbed and walk out to CR 524. Turn right back to your car.

HNZ

42

Cattus Island

Total distance: 3 miles

Hiking time: 1.5–2 hours

Vertical rise: Minimal

Rating: Easy

*Maps: USGS Toms River/Seaside Park;
Cattus Island Ocean County Park
trail map*

Cattus Island County Park (1170 Cattus Island Boulevard, Toms River, NJ 08753; 732-270-6960; www.ocean.nj.us/parks/infopage.htm) preserves a small portion of the salt marshes and pine forests on Barnegat Bay. Located in the midst of New Jersey's most popular summer vacation area, which has been extensively developed, Cattus Island offers the hiker a variety of natural environments to explore, including pinelands, open marshes, holly forests, and bay beaches. The excellent views over vast marshes, across inlets, and out over the bay, plus the variety of wildlife found in the park, are further reasons to walk the trails in this 500-acre Ocean County park. Be advised that wood and deer ticks are found on the island. Take the usual precautions: Tuck pants into socks, spray with tick repellent, and check for ticks after the hike. Staying on the trails is also very important.

Cattus Island was first settled by the Page family, who moved here in 1763. Timothy Page, born on the island during that year, served in the local militia during the American Revolution. Most probably he was a privateer, essentially a pirate licensed by the Continental Congress. During the war, British ships were lured into Barnegat Bay through Cranberry Inlet only to be attacked and their cargoes sold for profit. Cranberry Inlet, an opening to the Atlantic near present-day Ortley Beach, existed between 1750 and 1812. It was opened and closed by strong storms.

After the death of Timothy Page, the family house burned down, and the property was sold to Lewis Applegate. He moved

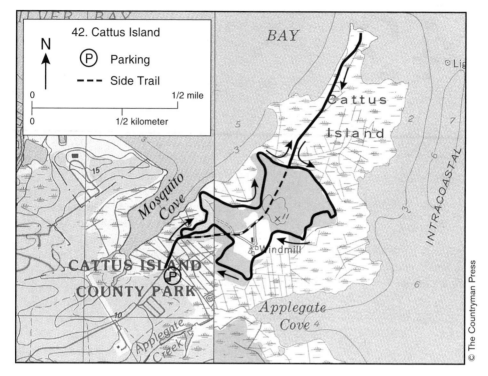

there in 1842 and developed the south-eastern section of the island, now named for him. He built a sawmill and a port for lumber boats. The island was sold again in 1867 and was slated to be developed as a resort, but the 1873 depression canceled the project.

In 1895 the island was purchased by John V. A. Cattus, an importer and Olympic-class athlete. He used the island and its buildings for weekend vacations, not as a full-time residence. Cattus loved boating, owned many boats, and built a hunting lodge on the island. After he died, the land was sold in 1964 by his sons to developers. New state laws passed in the early 1970s that limited development in wetlands and along the coast discouraged the developers, and they sold the land to Ocean County in 1973. The property was acquired with county tax dol-

lars and state Green Acres funds. In 1976 the park opened to the public, and the following year trail development began.

Before beginning the hike, follow the asphalt path to the nature center. Sign in, take a look around, and pick up a map of the park that shows both trails and terrain. The nature center has a number of displays and maps that pertain to Ocean County. The center is staffed by naturalists and a large number of volunteers, both young and old.

HOW TO GET THERE

From the Garden State Parkway exit 82 (Toms River/NJ 37), take NJ 37 east 4.4 miles to Fisher Boulevard. Travel north on Fisher Boulevard for exactly 2 miles and turn right onto Cattus Island Boulevard (just after the Bellcrest shopping plaza). The park entrance road is 0.1 mile ahead on the left.

Cattus Island

Another 0.5 mile will bring you to the large parking area near the Cooper Environmental Center.

THE TRAIL

After a visit to the center, walk around it past the directory and bear to the right. Pass through a wooden gate and onto a sand road marked sporadically with white. This road, more like a causeway, penetrates the salt marsh that surrounds the slightly higher and drier land ahead. Cattus Island is not an island in the true sense, but if it weren't for this road, access would be very difficult. The body of water to the left is Mosquito Cove. The sand road leads straight ahead into the woods and eventually out to the tip of the island, which extends well into Barnegat Bay. Our hike utilizes this sand road and footpaths on either side of it.

Make a left turn onto a blue-blazed footpath, called the Island Loop, just after leaving the marsh. This path winds through a pine forest, makes a small loop out to the shoreline, then swings out again to the grassy shore of Mosquito Cove at the old Boathouse Landing. Here, rising from the water, are the last remains of the old boathouse and a dock.

Leave the dock area and continue following markers through a forest of oak, pines, and enormous thickets of greenbrier. The walking through this aromatic woods is very pleasant. Pass near the gnarled trunk of an old cedar and enter a holly forest, green in all seasons. Notice that the red berries do not occur on all the holly trees—only the female trees bear fruit. These bright red berries are found on the tree year-round and the bird population is well supplied with food. Not far ahead, the trail meets the yellow Cedar Line Short Cut Trail. A right turn here leads immediately to the sand road again. Turn left on the sand road, heading northeast.

Walk the white-blazed sand road causeway, bordered by salt marsh on the right and wet lowland forest on the left. Here are stands of pitch pine, and also those of red cedar, and other plants capable of living in this moist environment. Towering over the marsh to the right is an osprey nesting site. Other water birds, such as the great egret, may be feeding in this area. After 10 to 15 minutes of walking, the road ends at the narrow, sandy beach that forms the northern tip of Cattus Island. You may wish to walk along this narrow strip of sand to the final point of the island. After this short exploration, return to the sand road and retrace your steps to the junction with the yellow Cedar Line Short Cut Trail. Bear left here.

The yellow trail again penetrates the drier woods of Cattus Island. It winds through a forest of holly and some rather large oaks. You will pass two large, twisted, gnarled, and quite dead cedar trees on the right. Deer are plentiful in this area, their footprints in the sand a common sight. After penetrating a dense pine forest, you will reach an extensive vista of black, muddy salt marsh, sliced by drainage ditches, and the forest beyond. From this vista, the trail swings to the right and ends at a junction with the blue-marked Island Loop Trail.

Follow the blue markers straight ahead (do not turn left) to an open area lined with bayberry bushes. The large clearing and the park benches under tall cedars mark the site where the island's former residents lived. From the clearing, follow blue markers back into the woods on a curving forest road. The trail makes a series of tight turns through holly trees, only to reemerge near the edge of the salt marsh. From here you will see Applegate Cove on the left and, to the right, the Cooper Environmental Center. After many small turns, the trail emerges onto the sand road again. Make a left here, walk down the straight lane through the marsh, and journey back to the nature center and parking area.

BCS

43

Island Beach State Park

Total distance: 3.5 miles

Hiking time: 2.5 hours

Vertical rise: Minimal

Rating: Easy

Maps: USGS Barnegat Light; DEP Island Beach State Park map

Along the 127-mile boundary between New Jersey and the Atlantic Ocean are a number of long, thin barrier islands. Separated from the mainland by large bays, these islands are part of a chain that runs from New England to the Gulf Coast of Mexico. The constant movement of sand pushed by the ocean waves, called littoral drift, both maintains and changes these relatively fragile land forms. Severe storms often open or close inlets, wash out beaches, and even extend barrier islands, creating new land. With the exception of Island Beach State Park (PO Box 37, Seaside Park, NJ 08752; 732-793-0506, http://www.state.nj.us/dep/parksandforests/parks/island.html), most of these islands have been developed with row after row of summer beach homes, boardwalks, and restaurants. If it were not for this park, many New Jerseyites would have no idea of what the shoreline in its natural state would look like.

Island Beach State Park occupies the southern end of a long spit that is joined to the mainland near Point Pleasant. This section of the spit was an island at one time; an inlet connecting the ocean and Barnegat Bay was once located near present-day Ortley Beach. This inlet, known as Cranberry Inlet, was created and destroyed overnight by storms in 1750 and 1812. More recently, in 1935, a storm opened up an inlet just south of the present park entrance. Local rum runners wanted it to remain open, but the owners of the tract at the time had it closed.

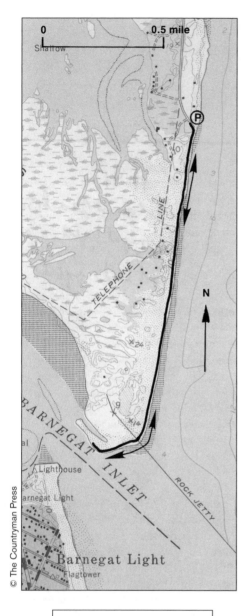

0   0.5 mile

Shallow

N

BARNEGAT INLET

TELEPHONE LINE

Lighthouse

Barnegat Light

arnegat Light

ROCK JETTY

Barnegat Light

Flagtower

© The Countryman Press

43. Island Beach State Park

Ⓟ   Parking

Originally, Island Beach was owned by Lord Stirling, owner of vast acreages in New Jersey during the 17th century. During this period, the island was called Lord Stirling's Isle. Not much happened here during the next 100 years. These beaches were remote from industrial areas and were occupied only by squatters who lived in part from materials washed ashore. In 1926 Henry Phipps purchased the island with a shore resort in mind. He was able to build three large homes (one of which, mentioned earlier, is used by the governor of New Jersey as a summer residence) before his project was halted by the stock market crash and Depression. During World War II, Island Beach was used by the army for rocket experiments and, as such, was restricted to the public. The squatters and leaseholders who lived on the island were forced to leave, though they were allowed to return after the war. In 1953, after much talk about preserving the area, the state purchased the land from the Phipps estate and opened the park in 1959. The island residents who held leases were allowed to live there as long as they were alive.

The 3,002 acres of the park are divided into three sections, the northernmost and southernmost being natural areas, the central section public beaches and concessions. Located 1.2 miles south of the entrance are the park office and a nature center. A short, circular, self-guiding nature trail, which begins at the Aeolium (the nature center) is a good introduction to the park's vegetation. Farther ahead on the left is one of the original homes built in the 1920s as part of a planned development; it's now used as a summer residence for New Jersey's governor. Beyond this house are the two large beach areas with their huge parking lots.

Island Beach dunes

HOW TO GET THERE

From exit 82 on the Garden State Parkway, take NJ 37 east through Toms River and over the Barnegat Bay Bridge. The entrance to the park is 2.5 miles south of the bridge at the southern end of NJ 35. There are many signs directing you to the park along the way. You will find that a fee is charged at the entrance gate. In 2005 this was $6 weekdays or $10 weekends from Memorial Day through Labor Day; $5 daily the rest of the year. You should also know that although a large number of parking spaces are spread along the 8-mile road in the park, they often fill up quickly during peak season, and late arrivals are turned away at the gate. In fact, use of the area is so high that computer signs on the Garden State Parkway advise of the park's opening or closing. The best time to explore Island Beach State Park on foot is definitely during the off-season, especially during the week.

To begin the hike, drive the full 8 miles south from the park entrance to parking area A-23, the last one on the paved road. This area is very popular and may be filled on sunny days, even during the off-season. If so, park at area A-22 or A-21 and walk the extra distance along the road. The area between A-19 and A-20 is a bird observation area.

THE TRAIL

From parking area A-23, walk through the gate toward the shoreline. You will be walking in a southerly direction toward the Barnegat Inlet and Lighthouse. You can walk either on the beach buggy tracks or along the water's edge, both far easier to walk on than the soft sand. The compacted sand along the water is probably the most interesting choice because it offers a fascinating variety of ocean debris that is constantly being reorganized by the tides and waves. Here are shells, dead fish, crabs, and driftwood. You will also encounter seagulls and fishermen with their beach buggies and campers. You will never be bored walking along what you may at first think to be a monotonous stretch of beach.

After about 1.5 miles, you will reach the southern tip of Island Beach. This is Barnegat Inlet, where the Atlantic Ocean meets Barnegat Bay. Barnegat Lighthouse, built in 1858, stands across the inlet at the northern tip of Long Beach Island. In Barnegat Inlet, the ocean currents are steadily moving sand southward toward Long Beach Island. The accumulation of sand from this drift is awesome when you consider that the end of the road, more than a mile back, was once much closer to the end of the island. The Army Corps of Engineers struggles to keep this inlet, which is constantly filling with sand, open to navigation. It was hoped that the inlet would be stabilized by the two jetties, but even these structures don't prevent the sand from filling the inlet. During low tide, a sandbar or breaking waves are often visible between the two.

Walk west along the jetty toward Barnegat Bay. To your right is a protected bird nesting area and, beyond that, the dunes. The stability of the entire state park depends on these dunes, which are in turn stabilized by dune grass and other plants such as seaside goldenrod and Hudsonia or beach heather. These plants are very tolerant of the salty sea spray, which kills other species. Continue walking westward until you are nearly opposite the lighthouse. Comparing the present topography with that of the geological survey map reveals the incredible changes constantly taking place here. To your right are the Sedge Islands, a large area of salt marsh inhabited by countless birds and visited by many kayakers. Also to the right are the higher backdunes, separating the foredunes and the bay, which support a thick barrier of holly, bayberry, and other shrubs that cannot tolerate salt spray. You can also see a residence from here, one of several at the southern end of the park.

A small promontory made of jetty stone juts into the inlet, most often a private spot for lunch or simply for viewing the bay, ocean, and inlet all at once. To the south, the lighthouse and a steady parade of fishing and pleasure boats are a sharp contrast to the wild, virtually inaccessible Sedge Islands to the northwest. When you are ready, retrace your steps from this spot to the ocean shoreline and then to the parking area. The first large gap in the dune fence that parallels the shore is your access to parking area A-23.

BCS

44

Wells Mills County Park

Total distance: 4.5 miles

Hiking Time: 2 hours

Vertical rise: Approximately 200 feet

Rating: Moderate

Maps: USGS Brookville; Ocean County Parks & Recreation Wells Mills trail map

Wells Mills County Park (Box 905, Wells Mills Road, Waretown, NJ 08758; 609-971-3085) is located at the site of the former town of Wells Mills. Here, sometime in the late 1700s, James Wells established a sawmill. He created the lake, which drove the mill, by damming Oyster Creek. Others settled in the area and over the years the ownership of the mill was passed along, each owner benefiting from the local abundance of Atlantic white, or "swamp," cedar. This wood is not only strong but also extremely rot resistant and was used to build ships. Shingles and house-building lumber were other products of the mill.

During the 1870s Christopher Estlow and his sons operated two mills in the area, which explains why the name of the hamlet, and now the park, is plural. In addition to the sawmill business, Estlow's grandson Tilden mined clay, which was sent to Trenton to be made into pottery. In 1936 the property was sold to Charles M. Conrad and his brother Grove. A year later they began constructing the cabin that stands today on the shore of the lake at the boat docks. By 1979 the Conrad family found a buyer for all of their 200 acres in the New Jersey Conservation Foundation. This private organization moves quickly to purchase land that might otherwise be developed. Later the land is sold to public agencies, in this case Ocean County. Additional acquisitions by the county have increased the size of the park to about 900 acres.

The staff of the Ocean County Park System has created an excellent trail system. Several color-coded paths explore the park,

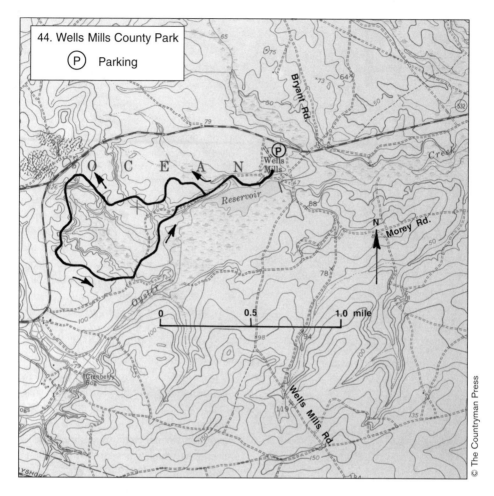

44. Wells Mills County Park

Ⓟ Parking

one of which totals 8.4 miles. The first section of this long trail, the Penn's Hill Trail, will be used in this hike. The park system has wisely kept hiking trails and multiuse trails (on which mountain bikes are permitted) mostly separate. One of the surprises you will find here is the frequent ups and downs. Most of the New Jersey pinelands are flat. Here, and also just to the north in the Forked River Mountains (privately owned), the flatness is broken by small hills.

Expect to encounter ticks here–mostly wood ticks but also deer ticks. They are worse in summer, less of a problem in cooler weather. Take the following precautions: Wear light-colored pants and socks, tuck the pants into the socks, and then spray your legs and feet with industrial-strength (containing DEET) tick repellent. If you stay on the trail, chances are you may not pick up even one tick. If you bushwhack off the trail, you may collect quite a few. After your hike, de-tick yourself thoroughly.

HOW TO GET THERE

Wells Mills County Park is on the eastern edge of the Pine Barrens, not far from the Garden State Parkway. (*Note:* at the time of

Pine cones

BRUCE SCOFIELD

this writing construction was underway to make exit 69 a full interchange allowing traffic north and south to exit at the same point. When this has been accomplished, see directions for coming from the south below.) Coming from the north, take parkway exit 74 (Forked River/Waretown) and drive east for 2 miles to US 9. Drive south on US 9 for 3 miles and then turn right (east) onto County Road 532 (CR 532). In 2 miles you'll cross over the parkway; in another 2.5 miles you will find the entrance to Wells Mills County Park on your left. If coming from the south, take parkway exit 69 and drive 2.2 miles west on CR 532 to the park entrance. Follow the entrance drive past the maintenance building to the large parking lot.

THE TRAIL

Walk toward the rest rooms and fountain, then follow the paved path to the nature center. Be sure to sign in at the directory just past the rest rooms, and be sure to stop in at the nature center to see the displays illustrating the natural and human history of Wells Mills.

When you are ready to start hiking, leave the center and face the lake; you should see a tree with three white paint markers to your right. This is the Penn's Hill Trail (Trail #4), which first follows the shoreline of Wells Mills Lake and then circles through a remote and hilly section of the park.

Follow the white markers of the trail, which shares its route briefly with a yellow-blazed trail, keeping left and close to the shoreline. Notice that the marking system in this park uses one blaze to indicate that you are on the trail and two markers for a turn, with one of the upper markers indicating the direction of the turn. Walk between the cabin and the lake; you can get a good view of the lake from the floating docks. After you pass the cabin, the white markers lead you first under some holly trees, then through a deep woods of cedar and laurel. Here the trail turns away from the lake on a wood-chip bed, passing a junction with a red trail on the right, a fire ditch, and then a junction with a blue trail. Turn left here onto the sand road. This is Ridge Road, and it is open to mountain bikes. You'll cross over a small creek on a stone-lined bridge, and then pass a side trail on the left that leads out to an observation blind on the lake. Not far past this junction, the white markers of the Penn's Hill Trail turn right onto a footpath, leaving Ridge Road.

From here the trail winds through a forest of pitch pines and scrub oak with an understory of mountain and sheep laurel, crossing several fire ditches along the way. The well-maintained trail snakes its way deeper and deeper into the pineland forest, crossing over wet areas on "narrow-gauge" bridges. About 20 minutes into the hike, the trail reaches the top of a small rise called Raccoon Ridge. This is the 1-mile point, as noted by a sign. From here the trail alternately rises and falls, a highly unusual pattern for the Pine Barrens. In some sections you will find sweet pepperbush growing alongside the trail, in others highbush blueberry.

After a short climb, the trail attains a small ridge. This is Penn's Hill, which is about 150 feet above sea level and about 100 feet higher than the surface of Wells Mills Lake. Although this relief seems inconsequential when compared with the mountains of northern New Jersey, it is unusual in the Pine Barrens. As you come down the hill with a swamp on the left, you'll pass the 2-mile marker. Just ahead the trail crosses an arm of the swamp on boardwalk. Although this section of the hike is actually near a road, it feels quite wild and remote.

Over the next mile the trail climbs Laurel Hill, descends, and then walks along what is called Laurel Ridge. Like Penn's Hill, neither of these high points is much more than 50 feet above the surrounding woods, but they do require some effort. Along the way you'll walk through a small clearing, use some wooden stairways, and straddle a few wet sections made worse by trespassing mountain bikes. At the 3-mile point you should arrive at a major junction. Turn left here, leaving the white markers, onto a sand road that is open to mountain bikes.

Follow the sand road, marked with yellow bike trail markers and the green blazes of the Estlow Trail, in a northerly direction. Almost immediately you'll enter a cedar swamp. The narrow, perfectly vertical cedars and the dark waters of the brook are a sharp contrast with your last 2 miles of hiking. After you cross the brook on a small bridge, turn right onto a footpath following the green markers of the Estlow Trail. This path slabs the side of a rise for about 0.5 mile, then reaches a junction with a wider sand lane. Turn left here, walk 100 feet to a much larger sand road, and turn right. You have now rejoined Ridge Road.

Follow the white markers past the trail to the observation blind and over the stone-lined bridge. Immediately after crossing, turn right, still following white markers back through the cedar swamp, past the cabin, and back to the visitor center.

BCS

45

Bass River State Forest

Total distance: 3.7 miles

Hiking time: 1.5–2 hours

Vertical rise: Minimal

Rating: Easy

Maps: USGS New Gretna; DEP Bass River State Forest Hiking Trails (sketch map)

Bass River State Forest is New Jersey's first state forest. Land acquisition began with 597 acres in 1905 (2005 was the centennial) and today it includes land parcels totaling 26,700 acres. The Garden State Parkway passes through the eastern parts of the forest making it very accessible by automobile. The 50-mile Batona Trail (see other Pine Barren hikes in this volume) terminates in the western portion of the forest. The focus of recreational activities in the Bass River State Forest is Lake Absegami which offers swimming and boating, and is surrounded by 176 car campsites and a number of cabins and lean-tos. Entrance to this section of the forest is via Stage Road and a fee is charged during the summer season. (The hike below utilizes a free parking area.)

A memorial to the Civilian Conservation Corps (CCC) is found in Bass River State Forest. The CCC was a New Deal program designed to get the many unemployed men, victims of the Depression, working on civic projects. During the 1930s some 3 million men served in the CCC and they worked on many park and forest projects that still stand today throughout the United States. Bass River State Forest had its own camp, one of the earliest in the nation. This camp, Company #225, planted 4,500 acres of timber and was noted for its valor in fighting fires in the Pinelands, including an especially tragic one on May 30, 1936. The CCC also dammed two streams in the forest and created Lake Absegami. The camp was later used by the military during World

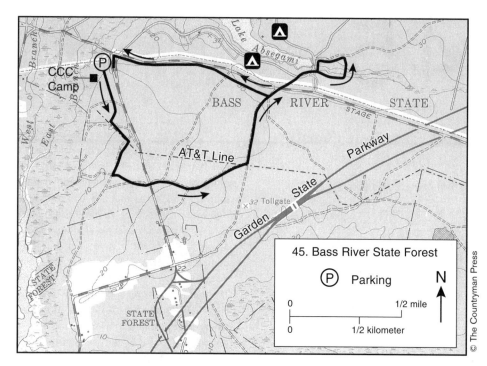

War II. Very little remains of this camp today, what there is will be visited on the hike described below. A directory at the parking area contains photographs of some of the corps back in the 1930s, making the memorial more personal.

HOW TO GET THERE

From the Garden State Parkway, take Exit 52 and turn right onto East Greenbush Road (CR 654) following signs to Bass River State Forest. Drive one mile and park at the CCC Forest Service Memorial on the left. There is parking for about 8 to 10 cars. The trailhead is at the northwest end of the small parking area.

THE TRAIL

The trail is marked with flexible plastic posts containing the trail blaze color and international symbols indicating usage. These posts are found only at junctions. Follow the

path away from the parking area in a southerly direction—you'll soon see a trail marker with a pink blaze (not to be confused with the Batona Trail) right away. For the next hundred yards or so the trail passes alongside the remains, mostly floor and foundations, of the former CCC camp that existed in this location. The first one you pass is labeled site A, it being the partial foundation of the kitchen/mess hall for the corps. The trail then swings to the left and passes several other foundations. Site B is unknown, but Site C is distinguished by a wide stairway and is thought to be either a medical building, officer's quarters, or an administration office. Just ahead is site D, a large slab of concrete which has small holes for drainage, was apparently the bathhouse. Site E was the trash pit and site F was where the five wooden barracks of the camp were located. As you walk along the pathway, notice that portions of the trail retain the former pavement. At the clearing, the pink-marked trail veers to the right leaving the camp area.

You now enter a typical Jersey Pine Barrens forest. The coarser-barked pitch pines (3 needles per clump) rise above a low understory of several common shrubs, among them highbush blueberry, leatherleaf, and sheep laurel. The trail next meets a wide sand lane, actually an AT&T line, onto which the pink trail turns left. After just a few minutes of walking, the pink trail turns right, leaving the AT&T line, and enters the woods on a 4-wheel drive lane. Notice how different the forest in this section is from that in the vicinity of the CCC camp. Here are white pines, distinguished by clumps of 5 needles and finer bark ridges. Pay attention to the route here—in the midst of the white pines the pink-marked trail turns left onto another lane and then heads in an easterly direction. As you walk the trail notice that white oaks are more prominent in this section of the forest. A debris shelter may be seen off the trail on the right. Follow the lane out to paved East Greenbush Road.

Cross the road and follow the pink-marked trail as it continues to head east in a pitch pine forest. A lane comes in from the right, and then the trail veers to the left onto a sand road. In places the sand is soft and limits traction. This is one of the characteristics of pineland hiking—a beach in the woods! Soon you will arrive at a junction with the AT&T line again, which is also a junction with a green trail. Follow the pink and green markers in a northerly direction straight across the AT&T line. Parts of this trail are on soft sand, other parts are more solid. After several minutes of walking you will pass through a crossroads (the trail on your left will be your return route) and come to Stage Road. Slightly to the right and ahead of you is the official entrance to Bass River State Forest. This is roughly the halfway point in the hike.

Cross Stage Road (be careful—people drive fast on this country road) and continue on the pink and green trail. Follow the trail across the power line right-of-way until you come to the red-marked trail. Turn right on the red trail, crossing the paved south-shore campground road. The park office will be on your right where you can pick up maps and other information. Just past the office, you will come to the paved north-shore campground road. Continue across the road onto the silver-marked trail with a surface of crushed cinders. This is the 0.5-mile Absegami Trail, which penetrates the Absegami Natural Area.

Follow the easy-to-follow trail through mountain laurel and other common pineland plants around a white cedar bog. Information posts are located along the way that explains the preservative properties of a bog. The anoxic conditions in a bog preserve pollen and other botanical remains as well as ash from fires or even distant volcanic eruptions. A core taken from the bog (3 inches equals about 100 years) contains botanical markers and ash particles dating back as far as 12,000 years, the end of the previous ice age. The bog itself, dark even on a bright day, is entered on a boardwalk. Here are densely-packed Atlantic white cedars rising from a carpet of sphagnum mosses on the moist ground. Leave the bog, and turn left at a junction. Continue to follow the silver markers back out to the paved road. Make a left here and, immediately, another left onto the south-shore campground road.

Walk back in a southerly direction towards the park office. Pass over the Falkinburg Branch drainage that feeds the cedar bog, and a wonderful view of the southern end of Lake Absegami. After crossing the

Old CCC camp at Bass River State Forest

drainage, follow the red-marked trail on your right. When you come to the paved south-shore campground road you will find good water at a pump at the sanitary dump station to your left. After crossing the paved south-shore campground road, continue on the red trail for a short distance then turn left onto the pink and green trail heading in a southerly direction.

Cross Stage Road (be careful) and continue on the pink and green trail. Where the green trail goes off to the left, turn right on

Coastal Plain

the pink trail which heads in a westerly direction. After a short distance, it turns left onto a smaller path. This long section of the pink trail utilizes a fire ditch paralleling Stage Road. It is not heavily used, but it is quite passable. However, at the time of this writing I had to carry a stick to dislodge the many spider webs running across it in places (the spiders are harmless). This is certainly preferable safety-wise to walking along Stage Road. Along the way the trail becomes lined with ferns. Cross the paved East Greenbush Road and follow the pink trail. After crossing East Greenbush Road stay on the pink trail which will turn left. Continue for about 100 yards where you will find the sign for the CCC Memorial, then turn left for the parking lot and back to your car.

BCS

46

Brendan T. Byrne (Lebanon) State Forest

Total distance: 8.5 miles

Hiking time: 5 hours

Vertical rise: Minimal

Rating: Moderately strenuous, some unmarked trails used—maps helpful

Maps: USGS Browns Mills; DEP Lebanon State Forest; DEP Batona Trail maps

At 34,000 acres, Brendan T. Byrne State Forest, formerly Lebanon State Forest, is the state's second largest forest. The original name, Lebanon State Forest, was after the Lebanon Glass Works, manufacturers of window glass and bottles, located here during the middle of the 19th century. The availability of sand and wood for charcoal supported the glassmaking industry until about 1867, when the wood supply became exhausted. About 150 men worked here, and a small town of 60 homes, a few shops, and a post office was established but later abandoned. In 1908 the state began to acquire land in the area. Also part of Brendan T. Byrne State Forest is deserted Whitesbog Village, the birthplace of the commercial blueberry and at one time the state's largest cranberry farm. The historic village is now being restored, and the not-entirely abandoned cranberry bogs are appealing to walkers. Cranberries are still harvested in some sections of Brendan T. Byrne State Forest by farmers who lease the land from the state. The reservoirs are used to flood the bogs in the early fall for harvesting. Machines are run through the bogs to shake the berries off the vines. The berries, which float, are scooped up and loaded, via conveyor belts, onto trucks that take them to processing plants.

The forest was renamed in 2002 to honor former New Jersey governor Brendan T. Byrne, who worked to designate the New Jersey Pine Barrens as a National Reserve. During his two terms as Governor of the State of New Jersey (1974 through 1982),

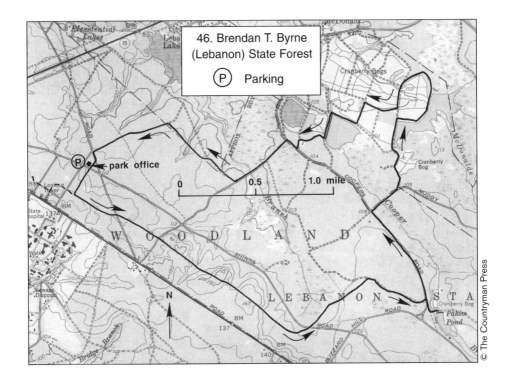

Byrne was a leader in the difficult and controversial effort to protect the New Jersey Pinelands. Pinelands is a politically correct name, though locals and scientists still respect the term Pine Barrens. With so many interests, public and private, involved in the large Pinelands region, the type of protection eventually settled on involved a combination of local, state, and federal agencies that would manage the Pinelands through land acquisition and land use controls. This unique arrangement required that the Pinelands be called a National Reserve, the country's first. Without such protective measures the Pine Barrens would surely have been developed commercially and for housing by now. The Pinelands National Reserve is said to be the largest assemblage of open space in the northeastern United States and has achieved recognition as a Biosphere Reserve by the United States

Man and the Biosphere Program and also by the United Nations Educational, Scientific and Cultural Organization (UNESCO).

Utilizing a section of the Batona Trail and the gravel and sand roads that crisscross the Pine Barrens, the hike described below takes in much of what Brendan T. Byrne State Forest (Box 215, Route 72, New Lisbon, NJ 08064; 609-726-1191, www .njparksandforests.org) has to offer. A section of the 735-acre Cedar Swamp Natural Area will be traversed twice and you will visit Pakim Pond, a good spot for lunch. The trail then uses sand roads to explore the shores of reservoirs and cranberry bogs. In this latter section your navigational skills may be challenged. Though long in mileage, this hike is not especially strenuous because the land is so flat; however, hot weather and biting deer flies could make it seem difficult, and, like most long hikes in the Pine Barrens, it should probably be hiked in cooler weather. Hikers are advised to stay on the trail and out of the brush, because ticks and chiggers have become common in recent years. It is best to wear long, light-colored pants tucked into socks, along with tick repellent.

HOW TO GET THERE

The main entrance to Brendan T. Byrne State Forest is on NJ 72, 1 mile east of the traffic circle where it intersects NJ 70. The entrance is on the north side of the road and is well marked with a large sign. Proceed 0.3 mile on this entrance road and bear right at the first intersection. The park office is just ahead on the left. Park here.

THE TRAIL

Take the blue access trail to the Batona Trail found south of the parking area. This trail, which is closed to mountain bikes, is labeled Batona Trail. After a short walk, you will meet the true Batona Trail, marked with pink paint blazes. Bear left here, heading southeast, parallel to, though some distance from, NJ 72. You'll be walking through a mixed pine and oak forest on a well-used footpath. The walking is pleasant and the trail surface, mostly sand, is soft and comfortable. After a short distance, the trail crosses a sand road and reenters the woods, continuing in the same direction. Here, stands of scrub oak, sassafras, pink and white mountain laurel, and blueberry bushes close in on the trail. Tall ferns line the trail in darker places. Farther along, the Batona Trail crosses another sand road, this one larger, and reenters the woods on a small sand road. Gradually the trail climbs to its highest elevation, about 150 feet above sea level. The land is dry here, and blackjack oak, scrub oak, and pitch pine predominate.

About 2 miles into the hike the trail veers to the northeast and crosses paved Shinns Road. Continue following the pink markers of the Batona Trail and enter a swampy area utilizing a corduroy log footpath and boardwalks in some places. You are now within the Cedar Swamp Natural Area, a dense jungle of Atlantic white cedars surrounded by the pitch pine forest. The cedar wood, which is soft but durable, is used in boatbuilding, for some kinds of furniture, and for shingles and stakes. The management of this tree is an important project in the forest. Below the tall cedars, the vegetation is dense and the lighting is dark. Plant life includes rare orchids, curly grass ferns, pitcher plants, and sundews. After leaving the Cedar Swamp Natural Area, you'll come to a junction with a gravel road—follow the markers and bear right through an area where cedars have been harvested. This gravel road is also marked with red, indicating it's part of a trail for the disabled. After you pass a few sand roads leading off to the right, the road swings left and meets an even larger gravel road, Coopers Road. Turn right and follow the pink and red markers into the Pakim Pond area.

Pakim Pond takes its name from the Native American word for cranberry. Its water is the reddish brown, acidic water typical of the Pine Barrens. Known as cedar water, it picks up its color and acidity as it moves very slowly through thick cedar swamps. Next to the pond is a swamp, a former cranberry bog. When the bog was actively cultivated, Pakim Pond was used as a reservoir to store water for the fall flooding of the bog. At Pakim Pond are rest rooms and picnic tables, but swimming is no longer allowed.

If you have time, you may wish to follow the 1-mile nature trail located here, which explores both the pond and the swamp. This trail begins just off the Batona Trail at

Pine Barrens pathway

the southern part of the dam. A guidebook, which explains the points of interest located by numbered posts, is available at the park office. Carnivorous plants can be found here, including the pitcher plant and at least two types of sundew. The pitcher plant has funnel-like leaves that are filled with water. Insects are attracted to the leaves by their odor and color and, should they fall in, are drowned and digested by the plant. The sundew is very small and grows in clumps in very wet but sunny areas. Its leaves, round or stemlike, have numerous sticky hairs that trap insects and then digest them. These plants can be found along the northeastern shore of the pond just off the Batona Trail.

After either exploring or resting at Pakim Pond, leave the way you came in and return to the gravel road. Do not turn left on the Batona Trail at the junction, though; stay on Coopers Road. From now on you will be following sand and gravel roads and will need to pay attention to the text and map.

Coopers Road, like most of the gravel and sand roads in the Pine Barrens, is straight, flat, and lined with pines. It can be very hot here and very buggy during the summer. After about 15 minutes (0.7 mile), you'll come to a crossroads. Turn right here, onto a smaller gravel road known as Muddy Road, marked with the white markers of the Mount Misery Trail, a trail on which bicycles are permitted. Along the side of the road are rhododendron, pepperbush, spicebush, and various species of blueberry. You will pass through a cedar swamp with towering Atlantic white cedars, densely packed, looking down on you from both sides of the road. After another 0.2 mile, just where the road begins to swing to the right, follow the white markers that lead left onto a sand road. This road has some soft "sugar-sand" sections, and the going may be slow in places.

Farther along, you'll pass an open area that is, in fact, a former cranberry bog in various stages of regrowth. Follow the white markers and the road as it swings around the bog and heads north (ignore the road going off to the left); then head west again where it ends at a T-intersection. Bear right here and head north toward the reservoir, which, like Pakim Pond, was used to flood cranberry fields. The scenery as you walk along the dam is beautiful, with the backdrop of pines and the green shades of water lilies and other aquatic vegetation. Wildflowers, not found in the shady woods, thrive in this sunny and well-watered environment. When you come to the corner of the reservoir, bear right, leaving the white markers. Now follow the reservoir's perimeter. The walkway heads east, then swings to the north, eventually leaving the reservoir with its dark cedar water, standing dead trees, and elusive pickerel. The sand road now winds through a quiet and remote pine woods with a forest carpeting of pine needles.

When you come to a junction with another sand road, keep left. Stay on this sand road (which is the white trail again) heading south for about 250 yards, then make a right turn on a sand road heading west. (From this junction, the edge of the first reservoir is visible.) An overgrown bog will be on your right and an open swamp, possibly with some waterfowl activity, on your left. From this point you will be working your way back to Coopers Road through a maze of old cranberry bogs, reservoirs, and sand roads. Don't be surprised if some large military aircraft fly by as well—these bogs are not far from Fort Dix and McGuire Air Force Base.

Take the second left turn at a T-intersection, and head south out to another reservoir. This was drained when we were here once and presented an awesome sight of blackish mud and gray tree stumps. At this junction, another T-intersection, bear right, heading west along the shore of the reservoir. Next bear left at the end of the reservoir and head south along the dam. At the next T-junction, turn right onto a sand road that first swings to the left and then comes to a fork. Take the left fork and walk through an area where sand has been excavated, staying on the main path which swings left and soon arrives at Coopers Road. Turn right on Coopers Road, then turn left on another gravel road only 200 yards ahead. There may be some yellow markers on this lane.

After a few minutes of walking on this lane, you'll pass a junction on the left with the red Cranberry Trail. (From this point on you can follow red markers back to your car.) Once again, you will cross a cedar swamp, now on a path separated from the road by a railing. Here the cedars are particularly tall and completely shade the road. Just after you leave the swamp, follow the red markers to the right onto a sand road that heads west. After about 250 yards on soft sand, the markers lead to a small sand road on the left. Take this road south for about 200 feet, then bear right and west again on a very straight sand road, still following red markers. This road is shady, surrounded by pine forest with an undercover of blueberries. Pass over a small mossy bog and then, after another 10 minutes or so, reach an intersection with a somewhat larger sand road. Bear left here, heading south with the red markers. Another 10 or 15 minutes of walking will bring you to a paved road. Follow the trail across the paved road and back to the park office and your car.

BCS

47

Carranza Memorial to Apple Pie Hill

Total distance: 8.2 miles (or 5.2 with car shuttle)

Hiking time: 4–5 hours

Vertical rise: 166 feet

Rating: Moderately strenuous

Maps: USGS Chatsworth, Indian Mills; NJWB #19; DEP Batona Trail; DEP Wharton State Forest maps

Walking uphill in the Pine Barrens is unusual. The entire region is just above sea level, and the very few "hills" are usually only 25 or 30 feet above everything else. There are a few exceptions, however, and this hike leads to the highest elevation in the Pines, a dizzying 205 feet above sea level and about 125 feet above the land around it. This is Apple Pie Hill, on which a fire tower is located. En route, the hike will take you over another hill, 139 feet above sea level, as a warm-up for the big climb. Another feature of the hike is a camping option. One of Wharton State Forest's primitive camping areas is located at the start of the hike and makes a great base camp. Camping permits are issued at the Atsion and Batsto forest services offices.

The Carranza Memorial, where this hike begins, commemorates the tragic crash and death of Mexican pilot Emilio Carranza. Carranza, only 23 at the time of his death, had been a Mexican hero for 5 years, his fame resting on both his aviation and military accomplishments. On June 11, 1928, he took off from Mexico in a Ryan monoplane, the same as Lindbergh's, and attempted a nonstop flight to Washington. He was grounded by fog in North Carolina but was still received with speeches and parades in both Washington and New York. Carranza was on the return leg of this goodwill flight when he flew into a thunderstorm over this remote section of the Pines and crashed. The local American Legion holds an annual observance of this event the first Saturday after the Fourth of July. Each year on this day wreaths are placed around the memorial—a stone marker made in Mexico that portrays a diving Aztec eagle.

HOW TO GET THERE

To reach the parking area at the memorial in Wharton State Forest, turn left (east) off US 206 just south of its junction with NJ 70. The sign here directs you to the town of Tabernacle and the Carranza Memorial. You'll reach the little town of Tabernacle and cross County Road 532 (CR 532) in 2.3 miles. Continue straight ahead through farms and a residential area into Wharton State Forest (Atsion Office, 744 Route 206, Shamong, NJ 08088, 609-268-0444). Seven miles from Tabernacle you will find the Carranza Memorial, which has ample parking, on the right. If you wish to do the hike as a one-way trip of 5.2 miles, leave a car on CR 532 where the Batona Trail crosses it about 7 miles east of Tabernacle and 3 miles west of Chatsworth.

THE TRAIL

Cross the paved road and head north into the Batona Camp. A sign here indicates the campsite, which is not far from the main road. After about 200 yards, you'll meet the pink-blazed Batona Trail, which connects with the camp access road from the right. From here to Apple Pie Hill and back you'll be following these pink markers. The 50-mile Batona Trail, begun in 1961 by the BAck TO NAture Hiking Club, is a foot trail only. Mountain bikes or motorized vehicles are not permitted on it. A map of the entire trail is available from the New Jersey Department of Environmental Protection, as well as at the Atsion and Batsto state forest offices.

Batona Camp is one of several primitive camping areas located in Wharton State Forest. The site is accessible by car and offers numerous spaces to pitch a tent, also pro-

viding a water pump and several pit toilets. If you wish to camp here, you'll need a permit, available from the Atsion Ranger Headquarters farther south on US 206 or from the office in Batsto. In 2005 the camping fee was $1 per night per person. Pets are not permitted in the campsite for overnight camping.

When you reach the end of the camping area, the Batona Trail veers to the right past a toilet and enters the woods on a footpath. Immediately, the typical flora of the Pinelands surrounds you. Highbush blueberries, which are found along the trail over much of this hike, make their first appearance. Blackjack oak and, of course, pitch pine surround you. Within a few hundred feet, the trail emerges onto a wide sand road, which it follows for a short distance. For the next 0.5 mile, the trail parallels this road, playing tag by using it for short stretches then cutting back into the woods on a footpath.

After a section that skirts the edge of a cedar swamp, the Batona Trail emerges onto the road for a final time to use its bridge. The brook you are crossing is the Skit Branch of the Batsto River. Like all Pine Barrens water, it is tea colored from the cedar wood that grows in it. From the bridge is a good view of the swampy brook and its plant life. If you look closely at the clumps of grasses growing in and around the water, you'll see hundreds of tiny sundew plants. If you look even closer, you may find a few miniature pitcher plants as well. These plants survive in this nutrient-poor environment by digesting insects that get trapped in their sticky leaves or no-exit entrances.

After crossing the bridge, the trail turns right and back into the woods on a footpath, this time for good. For the next 0.5 mile, Skit Branch and its white cedar swamp will be on the right. The many dead cedars, still standing tall in the water, were killed by fire.

Roberts

0   0.5   1.0 mile

N

Apple Pie Hill
Lookout Tower
205
150

124

103
98
114
100
139
100
89
85
100
111

T A B E R N A C L

Branch

Skit

75
80
98
70

NEW
OF
BM 87

Ore Spring

79

RR
BM 76
CENTRAL

Sandy
Ridge

Cranberry
Bog

Featherbed

campground

P
Carranza Memorial
BM
78
67
80

47. Carranza Memorial
to Apple Pie Hill

P   Parking

- - -   Side Trail

© The Countryman Press

Unlike pitch pines and shortleaf pines, Atlantic white cedars do not regenerate after a burn; only the water protects them from fire. In this section, the trail crosses a wet area on loose logs. Be careful, or you may sink into deep black mud. The next crossing is of the stream itself, again on logs and, once more, potentially perilous for your shoes.

The Batona Trail now leaves the wet area surrounding Skit Branch and heads into drier and higher territory. About 2 miles from the start of the hike, the first climb begins. The ascent is first noticeable by the change from soft white sand as a walkway to a harder gravel path. After a "climb" of about 40 feet, you'll reach the table-like summit of this un-named hill and, before you know it, begin heading downhill. Pay close attention ahead as the trail veers left off the path, crosses a sand road, and then reenters the woods.

One of the creatures of the Pines you may encounter on this hike, particularly in the drier areas, is the aptly named fence swift lizard. You may see a blur and hear the rustle of leaves, yet not get a look at this speedster unless you catch him sunning on a piece of dead wood. This rather attractive lizard has a gray-brown body and some very jagged scales along his head and back. The males have a dark marking under their lower jaws.

After crossing three more sand roads, the Batona begins another climb, this one more serious. Some views out to the horizon in the south appear between the trees. The trail winds along the hill until the summit and its fire tower appear. This rise is Apple Pie Hill, and at 205 feet it's the highest summit in the Pine Barrens.

Although the hill, which is accessible by car or truck, is the scene of many a wild party, the view from its tower is spectacular. To the south, a wilderness of green pines extends as far as the eye can see. To the west in the distance is the slight rise of Mount Holly. To the north are pines and, far in the distance, a water tower and a few other protrusions of civilization. In the east is a cranberry field–and more pines. To the southeast, a sand road runs from the hill in a perfectly straight line. For the most part, the view is one of vastness and wilderness that gives you an idea of the magnitude of the Pine Barrens.

Fire towers, which are frequently manned, play an important role in controlling the frequent fires (about 400 a year) in the Pine Barrens. The soil in the Pinelands drains the water so well that the oil- and resin-rich pine needles and dead branches are nearly always dry as tinder. There are no earthworms or bacteria to digest the dead materials on the forest floor, so the tinder accumulates year after year until it burns. The shortleaf pine and the pitch pine, the most common pines here, are two of only three pines in the United States that can sprout from buds lying deep within their trunks or large limbs, thereby assuring their quick recovery following a fire. The persistence of fires in the Pine Barrens, many of them started by arsonists, has ensured the dominance of these two pines in the forest. Ecologists believe that without regular fires, oaks would probably make up the bulk of a climax forest.

Because it is somewhat abused, Apple Pie Hill may not be the best place for a rest or lunch. We suggest that you find a resting place nearer to the first hill you climbed, which shows little sign of use other than from hikers. If you parked at the Carranza Memorial, this will be on your way back. If you left a car on CR 532, it is 1.1 miles ahead on the Batona Trail. Please note that this section of the trail is not on public land. Respect the landowners by staying on the trail.

BCS

48

Mullica River Wilderness

Total distance: 6 miles round trip (7 miles from visitor center)

Hiking time: 4–5 hours

Vertical rise: Minimal

Rating: Moderately strenuous

Maps: USGS Atsion; DEP Wharton State Forest map

Backpacking in the Pine Barrens is a unique experience for those more familiar with mountainous areas. The pines are not so dense or tall that they shut out a good view of a starlit sky. In fact, the effect is sometimes more like camping in a desert than in a forest. The pine needle cover on the sandy ground also makes for a comfortable bed. From Batsto, in the heart of the Pinelands, a 3.5-mile walk leads to the Mullica Wilderness Campsite in Wharton State Forest (4110 Nesco Road, Hammonton, NJ 08037, 609-561-0024, www.njparksandforests .org), a good choice for such an experience. This primitive camping experience offered by this hike is alongside the Mullica River at a designated primitive campground. It has a water pump and pit toilet, it is expansive enough for private folks, and is monitored by the forest rangers. You'll have to get a permit from the office in Batsto to camp here, however. In 2005 the cost was $1 per night per person. Pets are not allowed.

Batsto was the site of an iron forge that produced kettles, stoves, cannon, pipes, and other iron products during the latter part of the 18th and the early 19th centuries. Like Allaire Village in the northern extremes of the Pine Barrens, the iron was made from bog iron—accumulations of iron oxides leached from the sand by groundwater and deposited at or near the soil surface. During the Revolutionary War, Batsto was a major source of military iron, and its workers were exempt from military service. At its peak, the village that developed around the furnace had a population of nearly a thou-

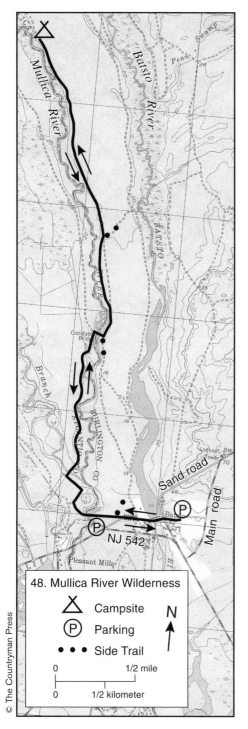

48. Mullica River Wilderness

△ Campsite

Ⓟ Parking

••• Side Trail

N

0   1/2 mile

0   1/2 kilometer

© The Countryman Press

sand. When the iron industry declined, a glassmaking factory was built, and the town produced window panes and other flat glass products for a few years. In 1876, after a major fire in the village, Joseph Wharton bought the property as part of his plan to own the Pine Barrens and sell its water to the city of Philadelphia. The state of New Jersey responded by passing a law prohibiting the export of water, effectively halting this project. Eventually the Wharton holdings were acquired by the state, forming the present-day Wharton State Forest. Information about the interesting history of Batsto and the Pine Barrens can be found at the visitor/interpretive center.

The route of this hike is the route of the Mullica River. Hikers will immediately notice its color. "Cedar water" is the usual name for it. The water of the Pine Barrens is dark, the color of tea, and comes in part from the tannins from decaying vegetation washed out of swamps and in part from the iron-colored sandy mud. Because the water in the Pine Barrens tends to stay fresher longer, sea captains used to sail up the rivers that drain the Pinelands and take on barrels of what they called "sweet water." The water table in the Pinelands is shallow, but the reserve of water is vast. As an aquifer, there is no equal to the Pinelands in the northeastern United States. Because the water lies so close to the surface, and the sand, which takes in the rain that falls on it, is not a good filter, the Pine Barrens aquifer is extremely vulnerable to pollution. For this reason, development—which constantly threatens this area—has been kept at bay.

HOW TO GET THERE

Batsto, a part of Wharton State Forest, is on NJ 542 and is easy to find—signs directing you to it (it is a major historical site) are strategically placed within a radius of 20

Sundew

miles. From the Garden State Parkway, take Exit 52 and follow the signs. If you plan to backpack and spend the night at the Mullica Wilderness campsite, it is advisable to leave your car overnight at the parking area behind the state forest office in Batsto.

THE TRAIL

The entire hike is within the Batsto Natural Area on sand roads and paths. Although you will be following a well-marked yellow trail, pay close attention at junctions as many paths and lanes intersect the main route. Markers are found on flexible plastic posts, and also as paint marks on trees. Sections of the sand roads utilized by the trail are very soft, with poor traction. The present route of the hike is a vast improvement over the route found in previous editions of this book. Formerly, hikers used the Mullica River Road, which they had to share with trucks hauling boats. The sand roads were very soft, to say the least, and boot traction was terrible. The present trail is for walkers only and it extends well beyond the campsite, all the way to Atsion.

If you are backpacking, or wish to also explore Batsto village and have parked at the main Batsto parking area, walk west on the main walkway through Batsto Village, across the dam on Batsto Lake, and go straight ahead until you arrive at a sand road. You will find a trailhead with yellow and orange markers here. If you are day-hiking and have parked among the trees adjacent to the west end of Batsto Village, just off 542, follow the lane that heads due north to find the yellow and orange trail on your left in about 100 feet. Turn left here and follow the path into a dark woods that leads out to the Mullica River. The trail next crosses the river on a magnificent wooden bridge built in 1999. Continue following the markers though the forest—posts bearing botanical identification information will be found along the way. At a junction, the trail

Coastal Plain

will turn right on a sand and pine needle walkway. Just ahead at a fork, the trail turns left. At the next major junction, the yellow trail turns right, leaving the orange trail. From here on you will be following only yellow markers. The trail now crosses a tributary of the Mullica on a wooden bridge. The next section of trail is particularly beautiful with swamp, river, white and yellow sand, stunted pitch pines, and a lot of open sky. The route next utilizes a soft white sand road on which tracks, evidence of usage by vehicles, hikers, and deer, can be found. The soft sand will slow down your progress and give you a taste of some of what is to come. A more compact section is just ahead.

About a mile into the hike you will arrive at a bend in the Mullica River that is noted as a scenic overlook on the forest map. A few rails stabilize the trail, keeping hikers away from the steep drop down to the river. There are inviting beachlike qualities to this river bend in the deep forest. The Mullica, along with the Batsto, Wading, Great Egg Harbour, and Rancocas, is one of the major rivers draining the vast water reserves lying just below the sands and forests of the Pine Barrens. Though the river widens considerably farther downstream, the Mullica here in the forest is typical of other rivers in the Pines. The river is not wide, but it can be deep enough in some places to be over your head. There are no rapids, but the current is strong. The fact that it runs all year along and through droughts at a constant water level indicates the extent of the aquifer underlying the Pine Barrens.

Continue hiking north on the yellow trail. In the summer the insects may be aggressive. Wildlife, including deer and flying squirrels, may be encountered. You may spot the red wasp, which looks like a giant ant, alongside the trail. Soon you will arrive at the Constable Bridge. If you're hiking on a busy summer weekend, expect regular deliveries of canoes to this popular boat-launching point. Next, cross over the Mullica River and continue following the yellow markers in a northerly direction, now on the east side of the river. After another mile you will reach the entrance to the Mullica River Wilderness area, a section of the forest where no vehicles (except the ranger's) are allowed. A sign here marks the boundary. About a mile from the beginning of the wilderness area is the Mullica River Wilderness Campsite, a good place for lunch—or for the night. There's a pump for good water here, and plenty of campsites within the limits posted and marked by a ditch. Along the banks of the Mullica are several beachlike areas.

After a lunch, rest, or possibly an overnight, leave the campsite area and walk south, following yellow markers and retracing your steps past the entrance to the wilderness area, back over the Constable Bridge, and back to Batsto village.

BCS

49

Parvin State Park

Total distance: 5 miles

Hiking time: 3 hours

Vertical rise: Minimal

Rating: Easy to moderate

Maps: USGS Elmer; DEP Parvin State Park map

In 1930, the New Jersey legislature began the acquisition of Parvin State Park with an appropriation of just less than $74,000. Nine years later, following 19 separate transactions, Parvin entered the state park system. During the Depression, a Civilian Conservation Corps (CCC) branch was established in the park. The men hacked out trails through the dense forest, using the wood to build bridges across the swamps. They cleared the main beach and picnic area and constructed the cabins—each with its own boat landing—along the shore of Thundergust Lake.

A German prisoner-of-war camp was located in a section of the park in 1942. When the European hostilities ended, the camp was converted for use by interned Japanese-Americans from the West Coast. The year 1952 saw the last nontraditional use of Parvin. Six years earlier, Soviet dictator Joseph Stalin had the Kalmyck people and some other Tartar groups transported to Siberia in retaliation for their revolt against the Communist government. Only about a quarter of the 400,000 people involved survived the ordeal, some of whom escaped to the United States. They came to Parvin in three groups, but stayed only a few months. Some are now settled in the Philadelphia area and in Howell Township in New Jersey.

This hike starts on the Parvin Lake Trail and uses the Long Trail for the rest of its route. Many of the trails in the park, even those in the natural area, are open to bike use, and some are also available for eques-

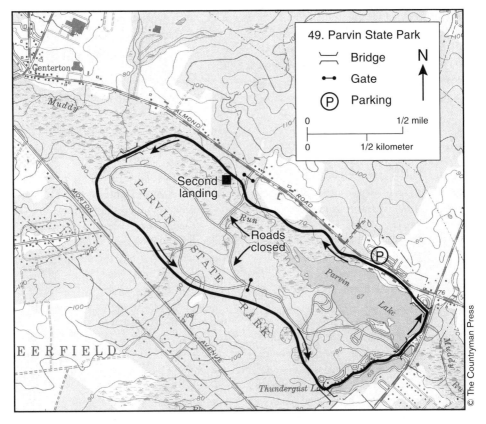

trians. If you live in the area, volunteers are needed to help maintain the trail system. Please contact the park administration.

HOW TO GET THERE

Parvin State Park is located in southern Salem County along the Cumberland County border. The park entrance is on County Route 540, slightly more than 1 mile east of Centerton or 6 miles west of Vineland. The surrounding area has many road signs to point you in the right direction. The office (701 Almond Road, Pittsgrove, NJ 08318; 856-358-8616) is located in one end of the park bathhouse, with a large parking lot across CR 540. Stop in the office for a free and worthwhile map booklet. The trails are named on the park map, and

there are some trailhead signs indicating permitted uses.

THE TRAIL

Your hike starts just outside the park office. Facing Parvin Lake and the bathhouse, walk to the right (west) along a brown dirt path and then beside a green chain-link fence. The trail is over flat terrain, and the walking is easy. It travels between the highway and the lake, passing a children's area and some picnic tables, and is marked with occasional green paint blazes. Holly trees and mountain laurel abound.

A few minutes after crossing a small brook on a tiny stone bridge, you will reach a small open clearing. Avoid both the trail to the left (which soon fades out) and the overgrown trail to the right. Instead, continue straight as the route swings closer to both the road and a few houses seen through the woods. Large pitch pines with their distinctive, thick, shingle bark are much in evidence. Ground pine moss abounds on the forest floor.

You may notice a short side trail leading left down to the edge of Muddy Run. Continue straight ahead, also avoiding the trail to the right. Shortly afterward, there is another path to the water's edge. Muddy Run is a typical slow-moving stream of south Jersey. A tributary of the Maurice River, its water eventually empties into Delaware Bay. In the 1880s, small ponds were formed by damming to provide power for gristmills and sawmills. One of these was owned by a family named Parvin.

Proceed ahead, crossing a series of small plank bridges to meet a paved crossroad. This road forms the main boundary between the developed area and the designated natural area of Parvin State Park—the latter to be left in a "forever wild" condition. A short walk to the left (suggested) along this road leads to both Muddy Run and an interesting bridge likely designed to discourage illegal motorbikes. Back on the main trail, continue straight ahead as the path gets a little sandier. In a few minutes you will reach an area known as Second Landing. Uphill to the right is a picnic area with a rain shelter and rest rooms. The shore of Muddy Run is just to the left. Because the trail now enters the heart of the designated natural area, the trail is basically not maintained and is less obvious. There are some blowdowns to climb under and over, and the footway may be wet in spots—a minor price to pay for the peace, solitude, and natural dignity here.

The League for Conservation Legislation, the New Jersey Chapter of the Sierra Club, and Assemblyman (later Governor) Thomas Kean deserve credit for the 1976 passage of the Natural Areas System Act. This landmark legislation, which followed in the footsteps of the Forest Preserve article of the New York State Constitution, allows the designation of areas to be left forever in their natural state. Except for trails, they remain fundamentally undeveloped, and the trees remain uncut.

Continuing ahead, avoid the nature trail fork to the right and proceed over two small wooden bridges onto the footway, now on land slightly raised from the surrounding marsh. This part of the trail has many small plank bridges but has otherwise not been maintained in many years. This path—like most of the footways in Parvin—was built during the 1930s by the CCC. Considering that more than 70 years have passed, it is easy to admire their fine, long-lasting workmanship.

The route through the natural area is obvious, even though indistinct in a spot or two. Don't worry, you can retrace your steps easily; but it is much more likely that after just brief hunting and pecking, you will regain the path. In one wet, open area, the trail does bend somewhat to the right, but otherwise it is mostly straight with gentle curves. The wooden posts seen occasionally along the route are long-neglected mile markers, which may even date back to CCC days.

Cross three or four small feeder inlets as the trail winds out and bends slowly left toward Muddy Run. Be sure to take time to observe the forest around you. Left alone by humanity, it has developed a distinctly wild feel. Birds seem to like the area—you will hear many, but see few. In about 20 minutes you will reach a substantial bridge over Muddy Run. Shortly after crossing it, and just as the main trail takes a distinctive turn

Oak and birch trees

to the left (red arrow), watch for and take the fainter path on the right (orange arrow). If you miss this spot, you'll soon climb gently to a paved interior park road. Just retrace your steps, find the correct path, and resume the hike. This junction, by the way, was–and may still be–incorrectly located on the park map.

Going ahead on the fainter trail, almost immediately you will spot a conspicuous downed tree with exposed roots. It's interesting to observe the complex web of the root system and the large hole in the ground left by its fall. Many times we have seen these otherwise unexplained dips in the forest floor after the tree has rotted or been carried away.

The trail continues as before with many two- and three-plank bridges. It soon comes to and parallels a small inlet creek flowing through the dense brush and forest. Cross a woods road. The trees begin to open up a little, and the trail resumes the wide, groomed look it had at the beginning of the hike. Through the trees to the right are glimpses of some houses as the trail nears the southern border of the park.

This part of New Jersey is known to have a considerable tick population. As you hike here, especially during the warmer months (June through September), be alert for the little monsters. The introduction to this book provides some basic advice on ticks and Lyme disease, which are widespread in New Jersey.

The footway becomes more distinct again, and the walking very easy. The plant community resumes the character it had early in the hike. The large pitch pines attest to the years the area has been undisturbed by logging. Young white pine trees add to the gentle feel, with their long, light green needles. Holly trees canopy the now-wide trail at one point. The holly is an evergreen

tree that, like mountain laurel, keeps its leaves throughout the year. The trees can be either male or female, and both sexes are needed before berries develop.

When the trail comes to a T-junction, go right, crossing over a sandy road after a minute or so. Continuing ahead, you will pass some indistinct trails, one on the right and one just beyond it on the left. About 15 minutes past the T, at another junction, take a 90-degree right turn over a small mound of dirt. Should you miss this turn, you'll shortly be at a paved road and can retrace your steps.

The path is again raised from the surrounding forest floor. Crossing yet another trail, continue straight as the path gets a little narrower. In less than 5 minutes, the main trail swings sharply to the left, while a fainter trail goes straight. Take the latter. Off to the left, through the woods, you can see some of the cabins in the Thundergust Lake area. You will quickly arrive at a nice wooden footbridge over Thundergust Brook, a pleasurable place to pause as the hike draws to a close. Eighteen rental cabins are available from April through October. Each is well equipped with a fridge, stove, toilet, shower, and electric lights. They sleep four but can accommodate six if you're willing to bring the extra cots.

This route does not cross the bridge, though. Take a left onto the trail along the near shore of Thundergust Lake, passing the cabins and sandy boat-launch beach. Stay between the lake and service road, passing a wooden fishing platform and small brick structure. As the trail approaches the main highway, you'll notice a dam with a wrought iron railing on your right and the campground entrance road on your left. Walk on the road into the park past the 20 MPH sign. Shortly afterward, in a split-rail fenced area, turn right onto a footbridge over a small section of Parvin Lake. The park office and bathhouse, where your hike began, are now visible.

From here, no formal directions are required. Just continue through the more developed part of the park, always remaining close to the shoreline. The outlet dam of Parvin Lake is especially interesting with its Art Deco lines and unusual curved spillway. Two bridges, one concrete and the other wooden, cross what appear to be streams, but they actually take you on and off Flag Island.

You will be back to your car before long. Stop at the office (nice rest rooms!) and tell the staff there of your excursion through the outer areas of Parvin. They don't get all that many hikers in the area and may enjoy hearing your anecdotes.

HNZ

50

Belleplain State Forest, East Creek Trail

Total distance: 7.2 miles

Hiking time: 4.5 hours

Vertical rise: Minimal

Rating: Moderate

Maps: USGS Woodbine, Heislerville; DEP Belleplain State Forest map

Located in the southern tip of the Pinelands, Belleplain State Forest (PO Box 450, Woodbine, NJ 08270; 609-861-2404) is a popular camping spot containing a few hundred family camping sites, 14 all-season cabins, five yurts, two group campsites, which can each accommodate 75 people, a group cabin for up to 30 people, hot showers, and flush toilets. Belleplain has, in fact, more campsites than any other state forest in New Jersey. Central to the camping areas in this recently enlarged 23,000-acre forest—90 percent of which is part of the Pinelands National Reserve—is Lake Nummy, a transformed cranberry bog with white sand beaches. It was named in honor of King Nummy, chief of the Kechemeche tribe and the last to rule in the Cape May area. For hikers, Belleplain offers many short trails in the camping area along with the East Creek Trail, a white-blazed footpath that will be used in this hike. Most trails in the forest are multi-use; there are even motorized trails.

Please note that from mid-January into June of each year, a section of the East Creek Trail may be closed for nesting eagles. Call ahead to check if the trail is open.

The East Creek Trail is a 7.2-mile circular trail, which you will hike clockwise. As some sections of the trail are poorly marked and almost under a swamp, we've revised the route to utilize a small section of interior road. While park staff have indicated that this section will be improved by 2006, sometimes even with the best intentions work can be delayed.

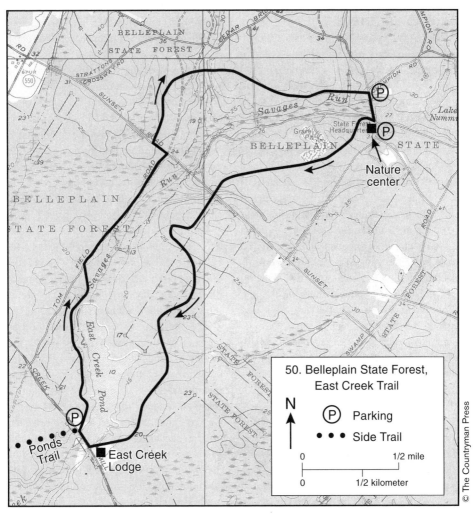

© The Countryman Press

50. Belleplain State Forest,
East Creek Trail

N

Ⓟ Parking

● ● ● Side Trail

0   1/2 mile

0   1/2 kilometer

Marked with white paint on trees and brown Carsonite directional posts, the trail was refurbished in 1996. Cut for nearly its entire length, it encircles the area drained by Savages Run between Lake Nummy and East Creek Pond. It generally traverses dry, oak-and-pine forests but frequently descends into deep, dark cedar brooks and swamps, more characteristic of the Pine Barrens to the north. Unlike the Pine Barrens, shore vegetation–particularly greenbriers and holly trees–is found throughout the forest, revealing the transitional nature of the region.

Be warned that the forest abounds in mosquitoes and ticks. Strong insect repellents may prevent unnecessary problems (see the Introduction). Those sections of the East Creek Trail that are used on this hike are fairly well marked, but not that well maintained. Some footbridges and planks are slippery, and a few areas very overgrown and/or under water. Expect to get your shoes wet and muddy.

HOW TO GET THERE

Take Exit 17 (Woodbine/Sea Isle City) off the Garden State Parkway. Follow signs for Woodbine and very shortly turn right (north) onto NJ 9 and go 0.6 mile; then turn left onto County Route 550 (Woodbine–Ocean View Road). After 6.3 miles, you reach the town of Woodbine (historically a sanctuary for European and Russian Jews), where CR 550 makes a left near Spirit Chevrolet, then a right at a blinking light. This is still CR 550–stay on it. It's another 1.4 miles to the state forest. Turn left at the entrance near the new park office, pass the entry station (a fee is collected seasonally), and drive 0.5 mile to an intersection. A right turn here will lead in another 0.5 mile to Lake Nummy on the right and the nature center on the left. Park at the nature center. If you are hiking during the peak summer season, you may need to continue on to the beach, where there is also a large parking area and a refreshment stand.

THE TRAIL

With your back to the lake and facing the nature center, the East Creek Trail starts about 100 yards to the right, near a sign for the campers-only trash recycling center. A sign indicating the hiking trail is just beyond.

Still following the white markers, begin hiking southward. The trail, a moss-covered footpath, penetrates first an open forest of young oaks, then a pitch pine forest reminiscent of the Pine Barrens. Where the trail parallels a fire ditch, the first of many along the trail, be alert for a sudden right turn where the ditch swings left. Clumps of mountain laurel, small pine trees and, in places, bracken ferns form the ground cover seen here and all along the trail. About a mile into the hike, the trail crosses a creek in the dark shadows of tall cedars. Here are the first of many holly groves and

tangles of greenbrier that threaten to overwhelm the trail. After crossing the small brook, reach and cross paved Sunset Road. Note this spot, because the hike returns over this just-traveled route.

The trail now follows the perimeter of an abandoned field filled with wildflowers, in season. The transition from field to forest is evident here, and wildlife, including deer and game birds, is abundant. After reentering the woods, the trail joins an old sand road, following it through a pine forest for only 100 yards or so before turning sharply left. Here is an old boardwalk, the first of many that will–hopefully–aid you through the wet sections ahead. The narrow trail now penetrates an older, deeper, and darker forest; some of the pines are very large. In the wetter areas, huge holly trees are found.

Beyond this low and wet area, the trail crosses another stream on planks at the edge of a dense stand of cedars. Then it recrosses where the same stream is wider, the cedars denser. The trees seem to be standing on their roots to keep out of the wet, green earth. Be careful while crossing on the planks, which were moss-covered and slippery on our last visit–although they may have been replaced. If the going gets wet, look to both sides of the trail for hiker-made bypass routes.

The next section of trail is very green, dominated by pine, holly, and laurel. This forest must be quite striking with a snow cover. After traversing more sections of boardwalk, the trail winds through an open section of trees killed by the gypsy moth caterpillars. Follow an old woods road through a forest of young pines before you reach an open area. Walk straight ahead, following markers, toward the building at the southern end of East Creek Pond. This is the rebuilt East Creek Lodge, available through the state forest for group use. The front of the lodge has a dock and many picnic tables; if it's not already in use, this makes a good spot for a snack or lunch. This location is the halfway point of the hike–about 3 miles from the start.

Nowadays, the view over East Creek Pond is a calm one–blue water lined with tall, green pines. If anything, the pond is underused, yet it is regarded as an excellent pickerel lake and does attract some anglers. A hundred years ago, however, this area was the scene of much activity; both a lumber mill and gristmill were located here.

When ready to continue, walk to the other side of the lake along the busy paved road, following white markers. The new parking area here was built to accommodate users of the new multi-use Ponds Trail to Pickle Factory Pond; it was dedicated on National Trails Day in June 1995. Still following the white markers, reenter the woods, heading north. The trail parallels the lake for a distance before it actually arrives at the shoreline near an inlet. Here is a wilderness vista of the lake. With the possible exception of anglers in boats, the entire panorama is of water and forest. From this point the trail turns left, skirts a wet section, then heads toward higher ground.

You now traverse a forest of young pines on both cut trail and woods road. As the trail nears the northern end of East Creek Pond, it meanders through a very dense cedar forest and, farther on, crosses a swamp on planks. At the swampy northern end of the lake, the trail makes a sharp left and meets, in 100 feet, a woods road. You will use this road for only a short distance, then bear left at the fork (a right would lead to a last look at the pond) and almost immediately turn left again, off the road and cutting back into the woods on a footpath.

After a short walk, arrive at gravel Tom Field Road, which is open to vehicles.

Because the next section of the hiking trail ahead was and may still be badly maintained and hard to follow, we can no longer recommend you use it. Instead, stay on Tom Field Road when the marked trail bears left from it. Follow the road north for 0.75 mile to its junction with the paved Sunset Road and turn left a short distance to again pick up the marked foot trail on the far side of Sunset Road.

North of Sunset Road, the trail traverses some higher and more open land, making for easier hiking. After about 0.25 mile, the trail, now heading northeast, descends and crosses Tom Field Road, then a smaller sand road. From here the trail once again enters a cedar swamp, crossing a brook on a wooden bridge and a wet area on a boardwalk. After a grassy road, the trail travels through a mature white pine forest, where some large holly trees may be seen as well. Ahead, it makes a final road crossing and heads toward Lake Nummy. This last section begins on fairly high ground but descends toward a large cedar stand. In the heart of this river of cedars lies Savages Run, the stream that drains Lake Nummy and feeds East Creek Pond. After keeping its distance from the cedars, the trail finally enters what may be the darkest and wettest of all the cedar brooks on the trail so far. Be careful here, for the trail can be slippery and very muddy in places. After emerging from the cedars, the trail bears left then right on a utility line cut; in a short distance it meets the paved road that crosses Lake Nummy's dam. If you parked at the main parking area, bear left and then right on paved roads. If you parked at the nature center, turn right, then left.

HNZ

Resources

Appalachian Trail Conservancy. *Appalachian Trail Guide to New York & New Jersey with 6 Maps,* 15th edition. Harpers Ferry, WV: The Appalachian Trail Conservancy, 2002.

Bennett, D. W. *New Jersey Coastwalks.* Sandy Hook Highlands, NJ: American Littoral Society, 1981.

Boyson, Robert. *Kittatinny Trails.* Mahwah, NJ: New York–New Jersey Trail Conference, 2004.

Brooks, Christopher & Catherine. *60 Hikes within 60 Miles: New York City: with Northern New Jersey, Southwestern Connecticut, and Western Long Island.* Birmingham, AL: Menasha Ridge Press, 2004.

Buff, Sheila. *Nature Walks in and Around New York City: Discover Great Parks and Preserves Throughout the Tri-State Metropolitan Area,* 1st edition. Boston: Appalachian Mountain Club Books, 1996.

Chazin, Daniel. *New Jersey Walk Book: A Companion to the New York Walk Books,* 2nd edition. Mahwah, NJ: New York–New Jersey Trail Conference, 2004.

Dann, Kevin. *Twenty-Five Walks in New Jersey.* Piscataway, NJ: Rutgers University Press, 1982.

Della Penna, Craig. *24 Great Rail-Trails of New Jersey.* North Amherst, MA: New England Cartographics, 1999.

Harrison, Marina with Lucy D. Rosenfeld. *A Walker's Guidebook: Serendipitous Outings near New York City: Including a Section for Birders.* Michael Kesend Publishing, Ltd., 1996.

Kjellstrom, Bjon. *Be Expert with Map and Compass.* Hoboken, NJ: John Wiley & Sons, 1994.

Kobbe, Gustav. *The New Jersey Coast and Pines.* Baltimore: Gateway Press, 1982.

Lenik, Edward J. *Iron Mine Trails,* revised edition. Mahwah, NJ: New York–New Jersey Trail Conference, 1999.

Mack, Arthur C. *The Palisades of the Hudson.* Edgewater, NJ: The Palisade Press, 1909.

McClelland, Robert J. *The Delaware Canal.* Piscataway, NJ: Rutgers University Press, 1967.

McPhee, John. *The Pine Barrens.* New York: Farrar, Straus and Giroux, 1968.

New York–New Jersey Trail Conference. *Day Walker: 32 Walks within the Metropolitan Area,* 2nd edition. Mahwah, NJ: New York–New Jersey Trail Conference, 2002.

_____. *Guide to the Long Path,* 5th edition. Mahwah, NJ: New York–New Jersey Trail Conference, 2005.

Perls, Jeffrey. *Paths along the Hudson: A Guide to Walking and Biking along the River.* Piscataway, NJ: Rutgers University Press, 1999.

Ransom, James M. *Vanishing Ironworks of the Ramapos.* Rutgers University Press. 1966.

Rosenfield, Lucy D. and Marina Harrison. *A Guide to Green New Jersey: Nature Walks in the Garden State.* Piscataway, NJ: Rutgers University Press, 2003.

Scherer, Glenn. *Nature Walks in New Jersey: A Guide to the Best Trails from the Highlands to Cape May,* 2nd edition. Boston: Appalachian Mountain Club Books, 2003.

Scofield, Bruce. *Circuit Hikes in Northern New Jersey,* 5th edition. Mahwah, NJ: New York–New Jersey Trail Conference, 2003.

Waterman, Laura and Guy. *Forest and Crag: A History of Hiking, Trail Blazing, and Adventure in the Northeast Mountains.* Boston: Appalachian Mountain Club Books, 1989.

_____. *Backwoods Ethics: Environmental Issues for Hikers and Campers,* 2nd edition. Woodstock, VT: The Countryman Press, 1993.

_____. Wilderness Ethics: *Preserving the Spirit of Wilderness,* 2nd edition. Woodstock, VT: The Countryman Press, 1993.

Wyckoff, Jerome. *Rock Scenery of the Hudson Highlands and Palisades.* Albany, NY: Adirondack Mountain Club, 1971.

Zatz, Arline. *Best Hikes with Children in New Jersey,* 2nd edition. Mountaineers Books, 2005.

HIKING MAPS

(Published by the New York–New Jersey Trail Conference)

North Jersey Trails 2-map set. 2005.
Kittatinny Trails 4-map set. 2005.
Sterling Forest Trails. 2005.
Hudson Palisades Trails 5-map set, 2006

USEFUL ROAD MAPS

Rand McNally/New York City, Metro Area Counties, Long Island. Latest edition.
AAA New Jersey. Latest edition.

Index

G

Game birds, 270
Gas pipelines, 189
Gateway National Recreation Area, 214–19
Geocaching, 19
Geology, overview, 13–16
German prisoner-of-war camp, 262
Ghost Lake/Ghost Lake Trail (Jenny Jump State Forest), 130
Giardia lamblia, 19, 166
Gilbride Road (Washington Valley Park), 183, 185
Glacial erratics, 73, 79, 83, 103, 116, 118, 130
Glassmaking industry, 248
Glenwood Fire Road (Wyanokie Circular), 77
Gouvernour family, 73
Governor Mountain hike, 70–74
Grand Loop Trail: Jockey Hollow hike, 156; Schooley's Mountain County Park hike, 139
Grand Tour Trail (Hartshorne Woods Park), 226
Grass ferns, 250
Graveyards, cemeteries: at Ringwood Manor, 62; in Watchung Reservation, 178
Great blue heron, 142, 200, 206, 216
Great Ebb Harbour River, 261
Great egret, 234
Great Swamp Wildlife Refuge, 15
Green Brook, 177
Green family, 61–62, 70
Greenbrier plants, 233, 226, 269, 270
Grey Crag (Palisades hike), 167
Griggstown Barracks, 202
Griggstown Causeway, 202
Gunnison Beach, 214

H

Hacklebarney Mine, 142, 143
Halifax Trail (Skylands Manor hike), 66
Hart, John, 194
Hartshorne, Richard, 224
Hartshorne Woods Park hike, 224–29
Hasenclever Iron Trail (Ringwood Manor), 63
Hawks, 13, 126, 184, 223
Headley Overlook (Mahlon Dickerson Reservation), 127
Hewitt, Abram, 60
Hewitt, Erskine, 61, 70
Hewitt-Butler Trail: Carris Hill hike, 82, 84; Torne Mountain–Osio Rock hike, 86; Wyanokie Circular hike, 78
Hickory trees, 202, 224, 226
High Point boulder, 78
High Point State Park, 14, 27–30
Highland Cut, 136, 139
Highlands Trail (HT); Mahlon Dickerson Reservation, 125, 126; overview, 16
Hiking: carrying food and water, 19: clothing and gear, 17–18; pace, 16–17; planning for, 17; ticks and chiggers, 20, 240; trail etiquette, 21–22; trail markers, 19
Hiking organizations, 22
Hinge-boats, 203
Hoffman Building (New Jersey Audubon Society), 158–59
Holly trees, 216, 233, 266, 269, 270
Honeysuckle plants, 217, 222
Hooks Creek Lake (Cheesequake State Park), 222
Horse chestnut trees, 200
Howell Works, 229
Hudson, Henry, 216
Hudsonia (beach heather), 238
Hunterdon County Department of Parks and Recreation, 132

Hunting: Black River Trails area, 144; overview, 21; Six Mile Run Reservoir area, 208
Hypothermia, 17

I

Igneous rock, 15, 189
Indian pipe plants, 72
Iris Trail (High Point State Park), 29–30
Iron industry, 60, 120–21, 127, 258–59
Island Beach State Park hike, 235–38

J

Jack-in-the-pulpit, 63, 223, 226
Jackson, Paul R., 171
Jacob's Creek, 193
Jacobs Ladder Trail (Appalachian Trail backpack hike), 48
Japanese barberry, 155, 160
Japanese-American internment camp, 262
Jenny Jump Mountain, 131
Jenny Jump State Forest hike, 128–31
Jockey Hollow hike, 153–57
Jockey Hollow Road, 156
Johnson Ferry House, 192

K

Kay, Alfred and Elizabeth, 142
Kay Pond, 142
Kay Pond (Black River Trails area), 142
Kean, Thomas, 264
Kearney House (Cornwallis Headquarters), 165
Kechemeche tribe, 268
Kidd, Captain, 216
Kingston to Griggstown hike, 198–202

Kittatinny Mountain: Appalachian Trail on, 14; Backpacker Campsite, 42; backpacking trip through, 39; Kittatinny Ridge, 35–36; trails on, 31–34

L

Lady's slipper, 37, 222, 223
Lake Absegami, 15, 243, 246–47
Lake George, 137
Lake Lookout, 109
Lake Nummy, 268, 269, 271
Lake Owassa, 48
Lake Rutherford, 30
Lakes: Crater Lake (Lake Success), 45; Cupsaw Lake, 66; Ghost Lake, 130; Hooks Creek Lake, 222; Lake Absegami, 15, 243, 246–47; Lake George, 137; Lake Lookout, 109; Lake Nummy, 268, 269, 271; Lake Owassa, 48; Lake Rutherford, 30; Parvin Lake, 262–63, 267; Ramapo Lake, 50–55, 58; Sawmill Lake, 29; Shepherd Lake, 65–66; Surprise Lake, 98; Thundergust Lake, 266; Wawayanda Lake, 107, 109; Wills Mills Lake, 241
Lamington River. See Black River
Laurel Hill and Ridge (Wells Mills County Park hike), 242
Laurel Pond Trail (Wawayanda State Park hike), 109
Laurel Ridge Trail (Hartshorne Woods Park hike), 224, 226
League for Conservation Legislation, 264
Leatherleaf shrub, 245
Lebanon Glass Works, 248
Lebanon State Forest. See Brendan T. Byrne State Forest hike
Lenape Indians, 168
Lenape Trail (South Mountain Reservation hike), 168, 170–73

White Trail (Mount Hope Historical Park hike), 122
Whitesbog Village, 248
Wick, Henry, 153
Wick House and Farm, 153–54
Wildflowers, 30, 72, 193, 200, 217, 223, 252, 270
Will Monroe Look, 77–78
Willcox, John and William, burial site, 178
Wills Mills Lake, 241
Wingdam Trail (Wawayanda State Park hike), 109
Winter hiking, 18
Women's Federation Monument, 167
Wood thrush, 229
Worthington State Forest, 14, 39, 42–43

Wyanokie Circular hike and trail, 75–80
Wyanokie Range, 82
Wyanokie Ridge, 75

Y

Yards Creek Reservoir, 42
Yarrow plants, 200
Yellow Dot Trail (Terrace Pond hike), 91
Yellow Trail: Cattus Island County Park, 234; Mullica River Wilderness hike, 261; Schuber Trail hike, 54; Six Mile Run Preserve hike, 210–11
Yellow/Orange Trail (Mullica River Wilderness hike), 260–61